A
Vermont
Son

Autobiography of Conrad Wells

Order this book online at www.trafford.com
or email orders@trafford.com

Most Trafford titles are also available at major online book retailers.

Printed in Victoria, BC, Canada.

ISBN: 978-1-5539-5432-3 (sc)
ISBN: 978-1-4122-5152-5 (e-b)

*Our mission is to efficiently provide the world's finest, most comprehensive book publishing
service, enabling every author to experience success. To find out how to publish your book, your
way, and have it available worldwide, visit us online at www.trafford.com*

Trafford rev. 05/10/2010

 Trafford
PUBLISHING® www.trafford.com

North America & international
toll-free: 1 888 232 4444 (USA & Canada)
phone: 250 383 6864 ♦ fax: 812 355 4082

Acknowledgements

Studebaker National Museum - So. Bend, IN.
Auburn - Cord - Dusenberg Museum - Auburn, IN.
The Herald of Randolph (VT).
Cobleigh Library of Lyndonville, VT.
The Secord Collection, Cobleigh Library
Harriet Fletcher Fisher, Lyndonville, VT.
National Automobile and Truck Museum of United States
- Auburn, In.
Jenks Studio - St. Johnsbury, VT.
Lyndon Institute - Mr. R. Hilton, Headmaster
Lyndon Institute Alumni Association
Caledonian Record of St. Johnsbury, VT.
Reminisce Magazine
IBM Corp - Archives and Media
Rudolf and Jean Day
Dick Monroe
Jim Cullum
Cliff and Ann Eaton
Jan and Al Floyd
Wes Herwig
Randolph Historical Society
Mr. & Mrs. Jack Saylor
Kemp's Trucks
Robert Day
Robert C. Jones
Edison Ford Winter Estates, Ft. Meyers, FL.
Nathalie Wells
Barbara Lindquist
My wife, Bunny - 2 daughters, JoAnne and Lisa for the
prodding and encouragement to start and continue.
Many attempts and much time has been devoted to giving
credit courtesy for photos and documents. In some cases,
original photo owner could not be located.

Randolph Center, VT. Photo - 2001, C. Wells

Main Street
Randolph Center, Vermont
Date 1930's

State School of Agriculture, Randolph Center, VT. Dr. Allen house on the left. Approx 1907. Top and bottom photos from a collection owned by Mr. & Mrs. A. Floyd.

Corner of Main Street and (now) Rt. 66 - Randolph Center, VT. Date unknown.

North Main St. Randolph Center, VT. Approx 1908. Top and bottom photos from a collection owned by Mr. & Mrs. A. Floyd.

Corner of South Main and South Randolph Road, Randolph Center, VT. Approx 1910.

*South Main St. Randolph Center, VT. approx 1910. Top and bottom
photos from a collection owned by Mr. & Mrs. A. Floyd.*

Sunset Hill Road, Randolph Center, VT. Approx 1907.

The Dormitory, State School of Agriculture, Randolph Center, Vt.

The Dormitory, State School of Agriculture, Randolph Center, VT.
Top and bottom photos from a collection owned by Mr. & Mrs. A. Floyd.

Agricultural School Barn prior to 1940.

Introduction

Volume 1, within these pages are my recollection of time from early age, to approximately eighteen years of age. This would cover time from the late nineteen twenties, up to nineteen forty seven.

The main reason for writing this is to compare life (and work) from the thirties (and up) to life and work near the turn of the century.

The topics are headed, so if you come across a topic of low interest, just skip to the next topic.

This book should not be used to establish historic dates, events, records or points of interest tied to a specific time. While a lot of thought has been applied to getting all of this information on paper, there are times when my recollection(s) or memory may not always be correct.

Some of the auto pictures may not be accurate within a year or so. Also, the auto pictures will give an approximate year in relation to the general era of the text.

While many names of present and former residents of Randolph (VT.) are sprinkled through the text, the real reason is that these people not only provided the author with experiences, but also in many cases, guidance. It is for these reasons, that I thank them by mentioning names.

Sprinkled throughout the text are selected song titles within a box – and by year. These titles came from various songbooks and pieces of music, I've gathered over the years and are part of my music collection. I thought it would be interesting to show some of the more common and recognized titles, most of whom are now called......."standards."

Lastly, very few persons can deliver, or draw upon childhood experiences from birth to the next 12 or 14 years of life. My life, at that time, would be no different – about as exciting as staring at a bowl of egg whites!

Partly for that reason, I would like to spend a few pages describing my home town of Randolph, Vermont.

It is my intent to follow up Volume I with either an additional volume, (or volumes) to recapture some of the many "paths" I've followed as time marched on. I've had many different jobs – many different careers and it is my pleasure to share these with you, along with some of the interesting people I've enjoyed over that period of time.

Table of Contents

1928 - 1946

xii

xiv

xvi

U.S. Veteran's Cemetery, Randolph Center, VT. 2001 C. Wells

Top and Bottom: U.S. Veterans Cemetery in Randolph Center, VT.
Photo(s) 2001, C. Wells.

1912 National Cash Register made for A. C. Wells in Randolph Center Store. Still in use in the same store by Al and Jan Floyd. Photo 2001, C. Wells

Sticker on bottom of cash drawer validating above information.

The Cash Register Story

During the time A. C. Wells owned the Randolph Center (VT.) General Store (1903 - 1921), he bought a new cash register from National Cash Register Co. This unit is pictured and as the label states under the drawer - "Made for A. C. Wells, Randolph Center, VT. in May 1912."

Apparently the cash register has been used by each subsequent owner through the years and to this day is still in continuous use!

Al Floyd, the current owner, had a spring break last year. He called the parts department in National Cash Register and asked for a certain spring for the given model number. The parts department couldn't locate the model number and asked Al to verify it to which Al replied the model number again. Finally, he asked Al how old the cash register was. Al's reply: "1912." To which a reply of dead silence! With this, the parts department politely declared they didn't have a spring! They don't stock parts *that* far back!

General

If the day I was born was typical January 26, 1928, it probably started out at 30 or 35 degrees below zero.

In Randolph, Vermont, the months of January and February started each day very cold. Thirty-five below zero was very common and it probably didn't get above zero for at least two to three weeks, all day long. Even my Dad, who was a coal and fuel oil dealer, never showed any emotion that was greater in January or February than he did in May or June. He was not a greedy person and the fact he made more money in January and February didn't fire up his emotions.

Randolph was not really much different than any other community. It had a population of about 2,500 in the village and another 2500 in the township which included Randolph Center, North, East and South Randolph. The Central Vermont Railroad passes through here as does State Route 12. The terrain is very hilly with Randolph in a "pocket" amongst the hills. The terrain also provided a wicked pull for the trains as they headed north. From Randolph to Roxbury was one of the steepest main line rail road pulls in New England.

Randolph Center was, at one time, seriously considered to be the Capital of Vermont. This would explain why the few houses are set back from the road with nice large lawns. This idea soon was put

---

Selected Songs
Composed in 1928

Button Up Your Overcoat
I Can't Give You Anything But Love
I'll Get By
If I Had You
It All Depends On You
Love Me or Leave Me
Marie
She's Funny That Way
Sweet Lorraine

2

aside because a railroad would have difficulty passing through with an elevation of approximately 1,400 feet. The "Center" had three churches, a graded school, a general store/Post Office combination. My father was the store proprietor and also Post Master around 1920. When my father and mother were married, they lived in the house next to the general store. The house is still there, so is the general store. One time, about 1990, when I patronized the store, there was a picture on the wall of "A.C. Wells General Store." Also, the current owner, Al Floyd, showed me a rack (for bolts, nuts, etc.) that my Dad had made some time around 1920!

A. C. Wells General Store, Randolph Center, VT.
From a collection owned by Mr. & Mrs. A. Floyd. Date Approx. 1918

Dad's first wife died at a very young age. Her sister used to come from Chicago and stay summers in the "Center." The old cottage was dilapidated and rotted— I don't know how it stood up at all. "Aunt Jo" had a daughter, Lucille, who was quite talented as a painter. She used to let my sister and me help her gather birch bark that she would paint deer and trees on. Later, she graduated to various wooden items such as bowls, plates, etc. In nothing flat, she'd have a deer or two on a plate which she could sell quite easily.

But, that's enough about Lucille except, later, I'll tell you an interesting story about her future husband Manuel Miller.

The countryside was peppered with farms of various sizes all of which were dairy farms. It was quite common, in the 30's and 40's, for the fire alarms to blast away and later hear the old American LaFrance fire engine work its way up the hills to Randolph Center or vicinity. Then combat a fire in a hay barn that probably was started by spontaneous combustion.

This American LaFrance was new in 1935. It had a 6-cylinder engine with pistons probably 5 inches in diameter. With no muffler and an exhaust probably 4 inches in diameter—it was loud. Unfortunately, it was teamed with a 3-speed transmission. Considering the truck with all the gear, weighed about 12-14 tons, its ability to climb hills was always fully taxed.

General Store operated by A.C. Wells 1903-1921. Residence of Mr. and Mrs. A.C. Wells 1921 Photo taken approx. 1985, C. Wells

4

One piece of fire apparatus in the whole town for years most always meant a total loss from any fire. The truck was housed right next to my father's coal office. With this close proximity, I didn't have to spend years getting to know any of the fireman and, of course, they knew who I was, even at an early age.

In the forties, Joe Durkee, Raymond Campbell, Elgin Ladd, Elbert Fullam, Stub Wood, and many more all volunteered when the alarm sounded. The alarm was in the tower in the middle of the roof. The alarm was driven by compressed air and the after about 20-30 blasts, the air pressure would always drop enough so the subsequent blasts were at least an octave lower which also gave the horn an eerie sound.

But, by counting the blasts, and looking at a supplemental code chart, you could determine or get an idea where the fire was. Most of the time, it was out of the village which usually meant an outlying farm.

Once in a while, a neighboring town might request assistance if there was a large fire there, or, help was needed. One such time was when there was a serious train accident in Northfield, which was 17 miles north. The engine derailed and struck a bridge.

Going back to the fire engine, it was very common for three, four, even five volunteer firemen to ride on the rear platform. I didn't know it at the time, but years later I was told that riding flat footed on the platforms was dangerous. A sudden bump in the road made the platform jump and if you weren't hanging onto the cross bar tight, you could get flipped off. I believe Joe Durkee found that out one night as he rode flat footed. As the engine raced the narrow Randolph Center Road gaining speed for the Slack hill pull, he got flipped—without injury!! From then on, all rode on the balls of their feet over the back edge of the platform!!

Early Telephones

It was easy to call on the phone. The telephone number at "our" house was 176. The telephone number for Randolph Coal and Ice Co. was 129. Later, in the thirties, this number was updated to 129 ring 2 because the Fire Station was also 129.

As many senior citizens know, all telephone calls went through a local switch board and a personal greeting by name was very com-

> **Selected Songs**
> **Composed in 1929**
>
> Ain't Misbehavin'
> Am I Blue
> Can't We Be Friends
> Honeysuckle Rose
> I Guess I'll Have to Change My Plans
> If You Were The Only Girl
> Stardust
> Sunny Side Up
> You Do Something to Me

mon with one or more of the operators. A good definition of a small town is—where you get the wrong number on a telephone, you still have a conversation!

The switchboard in Randolph was located on the second floor of the Randolph National Bank building and at night, you could see the operator(s) working the switchboard through the windows on Pleasant Street.

The telephone operators also controlled the fire alarm. Needless to say, with each sounding of the fire alarms, the operator was barraged with phone calls for the benefit of those who must have failed to learn counting in school, or who didn't have access to a fire alarm "code chart."

Gladys Wells

My mother came to town as a public school music teacher. She was born in Framingham, Massachusetts. Her father (who I never knew), was an engineer for the Boston and Maine Railroad. When I was a kid, I never gave her enough credit for her abilities and accomplishments. What did I know about "giving her credit"— I had a full time job just trying to survive her! She was quite smart, she graduated from high school at age 16 by skipping a couple of grades. But... she didn't have the common sense that God gave a croquet ball! And of course, the common sense part (or lack of it), always poked its head into my life, and more likely than not, created a derailment between the two of us. My mother was very strict and very decisive. If she said no— that meant no! — Not "ask me later" or "again in the morning." And, not very often did she ever forget what she had said.

My mother wore her hair with a pug. I learned or found out that any woman who wore a pug commanded *and* demanded respect with no crap sprinkled in! (A pug is taking all hair, pull it back and roll it into a ball. Then anchor it at the neck.)

She could play the piano and I mean really play it. She could hammer out Ragtime or Novelty numbers that amazed and entertained everyone. Having a lot of natural ability, she furthered her ability early in life.

At age 16, she would take a train from Framingham, Massachusetts into Boston. That took about a half hour, as it is only about 20 miles. Once arriving in Boston, she would head to one of the movie theaters and play for silent movies.

She played from 11 a.m. to 5 p.m., right straight through. Some movies came with a musical score which she had to "sight" read for the first time that movie played. Shortly, she would have it memorized. She had a terrific memory and she could sight read music remarkably well. Other movies came without a score, so she picked tunes or songs from her "memory bank" that were appropriate and, added to the action on the screen. Bear in mind, she started this job at 16— Imagine any 16 year old going to any city and working for hours. But, when lunch time arrived, she would eat a sandwich with the left hand and continued to play the piano with the right hand!

One last item about this, she was very choosey on which theaters she played. No "Old Howard" or "Globe" — No "Burley" Houses, only legit theaters!!

Some way, or other, she met and married some man from Maine who was a State Senator. They lived in North Central Maine in a very small town.

After a period of time, the marriage was dissolved and Gladys took a job in Randolph, Vermont as a music teacher. Some time later, she and "A.C." were introduced. And later, the two of them were married.

"A.C." Wells

Alfred Wells was born in Randolph (actually it was near East Braintree) and lived on a farm with parents I never did know. My father was forty-nine when I was born. My mother was thirty-seven. My only sister was 2½ years older than I.

Living on a farm from 1878 on, with his two brothers and a sister, was probably more a disappointment than a joy for my father. There was always wood to cut, barn chores and I can imagine dozens of other repetitive routines.

The kids would gather around the sugar barrel for a treat. No store nearby and no money either, to buy a treat. A lump of brown sugar was about the only sweet treat. Sugar came as brown sugar and in a wooden barrel.

Being hard as a rock, my grandfather chipped pieces with a hatchet, and the kids would reach for a piece. Ignoring the warning of keeping the hands out during the chipping process, my Uncle John ended up with a part of a finger missing!

"A.C." was well known in the central part of Vermont, and by the time I was born in 1928, he had worked at many occupations.

By assigning dates to the occupations, this is how it would look:

1884-1896	Peth School
1896- 1898	Vermont Central Railroad (the name was changed to Central Vermont later)
1898- 1901	Cooperative Creamery
1901-1903	Worked his father's farm
1903-	General Store- Randolph Center, VT
1913-1919	Sold road machinery for New England Road Machinery. Kept the store- others ran it.
1921-1950	Sold Randolph Center Store. Bought Randolph Coal and Ice Co. in (West) Randolph, VT
1915-1916	State Representative in VT Legislature
1931-1932	Senator in VT Legislature
1932-1948	Side Judge in Orange County Court

When I was born, my Dad was the Coal and Ice merchant. In the late twenties, he digressed to fuel oil. When he bought the business in 1921, it was about 50% coal and 50% ice. That started to change with the sales of ice dropping noticeably by 1930. Bad luck with a dam in Randolph, that never produced (after one year), also "Frigidaire" refrigerators were starting to become popular. As Frigidaire was one of the first (if *not* the first) refrigerators, for years that appliance was referred to as the "Frigidaire"!!

By now, you have enough information to conclude that my family background is such that my folks were well known, well respected, but, also middle of the road members of the community. It was necessary that my sister and I *always* speak to other people, *always* be ready to help others, *never* speak down or be offensive. Believe me, if any act or action toward others was offensive, the phone would ring at home or in "the office." This would be a community where everyone pitched in to raise the next generation.

I thought the world of my Dad, and I spent a lot of time at the "Coal Office" with him when I wasn't in school.

Saturday evenings he would return to the office—it was easier for people to pay bills. Many, especially mill workers, worked Saturdays, for a 48-hour week.

He had a small room with some woodworking tools and he used to "putter" around and make various items such as lamps, cribbage boards and even a full size desk. Many items contained woodwork that was inlaid.

Although my Dad never graduated from high school, he came

**Selected Songs
Composed in 1930**

Body and Soul
Bye Bye Blues
Embraceable You
Exactly Like You
Fine and Dandy
I'm Confessin'
On the Sunny Side of the Street

Example of two trucks starting life approx same time as author.
Top: 1934 Reo Speedwagon. Bottom: 1930 Mack (Chain Drive).
Both from the Kemps Collection. Photos Approx. 1995, C. Wells

very close. Three weeks prior to graduating, he had to return to the family farm and help out. This killed his chance for a diploma. But in subsequent years, he built a good base of experience and also possessed a great amount of logic and common sense. He spent a lot of time reading. (Remember, no TV in those days!)

Although we had more than one radio at home, he listened to the news at 6:00 P.M., which was "The Esso Reporter." Sunday night he listened to Amos and Andy while he popped down some popcorn! My mother would listen to Gildersleeve, Burns and Allen and Red Skeleton. Good music was never on, especially if it was popular, jazz or a vocal. Classical had a better chance of survival, but not with me.

But, anyway, my Dad was always in the office. The only exception, was when Orange County Court was in session. He was a "side judge" in the court at the County Seat in Chelsea, VT. Once in a while, he would stay overnight depending on the case or caseload. This side occupation entered his life from his age of about fifty-five to seventy. Even without a high school diploma, he was highly regarded by various attorneys, the court clerks and presiding judge(s).

Railroad bridge over Route 14 near Sharon, Vermont. A.C. was one Foreman on the construction of this Bridge. Photo C. Wells

A.C. Wells was employed by New England Road Machinery 1913 - 1919. The Linn Half Track shown here was imported from England and was sold by N.E. Road Machinery. From the Kemp's Collection. Photo Approx 1995, C. Wells

12

**Selected Songs
Composed in 1931**

As Time Goes By
Dancing in the Dark
Guilty
Heartaches
I Apologize
I Don't Know Why
Mood Indigo
Penthouse Serenade
Prisoner of Love

Incidentally, Vermont is the only state that uses a presiding judge and two side judges. This system simplifies many cases that would require a jury. The presiding judge satisfies all requirements to ensure that the case is legal in procedure.

When it came time to establish a verdict, if the three judges didn't render a unanimous decision, a two out of three vote would arrive at a guilty or not guilty verdict.

Quite often, he was appointed probation officer and oversaw some individual or individuals that required permission to stay out late on Saturday night or what have you. Once in a while, Saturday evening, one or two individuals would be in the office trying to separate various puzzles Dad had in a drawer. Success could be rewarded with permission to attend a dance or movie!

Randolph, Vermont

Coming in to town from the south on Route 12, you soon pass Gifford Memorial Hospital (on the right), which is now referred to as Gifford Medical Center. It is now affiliated with Dartmouth-Hitchcock Medical Center Hanover, New Hampshire. As the "Hospital" expanded, it eliminated a few of the adjacent residences and also acquired others for various purposes. This section of Randolph was known, for a time in the 1800's, as the fairgrounds.

**Selected Songs
Composed in 1932**

Ghost of a Chance
How Deep is the Ocean
I'm Getting Sentimental of You
Isn't It Romantic
It Don't Mean a Thing
My Silent Love
Night and Day
Try a Little Tenderness

*Ernest Rattee and Con - Rear of Esso Station, Randolph VT.
Photo 1933, Gladys Wells*

14

*Randolph Main
St, Looking North
near Playhouse
Theatre. Note:
Sowles Block and
Red Lion Inn.*

Depot Square

*Main St.
Looking South.
All Photos
Approx 1984,
C. Wells*

Continuing on Route 12 North, past some really nice, old (and large) houses you approach Main Street Hill. Going down for about five hundred feet, it levels out and the business district starts. After crossing one set of railroad tracks, which used to be three sets, you're now in Depot Square. The old Depot and Station platform is on the left. On the right are numerous multi-story brick buildings. Needless to say, stores on the ground floor with various business offices on the upper floors.

Continuing, past a variety of businesses on both sides—a couple of churches, the town library and now the "old" high and graded school which was built in 1911, and now has outgrown its usefulness.

Near the Kimball Library and across from the Bethany Church is the Chandler Music Hall. During the thirties and forties, it was used for town meetings, high school plays, and an occasional minstrel show and not too much else. I can recall exploring in back of Chandler Music Hall, even before being a teenager. There was a small building there. I didn't know it, at that time, but I, later (much later), learned what it was.

Rudolf Day lived in the house beside the music hall. The house can be seen in the photo. His father, Rev. Fred Day, was the Congregational minister.

Years later, he explained that in the small building was a generator which was used to feed electricity to Chandler Music Hall during the presentation of a play. Apparently the current required for all the lights on (and off) the stage; it was found more economical to generate power right there. I don't have the slightest idea if any trace of the building is still present.

It was a well-built building with excellent acoustics. On the right end was a large room – couple "offices."

On the second floor was a large hall with kitchen facilities and used for various community functions. The strange item is the floor. It is a spring floor, designed to be "springy," never seen or heard of another one – but this one was "different" to dance on! At this time of my life, I would be interested to know how it was built and how it was "designed to be springy."

At this point, Main Street Bridge is coming up. Let's hurry up and pass over this. This bridge is on the State list for replacement, but if its position doesn't rise to the top soon, it might not have to be

16

Main Street Bridge - Randolph. Note: Old foundation at left either a foundation for a previous bridge, or a foundation for a grist mill. Photo 2001, C. Wells

Chandler Music Hall, Note Bethany Parsonnage next door. Photo 2000, C. Wells

removed—Mother Nature will do it.

Here, you can go left on Route 12A, go right on Route 12, take your pick of two other directions or stop at Cumberland Farms on the right and grab a bottle of Root Beer.

The community also offers a golf course recently expanded to 18 holes, an unusual local movie house, laundromat and various and many other businesses and interests.

You have to realize that living in a small community of this size, you don't have all the "things" of a large community or that a city might offer. It is made up by the fact that you have people—people that are warm, friendly, helpful, considerate and caring. The relationships you had with your neighbors or others within the community were close enough to take the place of things.

One time (as an example), my Dad was very sick and in the hospital. My mother couldn't leave the telephone—it rang constantly with caring townspeople inquiring his condition and offering help.

Randolph, had (and still has), its share of "colorful" characters as most towns do, many of which I will try to introduce.

And, of course, there were a few poor souls who were alcoholics. At my age, during the thirties and into the forties, I accepted the fact that most every time I saw one of them he was probably drunk. I don't know if Alcoholics Anonymous was even around. It wasn't, that I was aware of, until after World War II.

The Herald

There was even a local newspaper called *Herald and News* in the thirties and forties. A stately gentleman by the name of Luther Johnson, better known as "L.B.," published the paper. For some reason it was also known as "Johnson's Juicy Jabber"! Later, another gentleman, John Drysdale, bought the paper and it jokingly became known as "Drysdale's Dry Dribble"! Its weekly publication is still there but some time changed its legitimate name to *The Herald*. Its publisher is now M. Dickey Drysdale (son of John Drysdale). Someone asked John once why a small town like Randolph needed a newspaper, "everyone knew what everyone else was doing" and John replied, "He knew it, but the paper also stated who was getting caught at it"!!

Prior to age eight, I was pretty much required to stay in the

**Selected Songs
Composed in 1933**

Bill Bailey
Don't Blame Me
Easter Parade
I Cover The Waterfront
I Won't Dance
Talk Of The Town
Lover
My Happiness
Smoke Gets In Your Eyes
Temptation

*Home of the local newspaper The Herald of Randolph.
Photo 2000, C. Wells*

**Selected Songs
Composed in 1934**

Blue Moon
Cocktails for Two
Deep Purple
I Get a Kick Out of You
Moon Glow
Solitude
Stars Fall On Alabama
There Goes My Heart
The Very Thought of You
What a Difference a Day Made

---

neighborhood, as you would imagine. I had enough freedom during the day where I could play with other youngsters—some my age and others, both younger and older.

It was about this time (age 6), that I happened to be at David Angell's house on Prospect Ave.– about three houses from home. David's father was a local doctor (M.D.), as was his father. Both had an office in the house almost directly across the street from the Wells' residence.

The elder, Dr. Angell was "Dr. Frank" who was rather short, stocky and apt to be rather curt and short on conversation.

He owned a 1937 Buick Coupe and each morning, out of a peaceful atmosphere, a door would slam. His garage was in a barn attached to his house and – never closed the "barn" door. He used to make house calls by horse and buggy. By now, that era had passed, but he parked his Buick in front of two or three horse stalls. As the barn door was open, you could hear the car door slam! This was followed by a roar of the straight eight-cylinder engine under the hood. This would be followed by a cloud of blue smoke, and accompanied by the neighbor's terrier who would quite often be barking at all the commotion of this gray monster emerging from the "barn." Dr. Frank always kept his foot on the accelerator, nearly to the floor, then gauged his speed with his clutch!

Let me take a moment to explain about "lurch." Older cars, such as those in the twenties (and early thirties), were built like tanks. They were heavy, boxy, and not very refined in many of their characteristics—like the clutch. The clutch was designed to work and to last. However, a *good* driver would double clutch as it was shifted, as an effort to make a smooth shift.

You could often tell the quality of a driver especially if there were two or three passengers. When the car moved, it was apt to "lurch ahead," such as described in many books! This was accompanied by two or three heads all flying toward the rear of the car in synchronization.

Dr. Messier, the local optometrist in Randolph had an older Buick (late twenties) and his approach to motion would be a good example of "lurching ahead." He would also "place" the gas pedal usually close to the floor, select either first gear or reverse, then just take his foot off the clutch! *Now, this* was a first class example of lurch.

One day the rear wheels did a short "lurch" and that was it. Later, one of the local garages presented him with a bill for a rear axle replacement and the mechanics chuckled over the fact that "the axle had damn near twisted a half turn before she leggo!!"

Back with David Angell— He and I were sitting in a tree in front of "his" house. His mother, Margaret, was bent over, operating a hand trowel. David had recently been given a BB Pistol. Probably a Buzz Barton! (Bear in mind BB guns of those days were lower power than today). He said "I wonder if my aim is good." His mother, knowing what he was aiming at, said something to the effect that it better not hurt!" "Bang" and with that, she straightened up, and that hand trowel was launched far into the air.

Neither one of us noticed that she was half up the tree. Then back down equally as fast with him under her arm. Into the house she headed, bellowing for me to follow. Once in the bathroom she washed his mouth out with soap. Well, this was new to me. My mother never did anything like that to me! She then instructed me to stop laughing or I'd get the same treatment! She couldn't be serious and not only that, it *was* funny to see the soap bubbles surrounding David's mouth. Well, it wasn't as funny when I got the same treatment!

It must have around this time, give or take a year or two, that the Catholic Church, right beside Dr. Frank's house, received a new cross for the steeple. Someway, Bill Austin, Ken and Phil McIntyre, my sister and I acquired the wooden 3 by 6-foot crate the cross came in. There was a fair grade down the back of Ken and Phil's house (next to Rodney Slack's). We nailed that box to two sleds and would all ride for fifty or sixty feet. As anyone sat in the box, about all you could see was maybe a head or two above the sides of the box. *This* was a blast until the trip where we didn't stop in the garden where we normally stopped. Everyone bailed out except my sister. We helplessly watched as she headed down a steep bank only about twenty feet away from the priest's garage. The Rectory for the Catholic Church was right in front of her.

"No—not the garage—the window, jump...jump," the three of us were shouting. *Crash* right through the window just as pretty as you would ever want to see! Golly it took that window right out—window frame, sash, glass and all. She ended up right in the middle of the garage – luckily, the car was not in the garage. Our neighbor, Rodney Slack, a senior citizen and handyman, repaired the window – new frame, glass and all!!

Catholic Church on Prospect St. Randolph Vermont (Note Cross).
Photo 2000, C. Wells

Drivers Get Tested

Here is a good place to explain that between Rodney Slack's house and the Catholic Church was Prospect Street, which in this spot was a hill—a very steep hill. It is on this hill, that the local Motor Vehicle Inspector would bring potential drivers. Here a procedure was tested where the "learner applicant" had to stop in the middle of the hill. The parking (or emergency) brake was used to keep the car from rolling backward. Then, by letting out the clutch, as the emergency brake is released, the car should start forward. That is, if enough "gas" is given. This, was a requirement if the car was a manual shift. And in the thirties and early forties, this meant all cars.

On test day, quite a few of us kids would sit on Rodney Slack's lawn and watch this "test" take place. There were a lot of failures!

The emergency brake was right between the two people in front, sticking up out of the floor. Often (quite often), you would see the inspector grab for the brake and yank it toward the seat. It was also surprising how many people thought the car would go forward even if the clutch was still depressed! So, they would give it more gas

Prospect St. Randolph - Scene for many "New" drivers to demonstrate their skills during a test. Photo 2001

...and more. Of course, this "episode" always generated lots of noise and a humongous amount of smoke. *Most all* cars in those days, smoked.

Somewhere about this time, I had acquired a metal car. I used to pedal this around the "terrace." The terrace was a circular street. At one place you could look down on the business district—a nice residential street with a concrete sidewalk. No elaborate houses but all middle income and nicely maintained. My parents built theirs after they were married and moved down from the "Center" to Randolph about 1924. It was a Dutch Colonial with a two-car garage under a large porch.

The porch had a railing around the periphery which, one day my sister and I were leaning over. We were tossing Concord grapes from the nearby vine down on Dad's car as he was about to back out.

One of the neighbors, Helena Huse, was walking by – sensed a serious accident about to happen and ran over, down the drive, just in time to catch my sister as she fell! Not only did Helena prevent a broken bone or two from the fall of about twelve feet, she also stopped our father from backing out of the garage.

We lived next door to Cedric Clark, his wife and daughter, on Prospect Street. Cedric was the station agent for Central Vermont

---

**Selected Songs
Composed in 1935**

I'm Gonna Sit Right Down and Write
I'm In The Mood For Love
In A Sentimental Mood
Just One Of Those Things
A Kiss To Build A Dream On
My Romance
Stairway To The Stars
These Foolish Things

Railroad. More about this later.

I do want to say at this time that, unlike so many people, I never had to worry or think about a place to sleep or where the next meal would come from.

There were rules to live by *especially* from my mother and failure to follow the rules brought stiff punishment. I never liked W.E. Lamson Furniture Store, because they always provided yardsticks as advertisements. At a very young age, I didn't know what the numbers on that stick meant, but I knew what the stick was for.

If the week went by with no yardstick punishments, Dad would take my sister and I down to Leonard's Drug Store on Sunday morning. Here, we could pick out a pack of gum each. My sister could stretch her pack out in time. Mine was apt to be in my mouth by the time we were back home (all five sticks).

Around this time in my life, I built a car with a gas engine. My father took old reel type lawn mower and after removing the cutter bars, he installed a "V" belt pulley on the shaft. From there I built a wood frame, a seat and steering wheel.

Someway, a businessman in town lent me a gas engine. His

Former Cedric Clark Residence on left. Presently the residence of Mr. & Mrs. Michael Reeves. Photo Approx 1980, C. Wells

name was Gordon Scribner and he owned a hardware store. Among other products, he sold Maytag Washing Machines. Due to the fact that many farms in the country did not have electricity, Maytag made washers with a four-cycle gas engine, if needed. These were a fixed-speed cast iron base and came with either one cylinder or later, two cylinders. After fixing this engine to the frame and devising a belt tightener, I could putt-putt around the neighborhood.

Dad walked very unsteadily. This was the result of wearing shoes too small when he was a kid and his toes curled under. He required special shoes which were custom made (and expensive). For this reason we never played outdoor sports, etc. but we talked with each other. Many people who would come into the office for reasons other than coal or fuel oil business. Various business problems, marriages, money problems were discussed and resolved or "put to bed." He always said, if I heard bits of conversation, I should never repeat, and I abided by his rules!

The office was next to the railroad tracks on one side and Salisbury Street on the opposite. It was about 20 feet to the tracks with a concrete passenger platform in between. Three sets of tracks and then was the coal shed building, beyond that was a dirt road and then two large oil tanks, and beyond that, was a blacksmith shop.

It was fascinating to be near the railroad tracks. Not only did I like to watch the passenger trains fly by, but by now, when they stopped, I would wheel the Railway Express wagon to the baggage car door and help load off and load on. My neighbor, Cedric Clark liked the help!

Right in front of the coal office, was the mail bag snatch post. Cedric would fix up the bag (with special delivery or airmail specials) and then allow me to climb the pole, swing out the arms and attach the bag to the arms, which were extended toward the track. This setup was for passenger trains that were not scheduled to stop. It was fun to watch, as the train would speed by doing about 60. The baggage clerk or the mail clerk in a baggage car would stand with the sliding door open. As he approached that snatch pole, he would raise a steel bar and peer through a little windshield. With a blink of an eye, that bag would be snatched by the steel bar and in doing so, saved time by not stopping the train for a one mail bag pickup.

Wells residence taken from Emerson Terr. Porch on right has a two car garage beneath. Present owner, Mr. & Mrs. Peter Flaherty. Photo Approx 1937, C. Wells

Prospect Ave. looking north. Cedric Clark house is in center. Photo Approx. 2000

Main St. looking south. Unused Main School on right. Photo Approx 1985, C. Wells

United Church of Randolph (Baptist and Methodist). Photo Approx 1985, C. Wells

Prospect Ave. looking south. Photo Approx 1985, C. Wells

28

Depot Square from Salisbury St., "Sowles Block" dead ahead. Photo Approx 1984, C. Wells

"Old" Fire Station & Village Garage. Also, Randolph Coal & Oil Co. Photo Approx 1984, C. Wells

RR Tracks looking east showing Coal Sheds & Spragues Dairy. Photo Approx 1984, C. Wells

A Locomotive Ride

An out of this world thrill would happen once in a while. Engineer John McKay was a friend of my Dad. When it got around that "the kid is the son of A.C.," he would occasionally stop one of the 400-size engines on track 2 right in front of the offices. The first time this happened, Dad said to me, "Want a ride?" Out the door, we went, looked both ways on track 1, crossed track 2 and he helped me onto the ladder. I couldn't believe it. I was inside a big snorting steam engine! Each day, a "way freight" rolled in from the south. (White River Junction was the starting point.) Its job was to bring in the loaded freight cars, "spot them" and pick up any empty cars. They would arrive from 9 a.m. to 11 a.m. and spend from 20 minutes to an hour. The engine was one of the 400-size. They were numbered from 450 to 490 give or take a couple.

This was some experience to sit in the cab, watch the firemen or engineer and listen to this monster snort. Once, John climbed down, approached the steam chest and then opened the little slide door. Reaching in, he came out with two baked potatoes. He and the fireman then had a hot lunch!

I learned early and first hand about journal boxes, waste material, hot boxes and other parts.

One day, "A.C." and I were outside watching a freight going north. A typical freight could have at least 80 cars. Some had up to 130 cars. Going south was easier, it was downhill.

Hot Box Signal

As the train went by, smoke was coming out of an (axle) box. This indicated a hot box and no freight conductor or engineer wanted this on their train. All cars in those days had bronze bearings that rode on the axle. It was lubricated by wool or cloth waste material stuffed in the box, which was lubricated periodically by a trainman. If they were dry, the bronze would heat up and the waste material would catch fire. This could lead to sparks and in the wooded areas start a brush fire. Also, many boxcars were made of steel *and* wood.

Now, as the cars passed, standing on the platform of the caboose, was the conductor. "A.C." gave the hot box signal. The conductor opened the caboose door, entered and once inside pulled the

THE BIG 702 IS GETTING some attention from the enginehouse crew at St. Albans. (Jim Shaughnessy photo)
ALTHOUGH THE CV'S 600-CLASS ENGINES were purchased for heavy passenger service, occasionally they were given freight assignments, especially near the end of steam operations. The 600 here seems to have been relegated to work train service, as company hoppers are being filled at the St. Albans ashpit. (Jim Shaughnessy photo)

Both Photos: Courtesy of Robert C. Jones

The 705 is caught at rest in the St. Albans roundhouse about 1940.
Philip R. Hastings photo. Courtesy of Robert C. Jones

TEXAS-TYPE 700 STANDS near the St. Albans
ashpit on April 6, 1939. (Author's Collection)

THE 469 IS PULLING a long freight into the Paln
yard on July 19, 1939. (The 470 Railroad C
Collection)

Photos courtesy of Robert C. Jones

cord. A few hundred feet later the train was stopped. They "broke"
the train, and shuttled that one car to a siding. Shortly, they were
on their way. Those type of journals are now replaced with roller
bearings and that type of problem has gone away.

THE SMOKE DEFLECTORED 600 pauses for water at Montpelier Junction, while the engineer takes the opportunity to check over his engine. (Author's Collection)

WE FIND THE 603 at Montpelier Junction in the 1940s, as a few inches of snow cover the ground. (Donald A. Somerville Collection)

188

Photos courtesy of Robert C. Jones

(Jim McFarlane photo)

Typical Central Vermont box car. Note the wood construction.
Courtesy of Robert C. Jones

Milk Processing Plants

At the end of Weston Street, United Farmers Cooperative had a milk processing plant. Here, milk gathered from various farms, in 40-quart cans, was weighed and combined in a large storage tank. Each day a tank truck would make a "pickup." This truck was a semi-trailer and was contracted by various trucking companies such as Dairy Transport, Appleyard's and one more named Cosgrove, which will be heard more from, later.

The cans were weighed prior to dumping, then washed, sterilized and returned to the farm. At the other side of the village, and at the end of Pearl Street, was the Whiting Milk Creamery. Here the incoming process was the same only the milk was shipped to Boston by railcar.

Whiting was a large corporation and owned their own rail cars. Each car had a bulk tank at each end with plenty of room for ice to be packed around the bulk tanks and also around various 40 qt. cans, that were also shipped to Boston containing cream, etc.

Of course, this meant Pearl St. had to have a source for ice which was solved by having their own ice storage building next to the creamery. This was a building with double walls, which were filled with sawdust. The ice was cut from a small pond on Park Street owned by my Dad, and later, by Wallace Hill.

The next progression for cooling, came when each car had its own cooling system "underneath." However, the cooling units could

An early version of a rail refrigerated car. Owned by Whiting Milk Co.,
it is described in the text. Courtesy of Robert C. Jones

only run when "parked" near a power source. Then, a heavy power cord was plugged in so the electric motor would run the cooling unit.

So, daily, an empty Whiting car was "spotted," a full one picked up and the empty was plugged in to chill. Once the two bulk tanks were at least partially filled, the cold milk also helped to cool down the car's "insides." Separate diesel driven cooling units for either rail cars or trucks were quite a few years distant.

When mechanical cooled rail cars did arrive, the ice storage building became unnecessary. Whiting then leased it (year unknown) to the Town of Randolph for a maintenance garage for sand, gravel, and snow equipment such as trucks, plows, etc.

Frank Darrah

Frank, was a local welder who had his residence and welding business on Central Street. He also came to the old icehouse to weld various pieces of town equipment. I don't know if he was a town employee or contractor.

One day, there were quite a few pieces of equipment in the building and Frank was one of two persons. There was a terrific explosion. I believe one other person was quite near the big entry door and was actually blown out the door! Shortly, the fire engine arrived. Enough of the building was still intact but was now engulfed. It was then, that Frank was seen crawling out the door!

Naturally, he was seriously burned from top to toes and his face was really burned. It took months for him to recuperate and many facial reconstructions, but he lived, came back and ultimately spent many years working at Cone Automatic in Windsor and I'm quite sure as a welder. It was believed a spark burned a hole in the acetylene hose; the gas rose to the roof and slowly built down until it reached torch level, then ignited.

I knew Frank very well, and had him weld a couple of "projects."

Walking The Rails

Naturally, as I spent time at the coal office, sooner or later, I was outside. And, sooner or later, I was "walking the rails." Now, at age nine and ten this isn't the greatest playground I could have found.

I think my Dad let me do this alone because I had learned to have high respect for trains, locomotives, and any rail equipment. The rails in front of the office were straight for two miles. I could see a train long before I heard the whistle. I also ran like hell when any

A "Frog" (in the center) is a vital part where two tracks cross, as referred to in the text. Photo 2001, C. Wells

came in sight or within sound. However, I still wouldn't let *my* kids be anywhere near tracks unsupervised. You never know what might happen.

But, as I walked these rails, soon I would come to a switch where the train would shift on to another set of tracks, such as shown in picture. And, a switch meant also, a crossover of tracks, called a "frog." Now, you can walk a short distance on two rails. But, soon you can't reach both rails, so you have to choose which way you want to go.

Today or rather many years later I would compare that to life, where sooner or later you have to choose one route, path or the other, be it a job, a girlfriend or what else life might offer in the way of choice.

Cinders Galore

I stood on the platform one day somewhere around age eight or nine and was watching a long freight starting up. It was really work-

The 707 filling the sky with black smoke as she slugs her way up Roxbury Mountain with heavy freight tonnage. (Whitney Maxfield Collection). Courtesy of Robert C. Jones

ing as it approached. I made a mistake and looked up as it passed. (Never look up when a steam engine is "working.") Black smoke comes out the stack and so do tiny cinders! Well, you guessed it, one dropped in my eye, and being hot, it stuck right there. A trip to "Dr. Frank" luckily fixed me up. He froze the eye and scraped it off.

Incidentally, the big 700 series locomotives also had "Booster Drives" on the "Pony Trucks" directly underneath the cab. This was controlled by the engineer and when it was turned on, gave additional assist to the big drivers by these steam driven "Pony Trucks," (which was a rare feature).

Early Agreement

On the south side of the tracks and next to the coal sheds were two large fuel oil tanks. These were owned by Shell Oil. Dad's competition, "Tug" Slayton used them, but they were on land owned by the Central Vermont Railroad. Land was leased by Randolph Coal and Ice Co. and subleased to Shell. The cost to Shell was five dollars

Pump House for Shell oil tanks is at left. Access to railroad tracks are just before coal sheds. Photo C. Wells

Randolph Coal & Ice Co.

Dealers in Coal

▼

A. C. WELLS, Proprietor   Randolph, Vermont

Nov. 5, 1929

MEMORANDUM OF AGREEMENT

TO be made by and between the A.C. Wells, Proprietor of the Randolph Coal and Ice Co. and The Shell Eastern Petroleum Products Inc. a Delaware Corporation;

In consideration of Five dollars per annum to be paid by the Shell Eastern Petroleum Products to the Randolph Coal and Ice Co. and the further consideration of cooperation between the contracting parties in keeping the driveway between the said coal company's yard and the loading rack of the Randolph Motor Service Inc. which said loading rack, the Shell Eastern Petroleum Products Inc. is about to purchase from the Randolph Motor Service, together with all other property owned by said Motor Service Co; clear for the use of the said coal company, except when in use by the trucks of the Shell Eastern Petroleum Inc. for purposes of loading said trucks; The Randolph Coal and Ice Co. thru its proprietor will agree to allow the Shell Eastern Petroleum Products, to use the track facilities of the Randolph Coal and Ice Co. as leased from the Central Vermont Railway, for the purpose of unloading tank cars. It shall expressely be agreed by the Shell Petroleum Products Inc. that all courtesy and cooperation shall be extended to said Coal Co. in unloading tank cars, in such manner and at such times so as not to interfere with the unloading of coal as received by the Coal Co.,

This agreement shall be made to run concurrently with the lease of the Central Vermont Railway to the Randolph Coal Co, as now existing and as it may be renewed from time to time.

Aforesaid agreement is only to be executed in the event of the Shell Company's purchase of the Randolph Motor Service.

Randolph Coal and Ice Co.

Witness...............   A.C.Wells
                                                          Proprietor.

Shell Oil Company Lease. Note the 1929 date and also, in the second paragraph, an amount of five dollars per year.

per year. As typical, Dad would say, "Well, Tug Slayton (the Shell Dealer), has to make a living too!"

Next to the Shell tanks was a building used for auto repair, then was a larger three-story building painted bright red.

**Selected Songs
Composed in 1936**

Easy to Love
A Fine Romance
I've Got You Under My Skin
It's Delovely
One For My Baby
Poinciana
Way You Look Tonight

*Depot Square, Randolph VT. Esso Station - "Old Fire Station".
Photo Approx 1985, C. Wells*

Gelatin As A Business

On the end opposite the street, but next to the tracks was a building with painted lettering stating, "Brigham Gelatin Co." This was a business run by Lew Brigham, the inventor of a process that

Brigham Gelatin Co. Photo Approx 1985

was quite secretive. He founded a process where a "mixture" would be poured on panes of glass approximately 20 inches by 20 inches. After discovery, he moved to Randolph and used this building on Weston Street. It was learned that the climatic conditions of Randolph were such that it aided this liquid to solidify faster. Very thin sheets would be "peeled" up from the glass after it solidified. Very bright colors could be mixed, as could combinations. These sheets were ideal to cover floodlights in store windows such as Jordan Marsh, Macy's, etc.

Later when Lew retired (he lived almost across from "our" house, on Prospect Ave.), his son, Stanhope, took over. It was very common to see Lew sitting in a rocker on his porch. He was most often seen with a white visor cap, very stylish clothes – even spats! In the driveway, was a beautiful blue 4-door Packard Sedan (Vintage approximately 1937).

In later years, it was common, by then, to see Stanhope come out, cross the tracks and head to the RR Station. Under his arm was a kraft paper wrapped package about two inches thick. Inside were

Coal Sheds. (Brigham Gelatin Co. can be seen also). Photo Approx 1985

many sheets of gelatin. By now, their use in producing "Technicolor" movies had become standard, and he shipped these packages to Hollywood by Railway Express. This, obviously, was the fastest way, at that time, but still took about a week.

He only employed two or three local women. Two of the women I remember—one was Muriel Durkee and the other was Ella Bowen. They would pour the mixed liquid on panes of glass and then smooth it out. I don't think anyone other than Lew Brigham (later, Stanhope) knew the contents or the mixing process. In later years, technology diminished the business.

Also, a few years after Lew had died and Stanhope was running the business, both Stanhope and his wife were killed in an automobile accident.

Local Fire Station

On the north side of the tracks, beside the coal office, was a large building that housed the fire truck and other fire equipment, the local lockup consisting of two cells for the "naughty people," an office

Former Fire Station and village maintenance. Photo Approx 1999

"New" fire station. Photo Approx 1999

or two for village personnel along with the village truck.

Right in the middle of the roof was a cupola, which served as a fire hose dryer. The upper floor was unoccupied. Right in the middle was a hose drying silo from the ground up, so the cupola on the roof served as a vent outside, at the end of the building were various pieces of equipment. Among these was the village teakettle.

Village Tea Kettle

The "village tea kettle," as Harry Tatro used to call it, was a 6-foot square two-wheel trailer. Right in the middle was a small boiler about 20 inches in diameter and 6 or 7 feet high. The rest of the trailer carried coal, shovels, etc. and a 50-foot length of steam hose coiled on stakes. During the winter, frozen water pipes were common. The village crew would go to the resident's house, remove the water meter or whatever and stick the small pipe on the 50-foot hose into the water pipe. Turn the steam on and gradually the pipe is thawed out!

Years later as technology advanced, an arc welder performed the job by attaching one cable to the pipe in the house, attach the other cable to the pipe in the street and "fire it up." This, of course was almost a "dead short" but, the pipe would heat up rapidly and Shazam, the pipe was thawed. You might say that the hum from the welder replaced the "whistle and chirp like sounds" that used to emanate from the "village tea kettle."

Sidewalk Snow Plow

In the early thirties, I can remember the village using a horse-drawn plow clearing the sidewalks. It was fun bumming a ride on the plow. One day was clear and so white, especially after a fluffy snowfall of 10 or 12 inches. With no engine roar, it was very different to hear the plow creaking with the changing weight of the snow and also so quiet (except for an occasional "poop" from the horse).

Also at this time, the village cleared the streets with a big "V" plow. This was mounted on the front of a big steel frame. By removing the bottom crosspiece of steel on the rear, they would drive a crawler type tractor into this frame. The crosspiece was then reinstalled. On the front, over the "V" plow, were mounted two large

Typical old sidewalk snow plow. Photo 1995, C. Wells

Old Cletrac Tractor Kemps Collection. Photo 1995, C. Wells

1930's "CAT" tractor. These are typical for show plowing 1920's - 1930's. Kemps Collection. Photo 1995, C. Wells

headlights on the frame and on each side was a big wing blade. With these down and with the "V" plow, they could plow a swath 14 or 15 feet wide. An operator drove, sitting in the inside with canvas covers, but the wingman had to operate the wings by chain falls outside and in the cold. This unit was effective but very slow. It would take forever to open all the village streets after a storm. But, this was an improvement, because prior to this, they had big snow rollers and would actually roll the snow in the streets to pack it down.

In 1935, the village purchased a Ford truck with a dump body. This was the first truck to plow snow. Prior to his, the trucks were not capable of snow plowing, which is very hard on the equipment. I remember very distinctly that Ford truck plowing because it really screamed. It was much faster and could open the streets quicker even though it had only a single one-way plow on the front.

Joe Durkee was the driver, and each time the plow needed to be raised, Ben Allen, sitting in the rider's seat, hand-operated a long handle to the hydraulic pump mounted on the floor. This was a slow process, but the method was much faster than the old Cletrac or Caterpillar "V" plow.

Chrysler Airflow

In 1934, Chrysler came out with the "Airflow" model. This was a radical change in design and features. The appearance was "different." After years of seeing a box on wheels, it was an eye popper to see an Airflow. It had a rounded nose with a long and graceful trunk, rear wheel covers.

Stanley Chamberlain, a local attorney, had one, and, having his son as a playmate allowed me to also realize some mechanical features. On the dash was a push-pull control for the overdrive. (An overdrive is common today.) It also had "free wheeling." If this control was pushed in, the car would coast if you "let up" on the gas. The transmission was disengaged near the driveshaft allowing the car to "free wheel" coast. Of course, this coasting with no engine compression was hard on brakes.

The Airflow was so advanced in design, the buying public was very slow to accept it. For that reason, Chrysler Corp. almost went out of business. Another Chrysler product was the DeSoto, which was very similar in appearance.

Useless Auto Information

Here are a couple of examples.

The 1935 Hudson Terraplane had an electric shift, and on the steering column. A little lever protruded out of a molding near the steering wheel. There was an "H" path this lever had to follow. When you wanted to "drop" from third to second gear, you moved the lever to 2ND. Nothing happened until you pushed the clutch, then it shifted.

Many cars came out with front doors that opened by swinging toward the rear. These quickly died out because of the danger if the door might open, going down the road. It would rip the door right off. Also, the women didn't like the antics they had to perform when entering (or exiting), even if they had long skirts on.

Chrysler came out in 1936 with "Floating Power." Most cars, up to this point, had the engines mounted directly to the frame which, when running, was apt to make the car have the "shivers" (terrible vibrations!). "Floating Power" utilized a different design – motor mounts – which were very flexible and minimized vibrations—a great improvement.

Most cars, until 1937, didn't have factory-installed heaters.

Early Thirties Fire Engine (left), 1936 Snub Nose (right). Both are Studebakers in the Studebaker Museum. Photo, C. Wells

1937 Cord. Photo, C. Wells

1936 Cord. Both cars shown here had Lycoming Engine, Optional Supercharger, front drive and electric shift. Photos courtesy of Auburn - Cord - Duesenberg Museum. Photos - 2001, C. Wells

Shown above and below, Mid Thirties Deusenberg "Boat Tail".
Photos courtesy of Auburn - Cord - Duesenberg Museum.
Photos - 2001, C. Wells

1935 Auburn. Photo, C. Wells

*Dash of 1935 Auburn shown above. (Note electric shift). Both photos
courtesy of Auburn - Cord - Duesenberg Museum.
Photos - 2001, C. Wells*

1934 Duesenberg

Duesenberg, year unknown. Both photos courtesy of Auburn - Cord - Duesenberg Museum. Photos - 2001, C. Wells

Car radios were unheard of until this era also. By 1937 they were showing up as factory equipment but prior to that they were scarce. Also, they had a remote head with the dial and on/off volume control cables (like speedometer cables) that either went from in-dash or under-dash down to a box on the firewall. City reception could be acceptable but where I was, the nearest (and only) station was WDEV at 550kc in Waterbury. Between the "Farm Report," and many other "unique" programs you might catch "Don Fields and the Pony Boys"!!

This was way too early for FM, so you were stuck with AM reception, which picked up every electric fence and thundershower for miles!

Jumping ahead a moment to 1938. Fred Copeland was another dapper gentlemen. He lived on Highland Avenue and was president of Randolph Savings and Loan. Fred wore the visor cap, a suit and most of the time, a topcoat. Also, he always displayed spats and an umbrella that doubled as a cane. He owned a 1938 blue 4-door Oldsmobile Sedan, but, this one had a hydramatic transmission. The only car I recall prior to the war that had an automatic transmission. I suspect it might *not* have been trouble free!

Left, 1937 Ford V8 4 door, Right, 1937 Nash Lafayette 4 door.
Photo 1946, C. Wells

1937 Nash

By now, I have progressed on to age eight. The year is 1936. My folks, somewhere about this time, bought a new car. This was a Nash, a Lafayette Model. Dad bought it through Pierce's Garage in Randolph. "Dud" Pierce was a customer of RC and Ice and in a small town, reciprocities were always present. This was a middle of the road auto. This had a factory installed hot water heater and displayed many nice qualities. It was a 4-door black sedan. Its 6-cylinder engine delivered about 20 - 22 miles per gallons and, over the years, proved to be reliable, comfortable and enjoyable. It was manufactured by Nash - Kelvinator at that time.

Randolph's Stores

In town, there were three grain and feed stores. Claflins was grain, feed and farm supplies. Dustins was similar. Catlins was right beside the RR track and when a carload of grain arrived, they (two-wheel) trucked it right to the store. Dustins had to unload it to a truck, drive to the store and then unload the truck. Claflins was a feed store and also a meat market with groceries.

Mother shopped at Claflins and Jerd's Market in the Stockwell block, at the intersection of Main and Pleasant Street. Later, Jerd's moved to Merchant's Row. Ed Morse also had a grocery store beside Lamson's furniture store at this time on Main Street.

When you bought groceries at this time, you stood in front of the counter. "One 5 lb. bag of sugar, please," would prompt Ed Morse or Roy Brag to go and fetch it. Returning, he would put it on the counter and likewise for each item desired. Morse's and Jerd's grocery stores both had home deliveries.

Jerd's horse once got spooked on Emerson Terrace and yanked the wagon over the bank! Even though a Tess rein had been put on the ground, the horse still ran!

Pelton's Market was on Merchant's Row but we rarely patronized it because Bill Pelton apparently wasn't a customer. I do remember being inside one time when Bill emerged from the rear of store. It startled me because he was wearing a gas mask! It seems that when he grinds his horseradish, it was so strong, gas masks were needed. I also remember one time Bill was out front on the sidewalk wearing his usual garb of straw hat, white shirt, apron and straw cuff protectors. Right beside his store was a canopy over the sidewalk to protect patrons of the Red Lion Inn whose entrance was there. (Although the Red Lion Inn has been closed for over a half century, I can vaguely remember eating in the dining room which was probably in the middle thirties.) A dog sauntered over, sniffed a canopy base, and proceeded to lift his leg. He-e-e-e ah-h-h shrieked Bill and that poor dog came straight off the sidewalk and peeled out.

As you may surmise, my mother was religious in her belief of patronizing our customers. She even kept track, on a blackboard, which barber I was to patronize next, of the three or four in town at that time.

Claflin's Store

Claflin's Store was diagonally across the street from the "coal office" and even at eight years of age, I spent time there most espe-

Claflin's Store, as mentioned in the text. Grain section is extension in center. Hugh Claflins 1938 Buick is on left - Wayne's 1946 Chrysler convertible at right. Note the two gas pumps, Hugh's house (in center). Photo 1946, C. Wells

cially when they received a carload of feed. Although I couldn't be-gin to move 100-lb. bag of grain, let alone pick one up, one great guy I especially liked, could. His name was Bill Washburn. I used to ride on the truck(s) because each car on the tracks had to be unloaded to a truck and then brought over to the store. Bert Ducharme, Thad Allen, Roy Bragg (shifted employment here), a couple others (I for-get who) were joined by Hugh and Wayne Claflin, the owners. The fact that Dad was insistent that I always "stay back out of the way," I'm sure it paid off by granting me leeway to even be around!

In later years, two well-known people joined the work at Catlin's. One was Freddie Knight in the grain store, (more about him later) and the other was Red Dalton who always dressed as a clown in the July 4th parade because he always was a clown! He was a butcher and obviously worked in the grocery store. (Claflin's was the largest grocery store in town, even when Grand Union or First National came to town in later years.)

1938 International. Claflin's store had two of these. Part of a collection of old trucks - Kemp Bros. Photo 1995, C. Wells

Learning the Hard Way

One day when I was eight (in the second grade), I was alone on the "porch" where trucks were loaded and unloaded, there was a two-wheeled grain truck standing alone with six bags of grain (600 lbs.) waiting to be wheeled inside. So, I reached up and pulled down on the handles. These two-wheel grain "trucks" are well balanced and requires little effort to pull down. Beyond the balance point, it takes great effort to stop the tipping action, as I found out!

Well, you guessed it. The cart didn't stop until the handle hit the floor. Unfortunately.......... my fourth finger on the right hand was more than pinched by the handle! I won't describe the appearance, but, this was serious!! Bill walked me over to the "coal office" where I was loaded in the car, and we went to see...... Dr. Frank! The last section wasn't broken, but it was flattened and was smaller than it *was*. I still have a scar the length of the end section.

Like most kids, I had a sled. And, one of the ways I found to play with a sled is to bend over it, run like hell, then collapse on it and ride a little way. Well, I was doing just that in the winter of 1936. Only, I was careless about the rope, which was trailing behind. While running, I stepped on that rope and the sled stopped dead. My face went down on to the sled and broke one front tooth diagonally. This was the beginning of quite a few problems with that tooth!

Also, by this time, I had an experience with an old non-steerable sled, while a group of us were sledding at Mari Castle, across from Gifford Hospital.

I could see I was heading in a poor direction – you had to steer by dragging one foot. In this case, I dragged both feet and still ended up in a ground level well, or a spring. Whatever it was, by the time I was fished out, I was soaked from head to foot!!! Of course, my sister thought that was *really* funny and ... still does!

Double Duty Grain Bags

By now, a lot of the grain and feed suppliers were shipping some of their "products," as usual, in bags, but not burlap bags. The bags were made of cotton and had prints on them. This allowed the farmers' wives and daughters to make clothing from the bag. A pretty good idea – especially with the effects of the depression still being felt. Now I know the origination of the saying "He (or she) has worn flour sacks for underwear so long, there's dumplings in their drawers!"

Third Grade

At age nine, I entered the third grade of Randolph Graded School. This grade in town was noted for its teacher whose name was Maude Eddy Stokes. Just the name mentioned was enough to evoke fear in the heartiest of school characters. As you might guess, Mrs. Stokes had a Pug also! And, of course, this is where she stored a pencil. It was here we learned the multiplication tables, many other subjects, *and* discipline.

Once a week, the door would open and in came a record player on a high stand with casters, pushed by Miss Mesh, our music teacher. Miss Mesh always wore a Pug, and hers *always* had a pencil sticking out! It was a wind up record player and I was apt to count until the time everything dropped down in pitch when obviously, it required a few more turns of the crank. Miss Mesh was a good music teacher and did succeed in her quest to show us what classical music sounded like. Although her quest was good, my acceptance of classical music was one of the places I found that my ears *must* have had a mute feature.

Passing to fourth grade was a must for everyone that ever graced the third grade and therefore Mrs. Stokes goal must have been achieved with practically no failures. *No one passed* to the next grade with an average below "C" No ifs, ands or buts!!

Learning Music

By this age, my mother insisted that I start to learn music and how to read it at home. My sister, Nan, was well on the way with the violin. I didn't really know what I wanted, but I did know what I didn't want! And that was a violin!! So we spent the first few months on music fundamentals with the help of a piano.

I didn't think my mother wanted anything more than to see or hear me play an instrument or to make music some part of my life. I was rattlebrained, but if that is what she wanted, I really had nothing to say about it. This is how it's going to be and to oppose anything was an exercise in futility. There were *many* times that the tears in my eyes wouldn't stop. My mother really meant well (and for me) but I was an individualist and if I didn't like something, no amount of coaxing, let alone forceful actions, made me any more receptive. The incentive for me was not there and from her an incentive was not needed, you just did it. For instance, I leaned toward popular music, you know, the sheet music stuff. This was not allowed *until* the 60-minute time limit of fundamentals was over. After that, "you can play or whistle what you want"! By then, with tears running down, what I wanted, was out of there. If I spent 20 minutes in the morning before school, 20 minutes at noon during noon hour, this meant I had 20 minutes left after school before I could even leave the house! (No exceptions.)

So for the moment, let's say that I was in the process of learning the fundamentals of music not only from Miss Mesh in school but also from my mother at home. As I recall, this was the schedule for about a year.

Hard Winters

I have to spend a moment about the winters and the snow. There was never a question about having snow for Christmas in the thirties and forties. It was more like having snow for Thanksgiving or even Halloween. Right after Labor Day, the temperature generally dropped. Snow could arrive anytime by the end of October. By Christmas or New Years, a temperature reading of 10 degrees or even zero was common. Two or three weeks in January and the temperature might never rise above zero all day. Also, nights would easily see 30 below for that two or three weeks.

On mornings like these at below freezing, milk, which was delivered at 4 - 5 a.m., if left on the doorsteps would freeze. In the days of glass bottles with flat caps, the milk would freeze and raise the caps off the bottles by two inches.

(These would be the days you would see the "village tea kettle" being fired up.)

It was hard on automobiles, as Ethylene Glycol wasn't around yet, or was not popular. I hardly recall even Alcohol being used in the thirties or early forties, but perhaps it was. The two trucks for

**Selected Songs
Composed in 1937**

Harbor Lights
In the Still of the Night
The Lady is a Tramp
Nice Work, If You Can Get It
Once In A While
Thanks for the Memory
Too Marvelous for Words
Where or When

the coal and fuel business only had water in the radiators. Neither truck had a heater except a two-inch hole cut in the firewall.

Randolph Coal and Ice

Also, starting in the early thirties the ice business had diminished greatly, but fuel oil sales by now had, increased. Also, so had gasoline deliveries to two or three gas stations. My Dad had two trucks by the mid-thirties. One was a 1935 Ford with a wooden non-dump body. I don't recall what the other was, but was probably an early-thirties something or other. This one handled all the coal.

The 1935 Ford mostly was devoted to fuel oil, kerosene and deliveries. He devised a unique system for the 1935. In the body were two removable tanks with 2 by 6 spacers between the tanks and along the outside of each. These spacers were used to deliver bulk jugs of motor oil to gas stations. If another truck was needed for coal deliveries, the Ford would back into the oil tank fill up building, and there, by a winch overhead, both tanks were raised slightly and suspended in air. Each tank only held approximately 210 gallons. As fuel oil sales picked up, he dropped the gasoline delivery service. I'm sure the safety factor came into this, as sooner or later gasoline was bound to show up in someone's fuel tank! The two tanks sufficed, as did the 1935 Ford for many years.

*1935 Ford Truck similar to one used by Randolph Coal & Ice Co.
Photo(s) taken 2001 (National Automobile and Truck Museum of
United States), C. Wells*

**Selected Songs
Composed in 1938**

Falling In Love With Love
Heart and Soul
I'll Be Seeing You
Jeepers Creepers
On Green Dolphin Street
Prelude to a Kiss
September Song

*1935 International Truck similar to one used by Jerds Market -
Randolph. Photo(s) taken 2001 National Automobile and Truck
Museum of United States), C. Wells*

The "crew," at this time, were Ernest Rattee and Elbert Fullam. The bookkeeper was Mary Chase who lived on Weston Street. Ernest and Elbert both lived on Forest Street. Later, when Mary Chase died, Harold Simmons assumed the bookkeeping duties. He lived on Forest Street and his wife ultimately was my seventh grade teacher.

Pierce's Garage

Going into my tenth year, I spent more time at Pierce's Garage. I could get there easily by going half way around the "terrace," cut by the edge of Louie McLean's garden, down the embankment path and come out on Main Street hill right across from the garage.

There was no parking lot. All the cars had to be parked on the street with the exception that there was a drive in basement or lower level right beside Pierce's Gas Station.

To get into the garage part, you entered right off Main Street and drove up a short ramp. The garage was close to the street. There was only room to park a couple of cars parallel with the road. As you

Former Pierce's Garage. Photo 1985, C. Wells

Typical gas pumps used through 30's - 40's - 50's.
National Automobile and Truck Museum of United States, C. Wells

drove up the ramp, the parts room was on the right (with windows along the ramp) and the office was on the left again with windows (and a door).

In the office you would find "Dud" Pierce, the owner, and Allen Hancock, the salesman. The mechanics, Glen Allen, Frank Lamb and later Arnold Rattee worked under hard circumstances. In those days, the lighting was poor, drop lights had to be used constantly, the floor was dirty, so were the windows and the various workbenches were all a mess!

"They" would send me into the parts room for various items or down to Lamson's Hardware Store for bolts or nuts, etc. Most of the time they would write it on a slip of paper what was needed. One time they sent me to Lamson's for a left handed monkey wrench. Another time, for a can of elbow grease! They all had a good chuckle when I returned empty handed.

One time, they had the engine suspended on a hoist and were going to roll the truck back so the engine could be placed on the floor. After one or two attempts and a couple of grunts, Frank Lamb suggested I check to see if it was in neutral. So, ...I did. That was the day I learned that a transmission *plus* an engine were needed to keep a vehicle from moving!

George Sprague owned a local milk bottling plant nearby. He and "Dud" got into a discussion one day about bottles and how if you drop them from an arm straight out and a certain way they would not break. I don't know how many bottles were in a case, but they went through more than a case and also generated quite a pile of glass!

Of course, at this age, I was getting more acquainted with other people in town. I don't think I hindered their work, like at Pierce's Garage. Also mechanics had never heard of the flat rate system back then, so it didn't hurt their pay.

Randolph's Gas Stations - 1938

Stopping for a moment and thinking about gas stations. I mentioned Pierce's Gas Station earlier. That was a Gulf Station. Continuing "down" Main Street going north, at the railroad tracks was a Shell Station, "Tug" Slayton ran. Off Depot Square was an Esso Station Ray Ordway operated about this time. Across the street at Claflin's store were some Texaco pumps. Through Merchant's Row at Pleasant Street was Allen's garage. He had Atlantic Richfield. At the corner of Randolph Ave. and Pleasant St. was a Tydol (Veedol) Station operated by "Fat" Mitchell. Tilson had a small station at the rear of his store. You drove in from Pleasant Street to the pumps. There was room for only one car at a time and the office was about like a cracker box!! He had Sunoco brand. Further north on Pleasant St. at the rear of the Stockwell block down four steps and into a ten by ten room, Harry Hudson (and later, George Manning) had two more Texaco pumps. On Main St., the Richardson family had Cities Service. At the bridge was another set of pumps run by the Pitkins (and later Louie Spaulding). They were Amoco pumps. Not all of these stations were permanent long-lasting businesses, but many were for years. In later years, across the bridge was another gas/convenience store combo that was started by a man, who, at the moment his name escapes me. Later, it was operated by Harold Rogers Sr., Dan Rogers (and his wife), also Elbert Fullam, the brand of gas was Cities Service and also Sinclair.

Allen's Garage

By the time I was born, Allen's garage was in operation and in full swing. George Allen had bought a big house at the intersection of Pleasant St. and Randolph Avenue. It was also right beside the Central Vermont Railroad. Actually, a secondary track started right beside his property and paralleled the main track down around the corner for probably a mile. So, it was nothing to be at the garage and see a big 700 series parked – waiting for its time to move on to the main tracks and head north.

Allen's Garage was a full fledged garage including gas pumps and racks and racks of parts, and also, parts bins.

On one rare occasion, I was also in the attic where there was a "gold mine" of Model "T" parts – many still paper wrapped.

At one time, he sold Nash automobiles – but, I can only remember Studebakers. I know he sold Studebaker trucks in 1937 to Jerd's Market and also, Gordon Labounty. In the late thirties and forties, there was a service staff of his son, Wayne, Elmer Sanford, Ellis Irwin, Joe Untiedt, also, Wilbert Bowen's wife – Helen(?).

Skipping way ahead to the early fifties, I was in the garage when I felt something nudge me in the leg. Looking down, one of George's Bull dogs stood there with a length of heater hose in his mouth! The nudge was an invitation to throw the hose, which he would fetch (forever!!!). I finally got sick of providing "him" attention, so I tried to take it out of his mouth, so I could hide it. He wouldn't let go – so I dragged him over to a bench and cranked that hose in a large bench vise!!! When I left, about 20 minutes later, he was still yanking on that hose, trying to get it away from that vise!!!

Once in a great while, a box car would be placed by the freight house – an auto carrier box car. I never saw the whole operation of unloading the cars. But, George Allen would occasionally order enough cars, at one time, so they would be delivered by this method. Car carriers on the road didn't arrive (that I saw) until after the war.

There were two layers – and it was quite an event to see those cars come out of the box cars through the ends, which were hinged.

Early Movies

Harry Hudson, who operated the *very* small gas station, was also known as the movie man. While there was a movie theatre in town at one time known as The "Strand," many people didn't make the journey into Randolph from surrounding communities. Harry owned a 1936 Chevrolet Sedan and on the rider's side carted a long round tube. It started on the running board at the rear door and continued to the top of the front fender. In it was a full size screen. He carried the film canisters in the trunk. A typical film reel lasted about 20 minutes so generally three canisters were needed for the main feature plus one for any short subjects. He would spot colorful posters advertising next week's or tonight's showing. He mostly used Grange Halls or Town Meeting Halls, etc. The communities of East Braintree, West Braintree, Brookfield, E. Brookfield, Rochester, Gaysville, Barnard, Royalton, S. Royalton, etc. looked forward to movie night by Harry Hudson.

MOVIES
Pierce Memorial Hall

Rochester, Vermont

Friday, 7:30   Saturday, 8:00

EVERYTHING I HAVE IS YOURS

Starring

MARGE & GOWER CHAMPION - DENNIS O'KEEFE

Next Week: "The Savage"

Ad from Herald of Randolph in 1953 similar to that described in text.

Camp Abnaki

When I was ten, clothes were packed for me and before I knew what was happening, I (or we) was headed for Camp Abnaki. This camp, for boys, was located in North Hero, VT. That means it is "in the islands," in Northwest Vermont and which is surrounded by Lake Champlain. I was there for two weeks, and I admit not unpleasant. Each day was tightly scheduled and tightly supervised.

For instance, every morning at 7 a.m. you were brought to life by the sound of Reveille over the P.A. System. Wear what you wanted, but, within 10 minutes you better be standing on the rocky shore of Lake Champlain wearing nothing! About 20 minutes of "swim" time was the normal routine. This was done with a "buddy system" where two people watch out for each other. Periodically, a whistle is blown, you have to find your "buddy" and raise your arms. My big problems were that I'm not crazy about swimming, *especially* in cold water, *more especially* at 7:30 in the morning and *most especially*, butt naked. So - o - o what to do?

My cabin counselor had a big steamer trunk at the end of the aisle in the cabin. The trunk inside faced the wall. I could hide behind the clothes hanging in it. (The other half had drawers, so that side was out.)

Anyway, when the cabin was inspected for stragglers - I was "straggling" behind those clothes and out of sight. That solved part of it, and, if you don't go through the gate to the dock, there's no buddy system for me. That took care of enough so I very seldom went skinny dippin' for those two weeks!

The food was good, but Sunday night was another problem. You couldn't get in the mess hall without showing a letter written to your parents. I still have one letter that I wrote, but I'm not going to display that! After all a letter from a ten year old is not much of a prize – it's more of a *sur*prise.

A show was put together by boy campers of Abnaki and neighboring girl campers at Camp Hochelaga. This was where I was introduced to "A Pretty Girl is Like a Melody," "Top Hat, White Tie, and Tails," and a few more Irving Berlin tunes. To this day, when I either hear (or play) one of those tunes I think of Camp Abnaki.

There were two or three outbuildings spotted throughout the camp. One type was designated an "een." There were no toilet seats,

68

only a trough about 8-feet long and mounted just off the floor. This looked something like a wide sink with a higher back splash. It was here that I realized splatter was *not* a problem. It was also here, I was introduced to the art of writing your initials or as time progressed - your name!

All in all I found that you were busy all day and maybe because sports were always present, I did participate in track. The ribbons displayed, will attest to some success and the lack of others, will also attest to an equal number of failures!

A ten year old's valuable acquisitions.

The Red Comet

I think also about this time (in the late thirties) that Oscar Gates used to trudge around the village carrying a small black suitcase. From this suitcase he sold fire extinguishers under the brand name of "Red Comet." These were quite different. They were made of glass and somewhat teardrop shaped. There was a bracket (metal) that was attached to the wall, door jam, etc. The glass "container" nestled into the bracket with the smaller end down. The bracket was heat sensitive with a small spring compressed behind a solder "seal." As heat from the fire would heat the solder seal the spring would smash the glass releasing the liquid onto the floor. The liquid was Carbon Tetrachloride.

"Our" house had a pyrenne hand pump fire extinguisher near the front door. The fluid was Carbon Tetrachloride (with a very distinct odor). At the time, it apparently was very effective at quenching a fire. More so than water! It now has been established that this "liquid," when heated, develops into a deadly gas, so for that reason, these types of extinguishers are no longer common.

Playing Cards

My folks were apt to have 12 or 16 people in during the evening for card playing. Cribbage was probably the main game. I can remember sandwiches, pastries, etc. The living room was large enough to set up four card tables easily. I think the most interesting part that I now think about is that name, religion or occupational title was not a plus for anybody or a minus. The conversation was not much different, mostly news in general, family or kids, etc.

However, I should point out that the word pregnant was never used at this house! Also, many other words! Mother was very strict in many ways! I never saw Dad have a beer in the house, let alone drink one!! No booze either!! Also, you *never* told anyone to "shut up," you didn't interrupt when someone was talking, you waited until they were finished. Break any of the rules (amongst others) and you were in deeeeep doo doo!

You may now have a premonition of how I will enjoy some fun times in the years ahead. But at this point in time, my first years, are going to be somewhat bland.

Freedom While Young

Certainly there were many places I just could not wander into at random, and, by ten years of age, I had freedom and could be anywhere and everywhere in the village. Most stores, I stayed out of and you just couldn't hang around inside. I also didn't hang around on the street. This held true especially "downtown" where the stores were. It's sad that most of this freedom, if not all of it, has disappeared from most every city and town in the country.

Central Vermont Railroad Station

I did spend time at the railroad station. Cedric Clark would sit me on the counter. The building was constructed with a protrusion so he could sit at his desk and look at the tracks in both directions.

If he sat on the counter, so could I! He could be talking or working, with two or three telegraphs clicking away and all of a sudden, take the pencil off his ear and start writing. I never could understand how he would know when to write or even when to listen with so many telegraphs clicking away all at once.

He would often let me hold the hoop for a passing train. A hoop was a round piece of wood about the diameter of a pen and shaped

Depot in Randolph. Note the angled window(s) so the station agent could observe trains. Photo 1985, C. Wells

with a "handle" which graduated to a large loop about two feet in diameter. At the crossover point was a spring loaded pinch point. An "order" was folded and placed under the pinch point. By standing on the platform and holding the hoop up, the fireman would stick his arm out, and as he passed by would pick that hoop up on his arm. He would remove the "order" and toss the hoop out on to the ground, which I would run to and retrieve! All this took place while you're standing only four or five feet back from the engine (and cars) as it sped by. But, Cedric would be standing right there as a precaution.

Freight Station

Sam Bullard was the freight agent and he always liked to have a visitor in the freight house. So did Eddie Smith, who would take me along as he delivered various and many boxes of freight or Railway Express parcels.

While we're "downtown" as it was commonly referred to, or "overstreet" as others referred to it, the business "district" had quite a few stores. One, "The Thomas Store" was a ladies' store. Beside Mr. Chadwick (the owner), the store, over the years, employed quite a few local women. Among them was Jane Wadleigh who always used her hair for a pencil holder (even without a pug), and later Ruth Cooper, also, Mrs. Phelps. Obviously, at my now "grown" age I didn't go in there at all. But I do remember the wood floors (that creaked occasionally), the wood counters, the many drawers, etc. in back of the counters, dozens of them, all oak and apparently custom made at the location. Potted plants (palm tree and all) were spotted around. Also, it had a vacuum tube system, for money, which always held my attention! Quite an unusual store for a small town! It survived for *many* years.

Lamson's Hardware

Lamson's Hardware Store for those days was also impressive. The amount of stock stashed there was amazing. The basement also was full of stock as was the second floor. The third floor was a work area where such things as heat ducts, etc. were made. The store had a small elevator but no passengers rode it.

"Section Gang" transportation before a modified truck could ride the rails. This unit was used in 30's - 40's - 50's. This was powered by a gas engine (controls can be seen). A flat belt would connect engine to wheels which always squealed. It was stored in a building between freight house and Windsor City Farmers Exchange. Kemp Trucks. Photo 1995, C. Wells

"Old" Freight station (before restoration). Approx 1985, C. Wells. Note: RC&O oil tanks on left.

The cellar also had a glass cutting setup down there and various pipes, pipe cutter, etc. They got the pipe down there through a 4-inch cast iron drainpipe buried in the rear door platform.

The story goes that Fred Warner was pulling a pipe (21 feet long) out from the cellar when a crash ensued. Of course the pipe protruded into the street and into the path of an oncoming car. There was a crash and Fred looked like a pinwheel spinning around with that pipe. Fortunately, he wasn't hurt but the car had to have at least, two headlights replaced.

Lamson's Hardware Store was staffed by Primus, who, with his son Bill, who also worked at the store, lived in a well-maintained older house at the corner of Salisbury St. and Franklin St. Also, John who lived on Highland Avenue. His son, Jack worked in the store. John was *well* experienced in this trade as was Primus. This is no downgrade to Bill or Jack. John, when asked for a rare item, would start to hum as the memory bank started a "pass and review"! Subconsciously, he would mutter "pommety - pommety - pommety" as he walked toward the rear of the store. For that reason, he was hereafter known as Pommety-Pom Lamson!

Very rarely did anyone ask for an item and fail to have that item put in their hands.

Lamson's Furniture Store

W.E. Lamson was a furniture store about two doors from Lamson's Hardware Store. (To my knowledge the two families were not related). There were also gifts, toys and books. At the rear of the first floor, there was also a large freight elevator beside the rear door. A ride on this was always fun, and it happened once in a while due to more furniture on display on the second floor. Never *did* get up to the third floor and it was a while before I found out why.

This was where Leslie did the embalming for his funeral business and that explained the "freight" elevator. He used his house on Prospect Avenue for funeral services. This house was a large residence with a big round window facing the street. The house had a circular drive with a barn type garage away from the house. He used the "garage" to store his hearse, flower car, etc. along with two (or three) personal cars. There were two or three horse stalls, also.

Music Shop, former Scribner Store (Wilcox prior to that) and Former Lamson Hardware. Photo 1985, C. Wells

Main Street. Photo 1985, C. Wells

Main and Pleasant Streets, Randolph 1929.
From a collection owned by Mr. & Mrs. A. Floyd.

Main and Pleasant Streets, Randolph. Photo 2000, C. Wells

*Depot Square 1929 From a collection owned by
Mr. & Mrs. A. Floyd.*

*Junction of Rt. 12 & 12A. Morse Grist Mill on right near bridge.
Photo 1907. From a collection owned by Mr. & Mrs. A. Floyd.*

Main St. Bridge, Randolph. Photo 1907.
From a collection owned by Mr. & Mrs. A. Floyd.

Elm, Forest and Central St. Randolph. Photo 1910(?).
Note: Elm St. was Greenhouse St.)
From a collection owned by Mr. & Mrs. A. Floyd.

Summer St. Randolph. Date unknown.
From a collection owned by Mr. & Mrs. A. Floyd.

Prospect Ave., Randolph. Date unknown.
From a collection owned by Mr. & Mrs. A. Floyd.

PROSPECT AVE. AND PROSPECT ST., RANDOLPH, VT.

Homeowners as of 1940's.
(L - R) Clarke, Priest, Huse, Austin, McIntyre, Slack. Photo 1913
From a collection owned by Mr. & Mrs. A. Floyd.

Former Lamson Residence, Prospect Ave. Randolph VT. Note: large
barn/garage. Present owner – Mr. & Mrs.Bill Brigham. Photo 1999, C.
Wells

Lots of Polish

Somewhere about this time Leslie hired me to polish the funeral vehicles. I was about ten years old. (I'm sure my Dad played a part in this.) I worked on the hearse first. It had to be washed, then polished with Dupont #7 and then the final coat was Simonize. This process took about three days – all by hand.

I received two dollars for doing the hearse! Believe me, I knew what the name Henney stood for. It stood for work. (That was the coach maker.) I then did one of the other vehicles the same way and finally the last one. I don't remember what I was paid for those!

Stores In the Village

At various times through the thirties, many other stores were present. Some were gone fairly soon, others lasted for years.

Grants Drug Store was on the street level of the Sowles' block. The Grants lived right across the street from us. (They were the first house on Prospect Ave.) And they also were next door neighbors of "Dr. Frank." They owned the drug store there for years, I vaguely recall a soda fountain but I was too young to remember it extensively.

If the public wanted a soda fountain, they could go next door to "The Spot." This was operated by the Neil Family. Later the Mazzolini family operated it. Here, you could have a soda, milk shake or ice cream along with various and many types of candy, including penny candy, boxed candies but not the cheap stuff! Whenever they made a milk shake, a half-pint of milk was removed from the flip top fountain. The cardboard top was removed, etc. You could not use milk from a quart bottle, Vermont Law, at that time, did not allow "bulk" dispensing!

This was a nice "spot" to meet someone, have a cool drink. The dark wood cabinets in back of the soda fountain even on the other side of store, again must have been custom made at the site.

Sometime around now, there was another drug store that opened by Fred Osborne. I think it was the same location that Dell Wood had a small Luncheonette, with a soda fountain. Neither lasted much over a year. It certainly would be tough to compete against the two neighbors described earlier. This site changed again in the years to

Depot 1900 Both Photos from the A. Floyd collection.

Date Approx 1940.

82

*So. Main St. and Depot Square. Date approx 1915.
Both photos from the A. Floyd collection.*

*Salisbury Street – Hugh Claflin house on right.
Approx date 1905.*

Sowles Hall on the right, with Grants Drug Store at street level. Double doors go "up" to the hall. (Note: steps referred to for band concerts). "Johns" Restaurant is at the left. Note the canopy for the Red Lion Inn (vacant). described in the text. Photo 1946, C. Wells

come. There was also a time that there was a Bell's Millinery Store. Later Jerd's Market and a Freezer Locker Store. (More on this later.)

Before we go to the other side of Merchant's Row, let's go upstairs over all (or most all) of the stores just discussed. Above these, was Sowles Hall. This block was owned by Dr. John Sowles, a dentist who lived in town and had his offices on Merchant's Row. Sowles Hall was a combination basketball court, exhibition hall and whatever it was called to do. Access to the hall was on the West end facing "Depot Square." There was a wide set of concrete stairs, probably 25 feet wide with a total of about 12 steps.

During the summer months, platforms were placed on the steps which gave a good place for the Green Mountain Band (Randolph Town Band) to present band concerts, Friday or Saturday nights, for about an hour in length.

"Beyond" the top step to the right was a storefront, for the most part occupied by Dell Scribner, who operated a pool and billiard room from about 1938 to about 1952. Prior to that Robert Mayo operated a funeral business, also "Bucks" Printing Business was here. On the left side was a store which for a time Conrad Sault and

**Selected Songs
Composed in 1939**

All The Things You Are
Bubbles In The Wine
Don't Worry Bout Me
I'll Never Smile Again
It's A Blue World
Over The Rainbow
What's New

"others" used as a barber shop, etc. In the middle was another set of stairs (about 10 feet wide) which went up a full flight to Sowles Hall.

Today, looking back, it's hard to believe all high school basketball games were played here including a couple when Randolph ended up as state champions. The floor wasn't flat – it had a noticeable "wave" to it. Must have put an additional "flavor" into dribbling a basketball! On the court sides were two coal burning stoves or space heaters which helped human body heat warm up the place. Imagine running into one of these in the "heat of the game"! There was a one-door fire escape on the track side which continued on to an iron ladder down to the ground. Equally scary!

I remember, on more than on occasion, donkey basketball was played in the hall, which meant the donkeys and all that gear had to climb the stairs (and come back down). Also, roller-skating was another sport held in the hall.

On the other side of Merchant's Row, Raymond Jarvis had a large bakery. Later, he moved to a smaller store a couple of doors away and First National Stores moved into his previous spot. The bakery was nicknamed "Rubbercrust."

Also, on Merchant's Row going East, a shoe repair shop where Paul Miner who worked not only on shoes, but also harnesses.

Next to Miners was Central Vermont Public Service, the electric headquarters where power appliances were sold and serviced and also where you paid your electric bill.

A very small storefront was sandwiched between Central Ver-

Randolph stores remained about the same mid late thirties, through the war into mid forties. Above are Main St. stores - east side. Although Morse's store at one time was "Pleez-ing" it is pictured as "Nation Wide". Photo 1946, C. Wells

mont Public Service and the U.S. Post Office. Oh yes, a door for going upstairs over the Post Office to office space. Dr. John Sowles had his Dental office(s) upstairs here. (Previously mentioned)

During Fourth of July celebration, a couple times, fences were put up at each end of Merchant's Row. Sawdust was spread over the pavement and street dancing took place. Patch's Gift Store and Photography Services were on that intersection, also Tilson's Insurance Agency and "Pep" Blanchard (who gave piano lessons) was there.

Before we leave, on Main St. in the "square," Tewsbury and Raymond occupied the big brick building with a fine clothing store and next door was Totman's Florist, who also had larger greenhouses on Sand Hill.

Next door was "Chic" Steele's Barber Shop where he was helped by Raymond Campbell and Merrill Campbell (who were unrelated). Of course, Merusi's small but everlasting fruit store with its soda fountain, magazines, etc. had a three-generation ownership with Louie, his son Emil and *his* son Primo before it succumbed. Further North on Main St. was Leonard's. (We previously mentioned The

Main St. Randolph. Note Barber Pole – left.
From a collection owned by Mr. & Mrs. A. Floyd.

Replica of Leonard's Drug Store on display at Randolph Historical
Museum. Courtesy of Randolph Historical Society.
Printed by RAVC Graphics 1991

Thomas Store, W.E. Lamson and Lamson's Hardware Store.) In the thirties Ed Morse had a small grocery Store (next to W.E. Lamson) and operated under the name of Pleez-ing and/or Nation Wide. Leonard's Drug Store was another three-generation store with Henry, his son Laurence, *his* son Larry, (I think operated it for a short time). This was unique and can now partially be viewed at the Randolph Museum.

Randolph National Bank was between the two Lamson Stores and further North was another hardware store owned by Walter Wilcox, later to become Scribners, which would be Gordon Scribner. (More about this later.) The last store in the big block was Mitchells Clothing Store, which was only men's clothing.

Next was the Christian Science Church property and at the intersection of Main and Pleasant St. was a wood building housing Stockwell's Clothing Store, McLeans Day Cleaners, Jerd's Market (who soon moved to Merchant's Row) and the George Rye Barber Shop.

George, for a while had another barber who worked there by the name of Harold Sault. Rumor, by the way of Dave Barnard, (and passed to me) has it that, someone asked George "if he hadn't been there quite a while"? (He had.) But George said "You see that big maple tree on the lawn over by the Baptist church?" The affirmative reply prompted George to add, "Back when I first started here, once in a while, I'd look out and see an Indian peeking at me from around that tree"!!

Hayward's Diner occupied a very small piece of land where the streets meet. This Diner was originally "Abares." When Percy Abare moved on, "Spud" Coffin took it over. Sometime along here, a fire ripped the place apart. After it was rebuilt, it operated under the name of

Replica of George Rye's Barber Shop. Courtesy of Randolph Historical Society. Printed by RAVC, 1991

88

Depot Square, Randolph. Photo 1928.
From a collection owned by Mr. & Mrs. A. Floyd.

Haywards Diner. Percy moved to Royalton and opened the Atlantic Diner at Route 14 and 107 by the Hop Vine Tearoom. Spud Coffin moved to Beanville and became an appliance dealer with the Frigidaire brand and later branched into furniture.

Spud had John James for a Frigidaire salesman and he was certainly well known, in the whole central part of Vermont. However, this is way ahead in time.

Green Mountain Inn

At the end of Randolph Avenue, facing the avenue, on a hill was a large hotel called Green Mountain Inn. This was quite a building with awnings over the windows and a canopy over the driveway and entrance. People named Kimball owned it and I believe lived in the smaller house adjacent to it. In the rear was a 9 hole golf course which now has been expanded to 18 holes.

At one time, James Cagney stayed here while he negotiated for one of the popular and well-known Morgan horses at the Green Mountain Stock Farm, in the middle thirties. The building later was transformed into Tranquility Nursing Home.

Country Club, Randolph, Vt.

Originally the Kimball Residence, later called The Country Club,
then the Green Mountain Inn. Also, Tranquility Nursing Home.
From a collection of Mr. & Mrs. A. Floyd.

Ray's Esso Station

Ray Ordway at this time (in 1938) operated the Esso Station.
For about 10 years prior, the Esso station was operated by Harold
Simmons, and his brother, Asa, operated an Esso station in
Bethel. Ray didn't do any mechanical work, only pump gas. If
someone asked him to check the oil - watching the hood get raised,
etc. was apt to be *quite* a procedure.

Ray was very short and very small. His handkerchief always
protruded so far out his rear pocket, it was always drooping. He
liked me to visit him, I'd hop out, pump gas, check the oil and tires,
if necessary, and he would only have to do some conversing with
the customer!

Of course, I did this without pay which probably pleased him.
One thing you *don't* do is to shut the cold water faucet off in the
utility sink by the desk!!! There was no refrigerator, so Ray kept a
quart of beer under the faucet and the cold water dribbling down
over the bottle seemed to perform adequately.

One other thing. I never touched (or drank) the beer and I suspect this may have pleased him also!!

On the south side of the railroad tracks, the business section is almost as it is today, meaning the building placement. Of course the businesses were different then.

Hotel Maples

The only significant difference is that the Hotel Maples is long gone. It was a large wooden building with a large porch covering the entire front. On the right was a driveway to a couple of garages in the rear. There was a also a canopy here (on the right side). You could park, climb a couple steps up to the porch, and after winding between a few rockers, enter the lobby to be greeted by either Henry or Lula Batchelder. The lobby was always quiet, the only sound coming from the big clock on the wall as it ticked time away. We used to eat here occasionally on Sunday at noon. Believe me when I say that this (for many reasons) certainly was not the highlight of *my* day, or even week! (not the hotel, or owners.)

My mother was so strict, I dared not move!

Up to Prospect Street

Up Main St. Hill (going south) and half way up, a left turn on Prospect St. would bring you to an *old* vacated house on the right. Just beyond, was Lew Brighams house. That old empty house must have bugged him! Windows were open, curtains flying, porch falling down, you know what it probably looked like.

Early Age Troubles

One day a few (three or four) of us went inside. We certainly didn't pick anything up or clean it up! We added to the mess.

Anyway, my Dad asked if I knew who went inside and made the mess. I told him I was one with so and so. A few days later we received a letter from Atty. Phil Angell (Judge of the Probate Court), we all had an appointment to be in front of him at a given date and time. My Dad ensured that I would be there. He didn't have to be there. Anyway, we were given a stern lecture about trespassing, vandalism, etc., etc. We never did anything like that again. But, that's how you learn!

A few weeks later, the house was demolished and removed, big garage/barn and all. It was *years* before I finally added that up, and I think that was my Dad's idea with Phil Angell carrying the ball!! (It worked)!

Braintree Hill Properties

About here is when my Dad bought two properties on Braintree Hill right at the top of Grant Flint's Road.

One just had a house on it. The other had a barn and a real old square house with about five chimneys on it. It was bad, but it really had gone beyond "bring back." Inside was an old piano which he salvaged the black notes and the ivories for inlaid purposes.

He bought the properties with the idea of creating ski trails down toward W. Braintree Road. Time, money and ultimately, the war, kept that idea from happening.

However, the old house was taken down rather quickly leaving the barn which was still very solid. Also, there was a good 6x6 building, fairly new, that Phil McIntyre and I got to place in back of

Balance of property on Braintree Hill once owned by A.C. Wells.
Photo approx 1985, C. Wells

"his" house near where my sister took her famous ride in the "cross" box! We used to sleep in it. Later, it ended back up on Braintree Hill serving a worthwhile purpose. (More on that later).

Rogers Esso Station

The Esso Station in Depot Square was now under the operation of Alton Rogers along with his wife. I still pitched in there periodically (without pay). They were nice people and did appreciate what help I gave. (I think anyway!!)

Learning To Drive

Also, the Montague golf course was now taken care of by Walter Ordway. After pitching in there a few times, Wally taught me how to drive the Model A tractor with the big steel rear wheels with short bolts protruding for traction. This was exciting for an 11 year old!

Webster's Saw Mill

L.W. Webster had a sawmill at the end of Pearl Street. Donald Laskey lived in the last house – his father, Pearl, worked for "L.W." as a truck driver.

Don and I used to climb the various piles of lumber stacked in rows beyond the sawmill. This was the "lower mill" and was used periodically to cut lumber only. Hemlock and spruce were the main logs sawn. I don't know what the crew did when the mill wasn't sawing. We used to watch the carriage run the logs by the huge circular saw (of course from a distance).

When the mill was idle, it was awesome to see the big one cylinder steam engine. It had a fly wheel about 10 feet in diameter and really snorted and hissed when it was working. The lumber was rough cut and stacked for a natural air dry process. Stacks and stacks of it!

By now, I had my twelfth birthday and also about now was when the work started bringing in some pay. Wow this was something! Before, anything was play and I did it for free. Now it was called work and I got paid!!

L.W. Webster (Lower Mill) Pearl St. Randolph. Photo approx 1994, C. Wells

Small model of steam engine referred to in text. Photo approx 1994, C. Wells

More lumber was stacked on the right side of the vertical road.
Photo 2001, C. Wells

Selected Songs
Composed in 1940

Bewitched
Fools Rush In
I Could Write A Book
Imagination
Lets Get Away From It All
Nearness of You
Taking a Chance on Love
Tuxedo Junction
When You Wish Upon A Star

U.S. Soil Conservation

One part time job was for the U.S. Soil Conservation office in Randolph. I was one of about seven or eight hired to plant trees at various locations in Orange County (VT) The supervisor was Rudy Day. He, and "the crew" would load into a 1937 Ford Sedan (the office had two or three of these). This was no easy job for Rudy, who is about 6' 5", to climb into this undersized car! The engine in this car was *not* the standard V8 engine of 85-horsepower. This was a V8, only it was a 60-horsepower! Ford probably sold one of these 60-hp for each 100 or more of the 85-hp. I don't think the cylinder heads were more than 12" long! Of course, they gave better mileage because the pistons were smaller. Rudy had quite a time driving it because his big work shoes would bridge over the brake and gas pedal. The clutch and brake pedal were about 2½" in diameter.

One day near the stock farm we were in mud ruts and then stopped. The ruts were so deep we were dragging. So we all grabbed the back end, picked it up and set it over onto high ground. Likewise for the front end – climbed in and away we went!

Covered Bridge in back of former Edson Gifford Farm in East Randolph, VT. Fur trees in back planted by soil conservation in 1940. Photo approx 1999, C. Wells

Once we arrived at a location, three bigger guys would operate a mattock to break the soil and turn it over. Two others would distribute the tiny saplings near the spot and three others inserted the sapling and packed it in.

A gopher hole or woodchuck hole was apt to receive six to twelve saplings, just to insure one of them would root!

The only place I *recall* where we planted, was in back of Edson Giffords house on a hill in East Randolph. Pay was $.25/hr and after a couple weeks was raised to $.35/hr. I recall we planted totally about 10,000 trees.

Ring - As a Token

About age 12, I had made the acquaintance of a girl, a cute girl. Now, this was or could be called smitten by her. I don't remember this, but it was brought to my attention as being true.

I wanted to express my feelings to her. I couldn't tell her – didn't know how! (Hey, I'm only a little kid!) I couldn't give her any gift, didn't have any money. *So*, I decided to give her a ring — a diamond ring which belonged to my mother! I didn't know what a diamond was. Anyway, my mother noticed at once it was gone, put things together to believe I had taken it.

In the meantime, somewhere I lost it in the snow. I don't know who found it or where, but it was found. Apparently my hormone engine had *started* and this girl knew how to work the "clutch"!! Knowing my mother, she probably warmed my butt enough so I could have melted all the snow!

This fall (of 1940, age 12) my mother had taught me all the piano she could stand. We had gone from music fundamentals to elementary piano. I had no desire to continue with this – it was not fun.

It was what I could later call, hell. It was so regimented and so forced. My mother would lay a yardstick on the black notes. If the "practice" session was not going adequately, she would come in from the kitchen, grab that yardstick and rap me across the knuckles!!

After a few raps and as I had grown older, one day I laughed! (It hurt, but I laughed). She snapped that stick in half, put the two halves together and rapped me again!

The way I was learning piano, I now realize, would be similar, as an analogy, to building a house. Instead of building the house, we're into a full-fledged background explanation of how nails are made, different sizes, etc., how wood is grown, cut, sized, etc. I didn't care about all that. I just wanted to see some pieces together! With the piano, we had to practice the scales, the notes, the fingering, the length of time for different notes, the staffs and all that claptrap.

Let me play a tune, a tune I know, kindle the interest and then minimize or eliminate the problem(s)! Boy, she wouldn't budge on any of that. But, she would let me change to trumpet.

Cornet Lessons

So, I was signed up with a Mr. Slack in South Royalton and he let me borrow (or rent) a cornet. This was a really stubby cornet and had a pouch it was carried in.

1916 Maxwell

At this time in 1941, friends Stan Gould, Billy Slack, Otis Smithers and I chipped in and bought a car! None of us was old enough to have a drivers license, but "Oatey" lived on Maple St. and in back of his Dad's house was a big garage/barn, which had a ravine in back leading down to a flat pasture.

We bought a 1916 Maxwell Touring Sedan. This was not quite a car, it was an absolute jewel. We bought this car from Allen Battles, a gentleman in town who ran a garage for years. We paid ten dollars for the car. He had this car in storage in a building across the street. It had not been on the road for years. For a 1916, this car had a regular clutch, a three speed

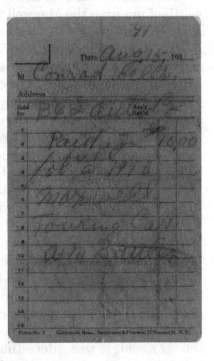

Receipt for 1916 Maxwell in 1941

"stick" transmission and a starter. Bear in mind, all model "T" Fords had to be cranked. Their electric starter didn't arrive until 1921. Also, all Model "T" Fords had a three pedal planetary transmission until 1928 when the model "A" arrived. (More on this later).

We couldn't drive it on the streets, so Max Shapiro drove it for us. Going up Main St. Hill, we barely made it to the top in second gear. When we went back to ask George Battles if that was typical, he asked us if we had the scissors stuck in the ignition switch?! Poking around, on the floor was a pair of plain steel scissors. He stuck them in the key opening of the ignition switch while saying something to the effect of "always going to take care of that." Anyway, the next time we tried Main St. Hill (with the same number of people) we literally flew over the top in third gear! I now suspect the electrical connection from the magneto to the coil, through the ignition switch, was very poor. Also, the battery was nearly flat – so the coil was putting out a very "insecure" spark! The scissors helped make a good magneto connection.

Through the summer and into the fall we all had our ten dollars worth of fun from the Maxwell. We had the top up, we had the top down. It ran great!

One day, we blew a tire. We certainly couldn't buy a tire or a tube. We used to collect coins so we could buy gasoline. I think a gallon of gas was eighteen cents! If we had fifteen cents between us, we'd walk "downstreet" and buy fifteen cents worth of gas in a one gallon maple syrup can. So if we had trouble with money like this, how could we possibly get a tire fixed. Stan Gould says, "I got an idea." "Oatey" Smithers father kept a few goats in the barn/garage in the rear of the house. In the barn were oats he fed the goats. So, we demounted one side of the tire after we removed the rim from the car. We stuffed as many oats as we could into the tire and then stuffed the bead into the rim. I wasn't very sure this was going to work because it wasn't hard enough until he turned the garden hose on into the valve stem hole. We waited for the oats to expand. Before the day had passed the tire was hard enough to drive on!! While I wouldn't recommend this especially for street purposes, it did last on the soft ground for a couple hours and then as they dried out and compressed, the tire bead came loose and while sitting in the rear seat, it was interesting to watch the fine stream of oats forming a pinwheel as we zipped along! Well, when this didn't work for long, we found that the rim alone worked on the soft ground. So we didn't cry too badly when the next tire blew!

The ravine was "L" shaped with a fair size field on the long side of the "L." One side of the "foot" part of the "L" was wooded, the opposite side was quite steep with only one tree.

One day we found some heavy wire and an old barn door "pulley." We secured the wire to the single tree and across the ravine to a tree near the bottom. What a ride we could get, after Oatey volunteered to try it the first time! You darn sure better let go at the right time. Too soon, - you were too high off the ground and too late - you would run right into the tree!! But, the ride was enough to utter a quick wh-e-e-e!

Scrounging around, we found enough decent lumber and built a camp at the bend of where we drove the car. We were always building a camp. Up on top of the ravine side, we built one previously, another up in a big pine tree and even one in an old cellar hole.

But this one, this one had a door, a window (opening but no glass) and four bunks. One night, we were allowed to sleep in this one.

Before we went to sleep, we heard a strange noise, and again, and quite repetitively. Next thing we knew, through the window opening, a cow ran a rough tongue up the side of Stan's head! The noise we heard was the cow chewing!

As the nights turned cooler, because fall settled in, we always tried to park the Maxwell up the ravine. At the top here was a place to turn around at the side of the barn. One cool morning, we noticed that "steam" was rising from a sizable area more to the rear of the barn - the area where the goat manure was dumped when the barn was cleaned!

From that day on, in cool weather we would park the Maxwell on the goat manure pile and the engine stayed enough warmed so it started easier. How surprising it was to stand there and feel the warmth float up your pant legs. I'm not positive but I don't think the Maxwell survived the winter well and by next spring, or at least early summer, we sold the car to Clark Hunt for four dollars and a quarter! What a shame – that car today would be worth thousands.

Mason's Lawn

About this year (in the summer) Stan got a job mowing the lawn at the Mary Mason Farm. The farm was operating at this time, but apparently the "hired hands" weren't require to mow this lawn. The house was large with an equally *large* porch that overlooked the "valley." It was on the road to "Peth" and the view could be beautiful, especially with the lawn and landscaping. There were *no* landscaping or commercial grounds keepers. The community really couldn't support one. The front lawn was terraced with small shrubs about every eight feet at the edge of each terrace. There was probably six terraces starting at the street *up* to the porch. Each terrace started at the driveway and went across the front and around to the side for a linear length of approximately eighty feet. We did the back yard, also which was a slight incline. No power mowers, we used two reel type mowers for all the grass and then hand trimmed. For all this, his pay was three dollars and mine was two dollars. It took all day!!

Gaspé Trip

Somewhere around this time, my folks took a one week trip with Dr. and Mrs. Eaton, who were good friends. They toured around what they called the Gaspé Peninsula in Quebec. They drove because the Eatons were enough older I doubt if either *could* drive. I mention this trip because its the only trip or vacation I ever knew them to take, together.

Dads Temperament

As a matter of fact, it's the only trip I ever knew Dad to take outside of Randolph except to go to Chelsea, VT, the county seat, for court purposes. I can't give an explanation why. I don't think they fought or got on each others nerves. As a matter of fact, I can't remember *one* occasion where I saw my Dad express anger, or even raise his voice to my mother *or anyone*! I'm sure there were times he might like to, but I also, don't recollect her ever being angry toward him.

THIS SNOWPLOW WAS built in 1895 and has a wood body and frame. (Jim McFarlane photo)

SNOWPLOW 4204 is a sister to the 4203 pictured above. It was rebuilt in 1954 and is seen here on a storage track in Brattleboro yard. (Homer R. Hill photo)

Courtesy of Robert C. Jones

Three Judges of Orange County Court - Chelsea, VT. A.C. Wells on left. Photo approx 1941, The Herald of Randolph

Local Murder

Sometime, around 1940, there was a murder in town. This was almost unbelievable! The victim was the wife of a man named Kenneth Norton. A suspect was arrested. The case was tried in Orange County Court, and, of course my Dad was one of the side judges. He didn't talk about the case during trial and little after the verdict of which I don't remember, other than I *think* he was found guilty.

Bert Starts Bide-A-While

On the northern "outskirts" of Randolph, which is Forest Street (also Route 12), was an old house. This is beyond where a brook crosses Rt 12. The house had been for sale for quite a period of time. No one made an offer until Bert Day finally bought it, price unknown. His idea was to remodel it into a residence. It had many nooks and points of interest and, I guess, woodwork that was of interest. I was never in the house. There were about 12 acres of land with it. Bert

Person in the yard is Barbara (Day) Lindquist.

Marietta and Russell Day - 1941.

loved ventures such as this, showed it to his wife and three children. Anyway, the next time he took them there to see the place, the house was gone!

Later, in its place, he built a new house, a two-story Colonial style house. It was named Bide-A-While. The pictures show two sides. The house was probably too far gone for a practical restoration.

Rogers Family

There was more than one Rogers family in the area. But, one family in particular comes to mind for numerous reasons. First, the total number of children. Second, of the five brothers that I know, were all blessed with great personality traits. They didn't let their mishaps or hardships show. They always had a smile. Third, all five were hard workers and, I mean *hard* workers.

Not trusting my recollection of 60 years, I gathered some info that I could trust. Robert and Bessie Rogers had sixteen children total with this breakdown:

1/ Harold
2/ Gladys
3/ Robert
4/ Bill
5/ Woodrow (Bucky)
6/ Don
7/ Duane
8/ Rita
9/ Nina
10/ Richmond
11/ Rose
12/ Clifford (Pete)
13/ Chester (Chet)
14/ Lucille
15/ Lawrence
16/ Betty

I first got acquainted with Bucky and Bill. I don't have the vaguest idea why or how I used to ride with them while they went after a load of pulp. I'm sure I wasn't over 12 years old, but, I loved trucks and these were large trucks at that time. I would ride in the middle. Each time, which ever one was driving, turned off the road, the road got smaller, narrower and bumpier. Soon, there wouldn't be any road – just a trail into woods or whatever until you came to a large stack of pulp. Actually it was long rather than large.

Both would start throwing sticks of pulp up on the truck. Shortly, one would jump up on the truck and pile it up. A cord is made up of 4 foot sticks, stacked 4 feet high and 8 feet long. One row on each side about 10 feet long and one row across the back 8 feet wide would total about six cords to a load. Stand on top of this, look down or around and this is like riding a bungalow through the woods! Riding up high when it is moving, it rolls, it pitches, it hesitates, it groans and it screams. All of this with only approximately 140 horsepower and a truck rated one and a half tons which is actually lugging around 11 or 12 tons!

Don Rogers Comes Home

Jumping ahead, sometime about 1945, Don came home on leave from the service. His daughter was to have a serious operation. He was on a 30 day leave. Knowing he didn't have a 1000 dollars to pay for this, he approached L.W. Webster in Randolph. "L.W." owned a wood working mill in town, which you will hear more about in pages to come.

Don asked "L.W." if he had any pulp to be "picked up" which meant brought from the woods to a rail car (a box car). "L.W." asked Don where he was going to get a helper. (There was a war on. All men were gone.) Don bluffed his way through this and asked "L.W." to get two box cars. Which came the reply, that only two days could go by before demurrage would start (a fine by the RR for tying up a car). The next morning, two box cars were spotted on a siding near Claflin's feed store. Don loaded the first car the first day – alone. This would be about five trips to total about 30 cords.

Up at 4 a.m. the second day, Don was loading the second car when "L.W." drove up. "Where's your helper"? Don said he'd be back at which point "L.W." said "Boy, you're going to have to pay the demurrage, you're only half through the first car in two days.

He would work between 12 and 20 hours a day. Don said *this* car would be ready by 3 p.m. to ship it out and the other is full now. It was said, Don did unload one truckload by hand in as little as 15 minutes. Standing there, you could hear each stick as it hit the end of the car, meaning he'd stand at the door, pull a stick off the truck and toss it half the length of a box car! No difference if it was about 3 inches in diameter or 15 inches!!

One time, Don drove a full load up to a box car at the same time Lemy Huntley and two helpers arrived. Don turned around to unload the second side, finished it – all alone – and was leaving at the time the other truck (with three men) was just turning around!

At the end of 30 days, "L.W." cut a check for 1000 dollars, held the check and said to Ken (his son) "Look at this – 1000 dollars in 30 days!! Look at this, Ken, 1000 dollars in 30 days!!" (I know he hated to part with it!)

With the check in his hand, Don went to the hospital and paid for the operation. There was no insurance and no green stamps even for cash. He could have borrowed it from the Red Cross, but Don didn't like the thought of indebtedness.

Incidentally, Don's weight went from 214 pounds down to 184 in 30 days!

When he was discharged, he was totally broke, but in 15 years he owned 3500 acres, couple trucks, nice car and some logging equipment – paid for. In addition he had a lumber mill that had been upgraded by technology so that production was increased and manual handling had been decreased.

And, skipping way ahead, Don cut and hand spilt 75 cords of wood, alone! He did this *at age 75*!!

Harold Rogers

Harold had his own trucks – hauled logs, pulp, lumber. He was also one of the first owners of hay baling equipment and contracted out to farmers to cut, bale and haul hay into the barn. A 14 or 16 hour day was normal, especially if hay was cut and rain was a threat. It was not uncommon to see his crew bailing hay at 11 o'clock at night - straight through from 7 a.m. to 11 p.m.

His wife rode on the side seat of the baler under a sun umbrella. Her job pertained to the twine tied around the bales.

He used to haul ash logs to American Fork and Hoe in St. Johnsbury for use in shovel, hoe and pitchfork handles.

The Ford dealer in St. Johnsbury had a picture on the wall in the salesroom showing Harold and a humongous load of logs.

Harold, during the war, had a Ford truck called a Baumis Warford. Its drive line was reengineered for all wheels to drive. This was something!

Circus Comes To Town

Periodically, a circus would come to town. This was always preceded by a rash of advertising in the local newspaper. Also, by driving on many of the roads you'd see various arrow signs taped to road signs. They always had an advance vehicle which planned the travel route from one location to the next. I imagine half the truck drivers didn't have a map or else couldn't read it if they did have one.

Once the circus arrives in town, they start the setup process at the location. Here is a good place to get a job. The pay is a ticket or two to the main tent show. The first time I was in line, the "Roustabout" looked up and said "Beat it kid. You're too young." (Probably 11 years old). By age 12, I'd grown enough to be accepted.

It was fun to see the big top get laid out and pulled up by the elephants. These guys knew how to do it (of course). You didn't have a name – everybody was "Hey you!" We worked all day and finally got our ticket(s). I could hardly ride my bike home, I was so pooped.

Sargent Roundy Corp.

This corporation was situated near the river which cuts through Randolph. To get there, a sharp turn at the south end of Main Street Bridge was necessary and from that, takes a steep dive under the bridge.

There were four or five buildings involved here – one, being the office, another being the foundry and moulding sand storage shed.

Another two or three were involved in product manufacture. They manufactured a corn planter which could plow, drop the seeds and then cover them. This was quite a machine when introduced, I guess in the 1920's.

They also produced milk coolers later in the 1930's which had a compressor unit run by electricity. The 40 qt. milk cans were lowered

Old office building of Sargent Roundy Corp. untouched since days of high activity. Photo 2001.

Buildings at the location of the former Sargent Roundy Corporation. Photo 2001, C. Wells

Left: one of the "original" buildings. Photo 2001, C. Wells

into this cooler and were surrounded by water. Any farmer selling milk quickly found out this item was necessary, by keeping milk at an acceptable temperature range as required by state law. I would say employees totaled about 50 to 60.

Once a day, the foundry would start "pouring" their castings with iron from the furnace being poured into molds. A shed housed tons of scrap iron waiting to be melted down. The molds were made of sand – a special type of sand which had to be "imported" from some midwestern state. Once this sand reached Randolph, it was trucked from the rail to S-R Corp.

Everett "Spot Cash" Sager

Everett lived next to the foundry property. He had contracted with S-R to do the transporting. The sand came in a box car (to keep it dry). "Spot Cash" hired me to help him move the molding sand. I was paid about $.25 an hour. He always wore a wrist band on each wrist.

As he opened the door on the box car, boards were nailed on the inside across the door opening. This will give you an insight on how full the car was. We dug away from the door and down removing boards as we progressed. *Each* shovelful was thrown into the truck. We worked down toward the floor and then toward each end, a wheel barrow was loaded and wheeled up a ramp and dumped. I couldn't handle a wheelbarrow, "Spot Cash" did that, I helped load it, but he fully expected my first shovelful to hit this wheelbarrow before he stopped with it!!

Incidentally, he was called "Spot Cash," obviously, because he carried a big roll of bills and paid cash – no checkbook for him, or, "Send me a bill"!!

When the truck was full we drove to the foundry. (Less than 5 minutes.) Seems this truck was a "Federal." It was not a common brand. But, it was not a dump truck – he had his own way of dumping this (when he could). (He later acquired a dump truck because of the need for flexibility.) He would spot where he was to dump the load, pace off so many steps, wrap a chain on each side between the duals and the other end hooked to the rear end of the frame! As he backed up, the front end would slowly rise and the load would dump!! Things had to be right to do this and as the shed filled, many loads had to be transferred by the wheelbarrow again.

If I was in school, and nobody else was available, he would do this alone. It was also common to see his wife and kids helping him nights and weekends. Remember, if the car wasn't empty and available for pickup in something like four days, he would have to start paying demurrage. And, we didn't lean on shovel handles and talk, we dug!

I have to admit, after this job was completed, I coaxed my Dad to go down to the foundry at 3:00 one day. This is the time of day they poured the molten iron. The furnace was hot and the steel was melted. Three or four men held large ladles and the molten iron would run and fill each ladle, then a long pole with a ball on the end would be stuffed in the hole to stop the iron. I don't know what the ball was made of, but it did the job.

The molds were in "halves" and then clamped together. The molds could be used until the clay must have hardened or became brittle, then new molds would be made by a mold maker. Obviously, molding sand needed to be replaced as it was consumed and that's where "Spot Cash" came in!

Coal Disappears

George Sprague had his dairy plant, near the Shell tanks. One day (when I was there), he came into the office and asked Dad if he knew so and so was backing under the coal silo(s) at night and taking coal? George said it wasn't his business, but thought Dad ought to know. The coal sheds were never locked nor were there locks on any valves on the fuel tanks! Later, someone else was known to be backing into the fuel oil shed. Dad was so easy going, he still didn't lock up and it turns out he knew who was "borrowing" both coal and fuel oil.

Randolph's Police Force (Or Lack of It)

I should say that up to this point, Randolph did not have any police force! Bill Somerville was a night watchman. He would go on rounds every hour and stick a key at given locations into the recording clock he carried. Each key (in a small box) had a number and would imprint on a coated disc in the clock. Thus, the key number and clock time would be recorded on the rounds. These were turned in daily. He didn't carry a gun and I don't know if he had the arresting authority but I'm quite sure he did not. Also, there was no ambulance, and as said previously, only a volunteer fire dept.

Strange as it *may* sound, by midnight most all activity had stopped.

Savage's Mill

Savage's Mill, at the end of Weston Street made various wood products. One product I really remember, was (during the war) they made "Billy" clubs. These were eighteen or twenty inches long and made from hardwood. They had a piece of rawhide at the handle end. They were dark stained and some, had the business end bored out and some lead inserted. There were thousands of these made.

Marcotte's Mill

Across Weston Street from Savages Mill, was Marcottes. This mill was basically a sawmill which turned out unfinished and finished lumber. This means mostly framing and dimensional stock, the owner lived right beside the millyard.

I'm really not equipped to say much about Marcottes, with the exception that I used to see lumber stock stored in the yard and in a couple of timber sheds. An educated guess would be that the number of employees was less than 10.

Salisbury Furniture

Another mill was Salisbury's Furniture Factory which made high quality furniture, most of which was bedroom furniture. It was made mostly, if not entirely, of maple. I can't get into names, but the present day funeral home was the main residence for the Salisbury family when it was originally built. The mill changed hands later. It employed (in 1940 - 41) probably about seventy- five people.

Former Salisbury residence converted to a funeral home by Rudolf Day approx 1940. Photo1985, C. Wells

L.W. Webster

L.W. Webster, on Pearl St. owned two mills. The lower mill was described earlier and cut lumber. The main mill (later called Branchwood) made bowling alley flooring (hardwood), kitty car seats (also hardwood), and bobbins, lots and lots of bobbins (also hardwood).

There were two sizes, one about 1½ inch diameter, the other about 2½ inch in diameter, and about ten or twelve inches long. They were used to wind yarn or cotton on in the textile industry. (Plastic was unknown at this time.) The closest thing to plastic was a material called Bakelite. It was hard and apt to stink! They shipped bobbins by the thousands, but, more on this later when I get a closer insight by a process called.......... employment.

Former L. W. Webster main mill on Pearl St. Randolph.
Photo 1985, C. Wells

Demeritt Canning Factory

There was a canning factory which took all the corn, farmers could provide. It was seasonal, and open for a short time each fall. It was called "The Demeritt Co." I think I could explain the process from the time the corn comes in on trucks, but that's a waste of space.

Between the two railroad crossings, on the south side of the tracks, the road went through from Main St. to South Pleasant St. Quite often, Catlin Feed Store would have a ramp across the road while unloading a car of grain.

Former Catlin Feed Store. Photo 1995, C. Wells

Former Johnson Printing Co. Photo 1995, C. Wells

Johnson Printing

Roy Johnson had a printing business in the building next to the feed store (on the Pleasant St. side). Roy was the son of "L.B," who, of course, was known as editor of "Johnson's Juicy Jabber." Roy's son, Peter apparently did not want to continue in the family printing business, and ultimately the building was vacated.

Walter Brown Pumps

Next to it, was a small building where a gentleman, by the name of Walter Brown, made pumps, also known to the "younger" generation as "Pump" Brown!. Tire pumps, water pumps (bilge pumps), etc. were the type, all of which were hand operated. Walter used to live on Emerson Terrace which was handy because he could easily walk to work, especially if he used the path on Terrace St. between the Huse Residence and the Mary Priest residence, coming out in the driveway of Henry Leonard's house on Pleasant Street.

On Main St. across from the theater is a building that Mary Merusi now operates the Beacon Printing business. Prior to that, Roy Haggett operated the Haggett Press. Before Haggett it was the building owned by Nelson Udall.

1941 Ford 4 Door. National Automobile and Truck Museum of United States. Photo approx 2001, C. Wells

Former Walter Brown Pumps - Also Clark Hunt Electrician.
Photo 1995, C. Wells

Nelson Udall

The ground floor, as I remember it, was only used for storage. There was an old touring car inside the garage. Dad knew Nelson, he repaired clocks and watches. Walking up the side ramp, and up a few steps, entering the door was a room about 10 x 12 that was finished off. The rest had partition studs up but nothing finished. Nelson was a bit scary to me as a youngster. As a matter of fact, I'm sure I used to stand behind my Dad, or hold on to his hand, even at age 10! He wore black sneakers, and always a visor cap. He was so thin, his eyes were very sunken. I couldn't understand him the few times I was there, but my Dad seemed able to.

One day, Nelson was shuffling down the sidewalk toward the stores. Carrying his usual white 5-gallon pail, he was crossing the tracks and as he approached the main track, the wind blew his hat off. He sat the pail down, turned around and stepped toward the secondary track requiring two or three steps to retrieve his hat. After his first step, a freight, pulled by a 700-size engine, went

Former Nelson Udall Block. Now, Beacon Press. Photo approx 1988.

Kimball Public Library, Main St. Randolph VT. Photo1985, C. Wells

whizzing by. The train had been blowing a whistle before it came around the L.W. Webster Corner. I saw this take place from a distance as did a couple others. He *then* waited for the train to pass, being missed only by a couple of feet!

Kimball Library

Mary Carr Dadmun was the librarian in the Kimball Library for years (and years)! When you entered the library, you were in a world of silence. She could read you the riot act with just a stern look on her face. Mrs. Dadmun lived in a nice Victorian house at the corner of Summer and Salisbury St. It was torn down making way for the post office. The year, I don't know, but it had to be in the seventies.

Flint's Socony

In the summer of 1941, I landed a job – a steady job. Harold Flint operated the Socony/Mobil station on Main St. He wanted help to pump gas, do grease jobs, oil changes and car washes. Harold had a pit, not a lift and he was insistent that I use an air lift under the cross in the frame. When in place, the car would slowly rise and then drop, to slowly start and rise again. In these days cars had many grease fittings. This air jack would help insure that the grease could fill in the whole bearing space.

He was very meticulous and that was an asset to him and a benefit to me. Seeing Harold work, and being very meticulous was a good example for me. He displayed good work habits such as neatness, being accurate, respect for customer's cars etc. I didn't realize it then, but this was an excellent number of habits I would adopt and help me considerably in the future.

Incidentally, there was a big house that was torn down to make room for the gas station. People by the name of Richardson lived there, and actually there were Cities Services gas pumps also. There still is a gas station there, but the gas brand has changed many times.

Here, my pay was $.13 per hour and after receiving my first pay check, I noticed he deducted a few pennies for social security! This worked out, as I remember, till school started and the job ended.

Kenneth Norton

On the south side of Randolph Village, on Route 12, was a "junk" yard operated by Kenneth Norton. "Kenny" was certainly a character. He was successful in operating this business, but he was equally well-known for the trouble he seemed always to be in. His father, Clint, operated a blacksmith shop. This shop was on Weston St. right beside Dad's fuel oil tanks.

Clint was easily recognized because he always wore "bib" overalls and a union suit with the sleeves cut off. In cold weather, he wore a union suit that the sleeves had not been cut off. On top of this was a shirt, with the sleeves cut off! More than not he had a day or two of whisker growth. To complicate this, he naturally, chewed tobacco. His wife, in a typical "housedress" of that era drove a late twenties "box" sedan, make and year escapes me. He didn't drive and would have no part of an auto. He was a horse man. If anyone was a *typical* blacksmith, he was it, especially with the heavy black work apron on!

Blacksmith shop, Weston St. Randolph, VT. Formerly Clint Norton and Henry Sault. Note coal sheds in background. Photo 1985, C. Wells

General area on Rt 12S, Randolph where Norton's "Junk Yard" was. Just south and opposite Justin Morgan Marketplace. Photo 2001, C. Wells

More specific location former Norton junk yard, Route 12. Photo 2001, C. Wells

One day I overheard Ken tell a group of his cronies about how earlier in the day (and on this day, it was zero or below), he owned a 1940 Lincoln Zephyr which was the only car of this "appearance" I ever saw. Meaning, black 4-door, long sweeping tail, "big white wall" tires and it had a V12 engine. It seems the car wouldn't start, so, with the hood up, Ken solicited Clint for help inside by merely depressing the gas pedal. In opposition, Clint said he didn't know nothin' about cars. Ken says "G - D - it," you don't *need* to know nothing about today's cars"! "Just sit on the seat and give it some gas, I'll do everything else out here." So with that Ken hooked up the jump cables, pressed the button on the underhood start relay, choked it and it started!

But, in doing so, Clint held the gas at least halfway, if not to the floor! (Ken thought he would at least let off on the gas, but he didn't. So, as it revved up, the breeze from the 8 blade fan was so hard, it ripped (his trademark) the corn cob pipe out of Ken's mouth, which then dropped into the fan and bent one or two blades! Ken was on his way around to the driver's door by now screaming, "Take your foot off the gas!" Clint didn't know what he meant!! Ken cut the ignition then the car settled back to earth as Ken was hollering at Clint "Don't you know enough to take your foot off the gas?," with Clint replying that he was told to keep his foot on the gas!!

About then Ken noticed that the fan had cut a nice 12 or 14 inch circle right into the radiator and to add more misery, the liquid from the radiator obviously had drained! So Ken's last statement, "A new radiator just replaced, four quarts of Prestone and a fan, all for the want of a G - D - 20 cent corn cob pipe!!" Then stormed off!!

(This was the first time I ever heard of anything like Prestone for a radiator – it was expensive.)

One time about 1941, he took four or five available men, loaded them on the southbound passenger train, and they went to Boston. While there is nothing unusual about this topic, sit tight. He bought an entire fleet of panel trucks from the Se- Lect Bread Co. They were a green or gray color and he and the four or five men made numerous trips. I remember the total was around forty trucks, most all Fords from model year 1935 to 1939. These were added to the many vehicles already reposing in the grave yard of vehicles. Remember now, by the 1990's standards this would be nothing but it *was* something in those days.

When I spoke with Ken about some part (probably for Pierce's garage), he was sitting in the garage in a rocker, smoking his corn cob pipe, at the junk yard. Beside him was a wood burning stove. But, from the hole in the top was a very small copper tubing extending up to a 5-gallon bucket with a spigot (in the line). I was looking at it, Ken explained that he burned used crankcase oil and with the spigot, could regulate the heat radiated. He also burned tires. Believe me, this stove could become cherry red, nearly to the top. While we were up in the yard, one of the yard men came running up and hurriedly explained that the stove was on fire! Well, it was put out before it burned the building! I was in awe of all the autos, parts, trucks, etc. in the yard. Model years were from 1920's to late 1930's.

Henry Sault - Blacksmith

Henry Sault also had a blacksmith shop in Randolph. Dad was quite often in need of special parts either for one of his truck bodies or one of the conveyors in the coal sheds. The blacksmith shop on Route 12 was the third building beyond the present fire station. It is constructed mainly of large flat pieces of ledge. He then moved to the building on Weston street near the Randolph Coal & Oil fuel tanks. After he vacated the building, Clint Norton occupied it as previously mentioned.

I have since heard the following incident from a famous comedienne, and tell it here as I heard it from Stan Gould somewhere in this time frame, of 1941.

Being in Henry's shop *quite* often, I felt comfortable and enjoyed watching him do his work whether it was horse shoes or a custom part. He had another man that worked with him for years by the name of George West. Henry was quite apt to sing or hum as he worked. Of course, Dad sold the coal for his forge.

This day, Stan had come with me, and we were standing there. George wasn't there that day and Henry was "out." A horse was standing there and a new shoe was on the floor. Stan picked it up and almost immediately dropped it back to the floor. (It was hot, but not red)! As he dropped it, Henry had come in

Former blacksmith shop operated by Henry Sault (and others?),
Randolph, VT. Photo 2001, C. Wells

the back door and saw it drop. Henry said, "Did you get burned?"
Stan said (rather embarrassed) "No, - it just doesn't take me
long to look over a horseshoe!!!

1939 Chevrolet Truck

By now, Dad found out that the snub nose Chevrolet truck
he bought in 1939 (and previously mentioned) was not really
suitable for delivering coal for two reasons. It was too heavy on
the front end also, there was a double lift body on it and
somebody laid it on its side when it became top heavy on an
incline.

Working for Randolph Coal & Ice

By now, I was big enough to actually work for Dad at the
"Coal Office." Starting out, I had a new pair of "Monkey Face"
gloves. These gloves had a hair like material on the backs of
them. I also had a shovel that was designated *mine*. I'm sure

both Ernest and Elbert had gone by this time. They both must be early fifties by now. The coal part would be tough on most fifty year olds. A new man named Glen Ducharme was here on the trucks and by now Harold Simmons was bookkeeper.

Gloves Get Hot

One day I was riding in the truck with Glen. Quite often after we loaded, he would proceed to roll a cigarette. Out would come a pack with papers, then the tobacco from either a Bull Durham bag with drawstrings on it or from a Prince Albert can. After smoothing the tobacco and then gently 'rolling' the paper - a swipe with the tongue and voila - a cigarette was born even if it did look more like a white twig!

Then a wood match would produce the usual wood match smell along with the tobacco aroma.

Only, this time, as I sat in the rider's seat with my new monkey face gloves on, he moved that match over towards them. I didn't suspect anything, but even before he got that match within two inches, that fine fuzz was on fire. And as quickly as they started, they were out! Scared the pewaddin out of me. But, no harm was done and he got a kick out of it!

Coal Shed Cleanup

One of the jobs that I had to do was to clean out the base of the coal elevator in the coal sheds. Before I elaborate, let me give just a general happening once a (RR) car of coal is "spotted" at the unloading spot. Beneath the center of any coal car are two hopper doors. Once these are opened (one at a time) coal floods over the track. There is a chute in the ground that slopes toward the building. There is a "gate," that regulates the flow of coal. Somebody has to stand here (in most cases) while unloading takes place.

At the base of this incline is an elevator with "buckets" that are filled on their way up. The gate allows the buckets to fill and, by how much. The buckets take the coal up one and one half stories and are dumped. They pass over the top pulley and then start down, upside down for the return trip down. The buckets dump onto a rubber belt conveyor that's on rails. This conveyor can be moved on the rails and reversed so the coal falls off either end into the correct bin. Dad had a big hand in putting the coal shed machinery together. I'm sure he put the "conveyor" in place, but not the bucket elevator. Trucks can back under these bins (most of them) and "get loaded."

Once the hopper doors are opened (and the track is flooded) the unloading must continue until that "pocket" in the rail car is empty and the tracks are cleaned up. Remember, the "way freight" will be in around 9:00 a.m. the next day, and will have to travel right over the tracks, at this spot.

Photo shows the approach to the unloading area. Photo 2000, C. Wells

The buckets slop some coal out as they are loaded and start the trip up. This coal dribbles, bounces and falls through to the bottom.

Glen backs the truck so I can hand load it. He can deliver fuel oil while I'm filling the coal truck with "slop" from the buckets. It takes about eight steps out to the truck, and eight in return for each shovelful!

Drinks are Strong

Interspersed with the coal to be cleaned up is apt to be a collection of two items: Vanilla bottles and Sterno cans.

In the thirties, a lot of "hobos" rode the rails. As they passed through town, if on a slow train, or if the train stopped on a siding, these guys would spot Claflin's store from the rails and hop off. After buying what they wanted they would head back to the coal shed to drink the "Good Stuff," and wait for another train. Many times the vanilla bottles didn't have the caps removed, they would bang it across something and break the necks off (with the caps still on).

126

Of course, Sterno is horrible stuff to drink, but it does have alcohol in it, which they would drink!!

Watering the Coal

Not far from the coal shed, and right in back of the Shell station was a round cast iron water tub. Not a tub on the ground but a fancy base, with the water tub at a height so the horse had to lower his head only a few inches to drink. There used to be many horses tied around here, wagons and all. The owners would be "over street." But now, there were still enough diehards to keep it operating. Ernest, Elbert and Glen, after coal was loaded, and driven to the "office" on Salisbury St., get weighed, and would then pull up to the horse tub.

By putting one foot on the tub rim and the other on the body ledge would proceed to scoop four - eight - twelve shovels full of water on the coal to keep the dust down. Of course, it had been weighed before watering, so the weight wasn't changed, also, water didn't stick to Anthracite coal.

The building on South Main St. in front of Dustin's Feed Store had the Randolph Savings and Loan and in the other half of the front, Rita Allen had a beauty shop (or hair dresser) operation, in the other half up stairs was available for office space, for tenants, such as the U.S. Soil Conservation Offices. Also, Dr. Holden had his Dentist office there. Later, Richard Mitchell (Dr.) had an optometry practice there.

Randolph Police Force

By now, I would think that Bill Somerville had retired and was replaced by Dave Barcomb. Dave had lost an arm below the shoulder by a shotgun blast in a deer hunting accident. The village still did not have a police force, as such, on night duty. Probably there were Sheriff Deputies to take care of a few repetitive bottle tippers.

Bottles were very common, but it was still customary to use a brown bag as a cover. Of course, to see someone put a brown paper bag to his mouth and then to tip it up wasn't much of a puzzle to figure out what he was doing.

Along the same line, Grants Drug Store used to sell Kotex

(naturally)! However, it was always wrapped with plain kraft paper. Couldn't sell that unless it was wrapped. Of course, any woman coming out of the store with a plain wrapped box, it didn't take much to see it was a box of Kotex. After all, it was the only product of its kind, it was a standard size, it was plain wrapped. Also, *very* rarely did you ever see a man carry a box out of the store. Who was fooling who?

Golf Clubs

Phil McIntyre came out of his house one day with a golf bag he was lugging. "Let's see how these work" one of us probably said. So with that, he found a ball and teed it up. These were strange "terms" to me, but Phil had seen Ed (his father) enough, so he set it up. I stood in back of him and there were *two* hits! One when he hit the ball and one when the club hit me in the head! (Probably the sound wasn't much different!) I didn't know what the sounds were, I was on the ground. I was also bleeding pretty good. The driver got me in the left eyebrow. I don't remember whether his mother or my mother came out (or not).

I was hustled over to see "Dr. Frank." You knew he was available by looking to see if the Buick was in the garage. Also, now you see why my folks picked that lot to build a house on!? Dr. Frank cleaned it up and then stitched it up. I don't know if he got paid for these trips or not. For all I knew, he just waited for me to come in! (I'm sure he was paid.)

1932 Nash

By now, Dad had got rid of the 1928 Whippet he had and acquired a used 1932 Nash Coupe with a big eight-cylinder engine. I know Dud Pierce was involved in the transaction. This car was comfortable (and powerful). Both this car and the Lafayette were garaged under a large porch on the rear of the house. One night, my folks were awakened by the sound of the Coupe trying to be started! In addition there was a crash as the garage doors (hinged at this time) were rammed by the car as it backed out! I didn't know anything about it, I slept through the whole thing, but later, the discussion was centered on who would do that, etc.

The car was started by pulling a knob on the dash. Apparently this engaged the Bendix Drive and then mechanically closed the switch for the starter. It was never found out who, or even if, it was a theft attempt.

Uneasy Europe

Also, by now, the town, the state, and the country was getting mighty uneasy about what was happening in Europe. It didn't bother me much because, I was only 13 and my whole world was only about five miles square, at least for that point in time.

Town Walter Truck – 1940

The Town of Randolph bought a new truck to plow snow with. The town, not the village used this truck to open up roads out in the "country."

The truck was a "Walter Sno Fyter." The nameplate on the nose said "100% Traction." This would take the place of the crawler tractor with the big "V" plow on the steel frame.

This really was a big step up in snow plowing. Both operators were inside now, the truck drove not only from the rear axle but, also from the front axle. It had a big wing plow which combined with the "V" plow could open a swath about 16 feet wide. This is what was needed in places like Ridge Road in Randolph Center. High up and wide open, snow would drift across the road even with snow fences erected, and a drift 6 or 8 feet high was common.

All the hydraulic controls for the plows and dump body were near the front edge of the seat. I'm sure that there was also a good heater in the cab.

Glen Ducharme was one of the drivers (before he came to work for Randolph Coal and Ice Co.).

Webster Fire

One day around noon (?) the fire alarm blew. Somehow I found out the code was for Pearl Street. Pearl St. is very close to the house and is where several houses are located. Also, L.W. Webster's Mill – actually two of them, was located on Pearl Street.

Both above and below are similar to Walter Truck, owned by Town of Randolph. Kemps Trucks. Photo approx 1995, C. Wells

I ran down to Webster's main mill and didn't have to go any further. A few people were standing around the main mill. There was a power house near the east end and also lots of logs stacked on the ground. To the right were the kilns and more logs. To the left was the main building, a three-story wooden building beside three sets of tracks.

There was also a railroad siding with a fair incline that went right to the main mill. I don't think there were sprinklers. Now, believe me, you couldn't build a better structure for a fire!

The powerhouse contained a boiler which burned wood scraps. All kinds of scraps such as chips, bark, shavings, unusable wood meaning defects such as knots, etc. As the boiler produced steam, a large steam engine consumed most of the steam and converted the "energy" into power for the mill in the way of belt power. There was no "OSHA" in those days! (Good thing, because there were pulley shafts, belts and more, of each.) As a belt came down from the ceiling, there was an engaging lever a machine operator would operate and "this" machine would come up to speed amid a few squeals as the belt would slip. These machines were various types of table saws, two-sided and four-sided planers, etc.

Of course, these machines were dangerous by themselves, and were fed by belts with minimal belt guards and also generated sawdust, shavings and dust. Ceilings were beams with posts, cobwebs and hardwood floors. (You guess if it would burn!)

When I arrived at the mill, there were flames centered around the "powerhouse." This didn't last long - it spread rapidly into one corner of the main building. By this time, Randolph Fire Dept. had arrived and was setting up. In 10 minutes, Bethel and then South Royalton Fire Department arrived. I think Tunbridge and Rochester came in, as did Northfield, and I think Montpelier and Barre sent a pumper each. They were 25 to 30 miles away. Believe me, Pearl St. looked like a lot of spaghetti with all the hoses.

One or two trains were halted as the fire reached a peak – the heat was terrific. By this time, I was one of a few carrying records, files and equipment, out of the office. The downstairs was pretty well cleared and by the time we "worked" the second floor, smoke was forcing in around the door connecting the main mill. I think we had to vacate before we had cleaned it out.

The fire also spread in the opposite directions and consumed at

*L.W. Webster
Fire Pearl St.
Randolph
Vermont. All
Photos by C.
Wells, 1941*

least one house, the dry kilns and numerous piles of logs on the ground. It was a mess! I had sent for a camera by including a Pepsodent Toothpaste box top and 15 cents. It came in the mail a couple days after the fire. So, I tried it out by snapping a few "shots" of the Webster fire in 1942.

Slowly it was cleaned up and rebuilt. As the business slowly got on its feet, more of the employees came back to work – and I would be one of them in about three years.

These days, there was no unemployment compensation, no disability pay, and no medical coverage furnished, also, no vacation pay or holiday pay.

Considering that, one thing I'm trying to accomplish here is to make a comparison of 1930 - 1940 living and the 1990's. That's with respect to life styles, changes in standard of living, jobs, etc. So many jobs were done manually, as compared to how it's done in the later years.

Gondola Coal Cars

With that covered and with my then present age, I realized Dad had ordered coal for the Vermont State School of Agriculture (the Aggie School) in Randolph Center.

One day, the "way freight" spotted a car of coal on the siding at Randolph Furniture Factory. This was a Gondola car which was long (standard width), but had sideboards about five feet high. This meant this had to be hand shoveled off!

One other item pertaining to this carload was that it was what was known as "steam coal." The composition of steam coal is *very* fine granules accompanied by chunks from plum size up to even larger than a watermelon. It was also soft coal known as Bituminous not that there was any difference in the way it shoveled. It did mean, though, that to even get started, it had to be loosened by a pick.

Starting at one corner, we picked and then shoveled down to the bottom of the car. When there, we worked our way toward the other end, and also, toward the other side. Once eight or ten feet of distance was covered, then I would start and work into the corner, and then toward the distant end. In this way, two people, offset could shovel and always be out of the way of each other. It wasn't bad shoveling once you reached the floor. Pick and loosen it up, shovel it using the floor. With five foot side walls, I couldn't see over the sides of the car. Also, I couldn't lift a full shovelful. I could only move part of a shovel, but, made up for it by trying to shovel faster. From a distance, you would see black masses flying through the air.

Typical Gondola Car (No pockets in bottom).
Note the wood construction. Courtesy of Robert C. Jones

Once the truck was loaded, a five mile trip up to Randolph Center and unload. Don't forget, this was not a dump truck. It was hand shoveled off. And, after the first few trips, the chute would plug up signaling it was time for me to start "mowing" away in the cellar.

So what's the big deal about unloading a car of coal. Well, once this one is done, there'll be four more to come. This school uses about 250 tons per year.

By this time, after the '39 snub nose Chevrolet truck had rolled over, that truck was traded off and a 1936 tank truck was purchased for fuel oil and kerosene delivery. That relegated the 1935 Ford to full time coal delivery. And, also ended the use of the two removable tanks. That's the reason there was no dump body at this time.

Each year (with an occasional exception), we did this order for the Aggie School and also, another two car loads of steam coal for the Randolph School building. At least it was done in either spring or fall, not in the heat of the summer.

Original Boys Dormitory at VT. Technical College, Randolph VT.
(Coal was chuted into cellar). Photo approx 1985.

Floyd Fuller

As 1942 rolled in, the springtime found me working on Floyd Fuller's farm. Floyd had a few hundred trees tapped for sap. He needed some help around the sugar house. He had two daughters, one a couple years older and one a few younger. The older one was Joyce and the younger one was Audrey. At fourteen, I didn't know anything about farming, about sugaring or much else, as far as that is concerned! His farm was about eight miles from Randolph Village so it was necessary to board and room on the farm.

This was in the spring. Cool nights and warm days in March makes the sap run. I don't profess to know much about "sugaring" as I write this, but I do know that buckets were hung on maple trees and ultimately the buckets fill with sap, which is 99% water. The weather determines how fast the sap flows. As the spouts are driven into a hole drilled in the trunk, shortly the sap drops from the spout into the bucket. This is where extra help was needed. Floyd had a team of horses which pulled a sled with a tank on it. The ground is partly bare and partially covered with splotches of

136

snow. The sled will work well on either.

Remove the bucket and dump the contents into the "gathering tank." Many times you cannot dump each bucket into the tank because the trees are spread too thin. So in that case, I wore a Dutchmen's yoke. This was a carved wood frame you wore on your shoulders. Suspended from each end, near your shoulders, was a 5-gallon gathering pail. Kneel down, and set the pail(s) on the ground. Then dump the tree bucket(s) into the gathering pail. Let's see, 5 gallons of sap at 8 lbs/gallon times 2 gather pails = 80 pounds. This isn't too bad, but don't forget you're walking over uneven ground, and quite often when you walk over snow, you break through and, of course, the sap slops. Then, you're wearing wet clothes! Anyway at the end of the gathering run, you know you've done something! So now, the sap is dumped in the holding tank at the sugar house waiting its turn to be "let in" to the evaporator.

Legendary horseman
Floyd Fuller.
Photo by Robert Eddy,
Courtesy Herald of Randolph

The evaporator is a metal pan with sides about 10 inches high and partitions inside. Underneath in a cast iron base is either a log fire or in some cases an oil burner. The cool sap comes in one trough and as it makes its way through the "trough" it becomes hot and finally boils. As the water boils out, the sap becomes thicker with less water. By the time it reaches the end of the last trough, it is well on its way to become maple syrup. The specific gravity is constantly read. When it's right (I forget the reading), the syrup is "drawn off." The color, density, etc. qualifies it to be a certain grade.

Once the boiling process starts, it makes sense to boil for hours, sometimes into the evening. On the farm with Floyd, the boiling was interrupted only for evening chores in the barn. It made for long days, especially if the "season" lent itself for large quantities of sap. After it was "drawn off," it was canned, sealed and label graded.

Nowadays, technology has lent a hand in more than one way, such as the collection of sap. Some hand gathering of sap is replaced by tubing, tying many trees into a "line" that ultimately ends at the sugar house holding tank. However the boiling process is still the same. Sugaring makes for a good supplement income to this farmer, but it is not a way to riches!

The barn chores were not that easy – if you weren't tugging on hay in the hay bay that refused to budge, you were tugging on silage in the silo that could be half frozen. And let's not forget cleaning the udders in preparation for the milking machines, *or* cleaning the gutters, because this farm wasn't large enough to have a gutter cleaner, that works at the touch of a "go" switch!

Milking at this time, on this farm, was done by machine. I "hung" the machines and started the process. Here, Surge milking machines were strapped on. Floyd "stripped" the cows after the machines were

**Selected Songs
Composed in 1941**

Chattanooga Choo Choo
Don't Take Your Love From Me
I Don't Want To Walk Without You
I Got it Bad
In the Mood
Jersey Bounce
There, I've Said It Again
This Love of Mine
You Belong To My Heart

through. Each and every dairy farm in Vermont, around this time, was quite apt to have a sign on the barn or milk house advertising either Surge or DeLaval milkers.

Floyd had a sense of humor that really helped. And his wife was equally nice along with the two girls.

It was different getting up at 4:00 a.m. and one of the biggest ways it was different was getting out of bed. I slept off the kitchen (which was the only room heated except what would drift upstairs through floor registers). The bedroom at 4:00 a.m. was like an igloo! By 4 a.m. the six blankets had allowed the bed to contribute something to comfort!

However, one morning, Floyd came in, woke me up and said "put some pants and a shirt on and follow." In his older daughter's room was my pajamas hanging on a clothes tree!!!! To this day, I don't know how they got there – I think he took them off me while I was asleep! (Believe me, I used to sleep – you could drive a "Cat Diesel" through the bedroom and I would never know it!

One morning as I entered the barn more asleep, still, than awake, I met a sight that sure woke me up.

One cow was lying down and had a couple extra legs protruding!! Boy, this made me go in circles, big circles, little circles. What the Hell is going on?! Before I could get my head to operate correctly with my feet and legs, Floyd walked in. It didn't take him long to spring into action. "Grab those legs, Con, and pull!!"

Surely he was joking! Lets face it, I *could* have been eight miles away, at home, or anywhere, and then who would have "grabbed those legs and pulled?!"

Let me say here, that a Doctor, a Gynecologist, a Veterinarian, etc. was on my same list of undesired professions, as a ballet dancer.

Anyway, we got the calf out and Floyd was cleaning it up. If Floyd hadn't been around right then, I would probably have kicked it right in the ass, just for crawling up in there!

And with that, I went out in the barnyard and made a deposit which, would have been much more appropriate in a barf bag!

Interesting thing – after he stopped farming, had retired and moved to Randolph Center, he started "floating" horses teeth. Jumping way ahead, to the eighties now, this is something his father did and Floyd learned it. Horses teeth wear down with use and whatever else. And at some point in time they have pain, discomfort, etc. Floyd could put his hand in a horses mouth and determine what and where anything was wrong. At the same time coax the horse to be patient. He would then file the teeth and correct any problem and of course, dissipate the pain. He was written up in several magazines over the years, also, newspapers. He traveled over most of Vermont and still did this over the age of ninety!

Freddie Knight

During the summer, a "crazy" guy by the name of Freddie Knight came looking for me. (Obviously, he found me!) Freddie was now a foreman for the Town of Randolph.

It seems a box car full of rock salt had arrived and he needed extra help unloading it. He estimated two maybe three days would be the right amount of time. So, terms were agreed upon and he and two or three others plus myself found the rail car. It was right near the freight house (and Main St. Crossing).

Freddie Knight was an employee at Claflin's Store. Now, he was working for the town of Randolph. (This was a different crew than the village of Randolph).

I had known Freddie for roughly six years. He was skinny as a hoe handle and should have been a clown. As we worked this guy could do stories, (funny stuff like Henny Youngman or more closely, he was a second Red Skelton). He could do the accents, the gestures, the facial expressions and work at the same time!!!

The salt came in a box car and was another "caper" like the molding sand with "Spot Cash"! So when the car was empty, some way I was paid, and the job vanished.

Periodically, I would see Freddie. Actually we were most apt to meet in the local grocery store – not supermarket – grocery store. We would stand in a sparse area and exchange a few "Did ya hear the one about."? Next thing you know, look around and six or eight people had gathered, and before long, most of *them* would be knee slappers!!

Jerd's Freezer Lockers

A while back I mentioned that Fred Jerd had a meat market/ grocery store in the Stockwell block near Main and Pleasant Streets.

140

Sometime back, the store moved to Merchants Row. As we passed Dec 7, 1941 and war was declared, many foods were among items getting scarce. Jerd's decided to occupy the adjacent storefront. In doing so, there were going to be freezer lockers installed in here. Home freezers were yet to come, but the need to freeze foods was now. Many people raised pigs, steer for beef, many kinds of fruits and vegetable could be frozen instead of canned. Birds Eye brand frozen foods had made a debut and was being publicly accepted.

This store was to be insulated with 2" cork and different sized lockable drawers would be installed on drawer slides. Each drawer was assigned to a customer and issued a key. What you stored was your business. Jerd would sell a side of beef (local), dress, package it, quick freeze and then store it in your drawer, or, you could furnish, such as deer or partridge, etc.

Armstrong Cork

Armstrong Cork did the room modification including installing the cork, building partitions etc. It also assembled the drawer frames and installed the refrigeration units with the cooler units etc.

Here, I got a job working on this project. I don't recall what the pay was or how long I worked over a couple of weeks. It was here I was introduced to refrigeration and a gas called ammonia. This was a gas used in refrigeration. Geezus, it was strong!! It would make your eyes burn!

Aircraft Wardens

This is a good time to point out and explain about Aircraft Wardens. There was no radar, no electronic aircraft detection. The "camp" that Phil McIntyre and I had (in back of McIntyre's house), had been "donated" as an aircraft lookout building. It was hauled back up to Braintree Hill and placed near the church in an open field. It was equipped with a telephone and various charts. Also, a couple of lawn chairs.

On the charts were silhouettes of U.S., German and Japanese planes. Any plane heard or seen (field glasses were used), had to be determined what plane it was, then telephone Albany N.Y. and relay the information. It was a 4 hour shift, 7 days a week. (I don't remember if it was a 24 hrs./day shift.) All able bodied citizens including Dad, Mother, and myself "pulled" many shifts. Apparently it worked!

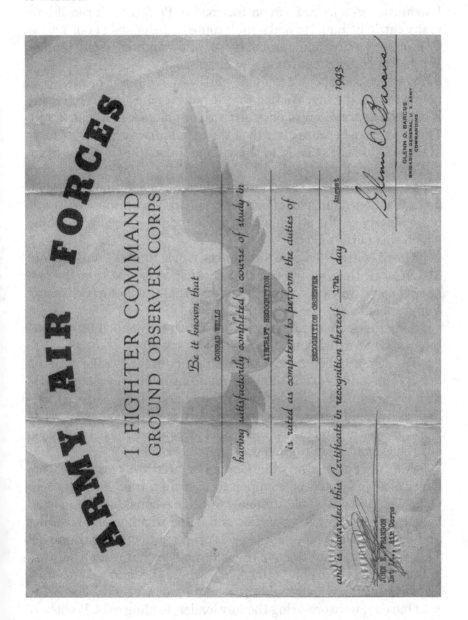

ARMY AIR FORCES

I FIGHTER COMMAND
GROUND OBSERVER CORPS

Be it known that

CONRAD WELLS

having satisfactorily completed a course of study in

AIRCRAFT RECOGNITION

is rated as competent to perform the duties of

RECOGNITION OBSERVER

and is awarded this Certificate in recognition thereof 17th day _____ August _____ 1943.

JOHN E. FRANSON
Int Ft, Air Corps

GLENN O. BARCUS
BRIGADIER GENERAL, U. S. ARMY
COMMANDING

Gordon Labounty - 1942

Stan Gould and I worked for Gordon Labounty on the farm. Labounty had a large farm on the road to Peth. I don't recall how many cattle he had. He had a milk route and stopped at our house. Gordon was a tiny man, probably 5'4" and weighted about 150 lbs. But he was a "wiry" guy and a workhorse!

We received about $.25/hour and we were hired primarily to help with the haying. We had to ride our bicycles "up" to the farm, it was about three miles on a dirt road, and most of it was uphill. This was good, because after the day we put in, we could coast most of the way down, at least to the village. I don't know about Stan, but everyday, I was "bushed"!

Leland Flint used to work the milk route in addition to Gordon. John Washburn did a lot of barn chores. Gordon's father (Will) was quite elderly but he still pitched in. He rode the mowing machine which was horse pulled.

There were also two (at least) work horses, and an old McCormack Deering tractor. It used to surprise me that the two horses could work as a team, *one* especially was forever losing compression!

Sometimes we used a hay loader which was pulled behind the hay wagon. We also "pitched on."

The senior Labounty also pulled the side delivery rake with the horse. This unit "raked" the field into continuous rows of hay. He also would pull the "tedder" with the horse. This "scattered" the hay so it would dry and was done before it was "winnowed." The worst job was to tumble hay (make piles) in preparation to be "pitched on" the wagon. Each tumble was a pitchfork full.

Stan and I pitched on while Gordon "mowed away" on the wagon. Quite often, it would be common to pick up a tumble, get it over your head and out would tumble a few horse buns! *If* the buns had been dropped a few days earlier and *if* the weather had been hot and dry, you were more apt to get sprinkled instead of thumped! This was always fun to have those tumble on you while you were hot and sweaty. We only "pitched on" where the land was too hilly for a hay loader, which could tip over quite easily.

One day, we were using the hay loader, loading oats. It was my turn to be up front and distribute the load while Stan pulled it away from the loader at the top. Oats would get all tangled up as they traveled up the loader. This one day, he was tugging on each fork full and I felt something hit my right upper arm. In looking back, he had stuck his pitchfork in my arm!! I said to him "your pitchfork is stuck in my arm!!" He said "I know it." I said "Well, get it out of there!!" He said, "I can't pull it out, its stuck!" So I said, "Well, pull harder." Anyway, this required that I had to ride down to the village and go see "Dr. Frank." He cleaned it up, and put a patch bandage on. Then I had to pedal the bike back.

We used to eat our sandwiches at noon in the walk-in cooler, in the milk house. This is where the milk was separated for cream etc., bottled and stored waiting for the delivery truck to go on its route. One noon we were in the milk house. Outside, a "whale" of a thunder shower was in progress. A bolt of lightning struck somewhere and came in through the faucets in the sink. This knocked Leland Flint across the room. Luckily it didn't kill him, but it did stun him.

It was cool there and we would sit on a 40 qt. milk can. Also, there was plenty of milk to drink along with Dari Rich. When the cream was separated from milk, the milk that was left, of course,

Gordon Labounty Farm (Now Kermit Labounty) on Peth Road. Note: Barn far right and highest barn dead center are described in text. Courtesy of Herald of Randolph

was skim milk. In those days, skim milk was apt to be tossed out.

Someone came up with the idea of adding a chocolate syrup mixture to it and called it Dari Rich. My mother wouldn't buy it because it was extravagant. She would take milk and add cocoa. (It wasn't as good!)

One time, right after we started to work, Gordon took Stan and me into the lower level of the barn. This one had to be nearly 100 feet long. On the lower level is where the cows were stanchioned. Also, there were pens for calves and a pen or two, for the bull(s). These pens were made of round iron pipe. The bull pen was at the end of the barn right in the middle. If you walked down the middle, there were cows on both sides, which faced each other. This, made it easier to feed them.

Then you would run right into the gate for the bull pen. Most farms, those days, which had over approximately 50 cows, kept a bull on the farm. In other words, enough cows to justify owning a bull. For farms under that number, some other farm would "truck" a bull over to their neighbor (or friends), so this bull could "entertain" the cows. At my *then* age, I would occasionally hear that term used. It always gave me the vision the bull must do something like pulling a rabbit out of a hat, or, do some card tricks!!

However, bulls were not to be trusted – their temperament was apt to be explosive. A ring in their nose *was always* attached to, by a short wood handle with a snap hook on it. This way the farmer could control the bull. Still, once in a while, you would hear about a farmer getting mauled – or even killed. For some reason, dangerous or unpredictable bulls carried a label of "Angry Bulls."

Believe me, this bull was angry. I'd heard about angry bulls many times before, but never did I see one that was like this up close. But, this one had a look in his eye that was scary. And we hadn't even done anything to antagonize him!!

One noon, Stan and I were standing in the doorway to the lower level during the noon hour and we had finished eating. As we stood there, a BB gun probably belonging to Gordon's son, Kermit was leaning against the door casing. We picked it up, cocked it and fired a couple of BB's. This was a Buzz Barton and BB guns then didn't have the power of today's BB Guns. You could actually see the BB travel as it left the muzzle. Naturally, one of us zeroed in on the bull. He was snorting (like a bull). "How about those long "things" hanging there, bet you can't peck one of them with a BB!" Bang, "See, I told you, ya gotta give it more of an arc"!

Bang! "Well, you're getting closer. You can hear that BB hit the steel pipe." My turn, Bang. "Hell you aren't any better than I am," (one of us probably said.) Bang – Splat ooo-eee-ahh!! eeahh! God, that damn bull pawed, snorted, pawed again and snorted some more! I was really wondering if that steel pipe was going to keep him from charging towards us – but it did.

I really don't think the bull tied us into the reason that he "smarted" in one area!!

For a couple of weeks, haying progressed. On this farm, there were three barns to fill, which is a lot of hay! Two of the barns had hay forks. The big barn had a good sized "clamshell fork" which had an electric lift, but once it was over the bays, it was quite high, and with about four bays, it was quite long. Stan and I found out one noon that you could get quite a ride. All you had to do was reach up, grab one set of tines with the left hand and grab the other set of tines with the other hand, then run over the full bay and you could ride over three empty bays.

About the second time I tried it, the edge of the full bay came up sooner than I expected and my right hand slipped off, only to be caught by a tine that stuck into my forearm. Bear in mind, I'm about 25' up from the floor of the empty bay or two we're riding over. Now, I'm hollering ow - ow being hung by a tine stuck into my forearm!! Strangely, it didn't bleed that much but we tied a handkerchief around the arm.

With that, I got on the bike and rode down to see "Dr. Frank"! Again, he cleaned it put a good patch on it and this time gave me a tetanus shot. I rode back up to the farm and we finished the day! (I still have the scar.)

When we pitched hay into a barn (with no hay fork), Gordon said, "all set?" Spit on his hands, grabbed a pitch fork and about buried us, it came so fast!! At the end of that day and about six loads of hay, Stan and I could only coast home!

We had been there about five days when the tractor was "spotted" and with a belt on the PTO (power take off) powered the silage cutter. What this does is grind up corn stalks (and leaves), mix it with molasses and shoot it up a long pipe on the outside of the silo and into the roof. This is candy for the cows which they are fed an equal amount of each day. After a few weeks in the silo it's probably looked forward to more than candy! It's more like a Manhattan!

This machine when its running is very noisy and very scary. It is dangerous with the knives rotating at that speed. Gordon "fed it." Stan and I either fed the stalks on the wagon to him or, we took turns mixing the molasses chunks with water in the open top big tank. We stirred it with a canoe paddle. The liquid dripped out onto the conveyor feed.

Courtesy of Herald of Randolph

The horse barn had a hay fork called a grapple fork. The wagon was driven into position under the hay fork rail protrusion at the peak of the barn. This hayfork rail was about 2½ stories up. The grapple fork had only two tines. You picked out the spot and stepped on the fork pushing it down into the hay. Once it is bottomed, you cock it which brings out a protrusion down at each point.

This fork was lifted by a rope and a couple of big pulleys. One at the peak and another at nearly ground level and then the rope is tied onto a vehicle. As the vehicle is backed up, the hay fork load is raised off the wagon and rises toward the rail projection at the peak. There it is "tripped" and the carrier, load and all, heads toward the big door and enters the barn.

This time, as I stood on the wagon about half the entire load was rising over my head. That grapple fork could really take a bite. Only the load of hay was so big, it couldn't go through the doorway into the barn. Leland tugged the line with the truck. It shuddered a couple times when all of a sudden the hay fork tripped meaning the projection at each point retracted and the load was starting down right at the wagon! I turned and jumped. As I left the wagon, the hay took my place with a big gust of wind and dust. No harm done but it scared the peewaddin outta me!!

Well, so much for work at the Labounty farm.

Randolph High and Graded School starting 1911 - now out of service. Photo 2001, C. Wells

Randolph Graded School

It's still 1942 and, obviously, I have passed from third grade to fourth to fifth to sixth and now I'm in the seventh grade. In the fourth grade Marjorie Walbridge was a repeat teacher as I had her for second grade. In the fifth, Carrie Eaton was quite elderly and fragile. In the sixth Dorothy Marshall made you realize this is for real and we really settled in. The seventh was taught by Kate Simmons. All these teachers provided me with a disciplined, and varied educational background. They were very thorough and, well prepared any student who had the desire to accept it.

Windsor County Farmers Exchange

Up to this point, there were three feed stores in town. A small "handcar" building was right next to the freight house and a vacant lot next to it had a building put up. It was at Windsor County Farmers Exchange.

148

Windsor County Farmers Exchange on "L" Street. Next to coal sheds (also railroad tracks). Photo approx 1999, C. Wells

I can recall some "stockyard pens" in this location, prior to the building being put there. The building would be used to sell grain and feeds. A freight car could be spotted right next to it.

Bob Noyes was the manager. He parked his car in the little alley. The thing that was different was this car was a 1927 Model "T," 4-door sedan. It was in excellent condition. On the passenger side of the cowl was a tank, about 3-gallon capacity. It seems this car could burn Kerosene. Remember, this is 1942 and gas is rationed. Kerosene wasn't. It was used for heating and kitchen stoves. Also, cars couldn't use it so it was more plentiful than gas.

What he would do is, start it on gas, retard the spark (as you could do on a Model "T," which would heat the engine up fast), and then switch to kero. This would work on this car, but it wouldn't work with a cold engine.

Inside, the building were the usual stacks of grain bags separated by type. I don't remember the types but, they were tagged.

Milking machines were in use. One of the necessary parts to a milking machine are the cups. These are steel but in order to work, they have a rubber liner. Apparently, these liners wear out and were turned in when a replacement was purchased. So, a big box of used teat cup liners was near the office door. With these, we used to throw them at each other while ducking behind stacks of grain – similar to paint ball of today! But let me tell you, it sure could smart if you caught one of those in the side of the head!!

Between the Windsor County building and the coal sheds was a small concrete building mostly submerged into the ground. I was told this housed a gas generator – a calcium carbide generator from which the gas was used for street lights on Main St.,, Depot Square, etc., prior to electricity being available.

Pleasant Street

Pleasant Street was known as "Back St." and out of the main stream of autos, there were a couple businesses. One was Henry Goodeill who operated a monument and stone cutting business. Also, Frank Woodard had a garage where he worked on cars and *way back* I can remember a big house with a garage/barn attached which was a livery stable.

Lawson's Hardware store had a fairly large storage building there with an upstairs that was a large hall. (More on this later).

1924 Overland

Going back to Woodard's garage. One day I was looking at "something" in the yard. It resembled a "short car" with no body, no windshield, front wheels and tires but no rear wheels. I asked "Mr Woodard" and he said it was the "old" golf course tractor. "It won't start and they decided to replace it rather than fix this one." It was a 1924 Overland or rather what was left of it!

I bought it for five dollars. Then I persuaded my Dad to have it "towed" up to the house.

There it was on the back lawn right on the grass. I raised the back end up and blocked it. The rear wheels were gone because they were oversize, like about 4 ft. in diameter. They were merely idlers and were driven by small matching gears mounted on the axles. It was necessary to grind the axles down so these gears would fit "other" vehicles. The golf course replaced the Overland with a 1930 Model "A."

> ## Selected Songs
> ## Composed in 1942
>
> Don't Get Around Much anymore
> I Had the Craziest Dream
> I'll Be Around
> I've Heard that Song Before
> In the Blue of the Evening
> Moonlight Becomes You
> Paper Doll
> Serenade in Blue
> String of Pearls
> Tangerine
> There Will Never Be Another You
> This Is the Army

I used to come home from school - finish what music or piano lesson was required and then go out and work on this doodlebug. Believe me, I learned a lot. This had a clutch and a 3-speed transmission.

One afternoon about two weeks after I got it, I was cranking it and cranking it, there wasn't a battery so I had to hand crank it. (Incidentally, any time a hand crank is used – be sure to keep the thumb with the index finger, not "around" the handle. In this way, if it kicks, the crank will get yanked out of your hand easily.) After about the second crank, the damn thing started! I about fell over and so did my Dad sitting by the window reading the paper! When it started, the neighborhood disappeared...... within the smoke!!

Anyway, I had to put a crate on the frame for a seat. But this is where I learned to drive. This and watching my Dad. I could sit on the box, work the clutch, shift the stick and by watching the axle(s), see the difference of different gears. I really don't know what "fixed" it, so it would run. But I did work on most everything under the hood. If I had questions about one unit - I'd ask various or many acquaintances that would offer suggestions. I was working on this while the other guys were playing catch or football!

Randolph Coal & Ice

By now, I'm sure that Harold Simmons has either retired or left. His wife (my seventh grade teacher) has died. In his place was Harry Tatro. Harry was known about town because he drove a 1932 Rockne, a car named after the football coach.

This year, when all the steam coal started to arrive, there was a difference. No gondola car spotted by the Randolph Savings and Loan Building or on the siding by Randolph Furniture Co.

The first car to arrive was a standard two-pocket hopper car. This would hold about 50 tons of coal. Also, it was spotted at the coal sheds.

Apparently, Dad felt that we could unload there provided that the "gate" was manned, and this attendant would smash chunks by holding a shovel at the gate. When a big chunk came, smash it with a hammer.

During the summer, two of the east end bins had been modified by installing false bottoms and adding outgo spouts for this type of coal.

There was still a minor problem. Once the hopper "door" is opened work had to continue until that pocket is emptied and the track is cleaned up. This would allow the freight to pass over this spot when it arrived. So, with that in mind, it was decided to start a pocket at 5 a.m. I hated getting up at 5 a.m. However, I did it. Dad was going to tend this gate, Glen and I would work the car.

We unlocked the pocket door, pried it open – no flood of coal. Glen used a sledge hammer and pounded on the side of the pocket. Slowly, coal would drop. The coal had to drop straight down and it still wouldn't fall unless it was coaxed. The car riding the rails settles the coal and compresses it. After pounding it with a sledge it starts to drop from a higher and higher point. Finally, by going up on top and using a pipe, a little hole showing through can be enticed to grow larger, finally, a pick is used to loosen, and a shovel guides the looser stuff down and out the hole. After one end is emptied the door is swung shut and the track is cleaned up adequately for passage. One pocket takes about 4 hours. Tomorrow we would repeat on the other pocket.

A couple more things, before we leave this. The second car that came in was a four-pocket car. I didn't know there was even such a thing. This had four pockets and required four early morning sessions. It held over 70 tons.

Randolph "Playhouse"

It was this year that I got a job in the local movie theatre in Randolph. By now, Jack and Barbara Robb had bought "The Strand" from Merton Carr and renamed it to "The Playhouse." Mert Carr and his wife lived on South Pleasant St. next to Bill Savage's house.

Jack and Barb came from "Down Country" (meaning South, – New Jersey or New York). They remodeled the place including an apartment in the rear where they lived, Really nice people.

Barb painted the mural in the front of the theatre and they both were present during movie time selling tickets, collecting tickets and ushering. My job was to come in after school, make popcorn in the lobby machine and turn on the warmer so it would be warm for the 7 p.m. show. Or, be ready for the Saturday afternoon matinee.

Playhouse Theatre, Randolph VT. Photo 1988, C. Wells

I used to attend the Saturday afternoon show when I was probably age eight. The ticket cost $.15. I never had popcorn or candy, I was happy just to see a movie.

Saturday was apt to be geared to the younger generation with movies like the Three Stooges, the Ritz Brothers, the Marx Brothers, Tom Mix, Hopalong Cassidy, Gene Autry, Roy Rogers, Smiley Burnette, Gabby Hayes, Sons of the Pioneers, Jimmy Durante, Bob Hope, and Bing Crosby.

There was also a Dick Tracy serial. It lasted for weeks. Each Saturday you'd see a 20 minute segment. An actor whose name was Victor Jory played the "Badman," and father of five or six sons.

Of course, there was Little Lord Fontleroy. Also, Our Gang. Even in mid thirties, the movies had sound, I think "silents" started to recede in the late twenties. Movies fascinated me and so did the projectors!

So, after a few weeks making popcorn, Jack asked me if I wanted to usher also, so I did that, and from that to "taking tickets" at the door and selling tickets. (This sharpened me in making change!)

One day they were gone and I was upstairs in the projection room looking at the projectors. I heard a strange noise only to find a pigeon flying around the main seating area. The window was open in the far gable. You could climb a ladder up onto the ceiling stringers over the main seats. Which I did, and proceeded to walk on the stringers toward the rear of the theatre. There were "collar ties" (which I then called braces) to hold on to. At the rear, the upstairs to their apartment was higher. So I climbed up and shut the window. Coming back I stepped on a 2 x 4 on their apartment ceiling and fell through! Ow-w-w! Geez! I didn't break anything, but only one leg went through and as it did, I thought I was going to get converted from a rooster to a hen!! Before I stopped wailing, I could swear my voice went up an octave!!

So, now what do you do? There was a sizable hole in the ceiling – damn stuff was only beaver board!! So I told them the truth of what and why. Jack didn't fire me – asked me if I wanted to learn to run the projectors? I sure did. So he explained that if the projectionist, Lawrence Berry was sick, it would be nice if I could fill in. So here was the plan. I would be in the projection room which Lawrence "worked" and I could "watch" him, etc. There were two projectors and these were big! Not any Keystone which would sit on a table.

These stood on the floor and were at least 6 feet high. The make was Simplex. There were two because a reel lasted about 18, maybe 20 minutes.

- As one was working, you load the other and set up - waiting for a changeover. By watching out a for inch square hole you could see the screen. Each projector had a 4 inch square hole in front of the lens. One was open for the projector working, one was closed. They were tied together, so as you slid the bar, one was shut out from "projecting," the other was "turned on" to projecting. You did this by watching the upper right corner of the screen for a black dot. With that, you turned on the sound amp and the drive motor switch for the "cut in" projector. Twenty seconds after the first dot, a second one signaled to slide the shutter which changed the source of film to the second projector. If you threaded a projector with the right amount of film lead, (number of frames etc.), the changeover would not be noticed.

Also, the light was generated by two carbon rods and these had to be watched, because as they "burned," they got shorter. Of course, you didn't want to run out of carbon rod half way through a reel. I recall that these projectors were 35 mm film size. So, for a while, I also, "worked" the projection room.

A couple of times when I finished at about 11:15, I would hop over to the pool room on a Friday night. I figured I had worked, now I should be able to play! However, my mother got wise on what I was doing. One night, I looked up from the pool table and saw my mother bearing down on me! Grabbed me by the ear, and headed for the door! That was around October or November. My punishment for being in the pool room was that after our evening meal has been completed, for each evening, I was not again allowed out of the house. That is, until spring!!! Boy, that hurt.

Typical 35mm Projector used for movies in 30's - 40's. Photo 1994, Courtesy of Edison Ford Winter Estates

However, coincidentally, just about that time, the State (some department) wrote my folks and said that I was too young to work these hours. So I went back to making popcorn.

So much for the Playhouse Theatre except I remember my pay started at $.15/hour and progressed through increments to $.35/hr as a projectionist.

This was a time when gas was rationed so most travel was very limited. Many people went to the movies and most times, I remember the lobby being full with waiting lines outside on the sidewalk.

Wallace Hill

As we advanced into winter, Stan and I both got a job with Wallace Hill, the iceman. Wallace owned a farm on Park St. right at the top of the hill. Wallace was friendly man and a hard worker. Ironically, he also owned an ice house that, in years past, my Dad also owned. Wallace still was cutting ice on the small pond and storing it in the ice house beside the pond. Believe me, in Randolph in the thirties, forties, etc., it really did get cold. I've touched on this before.

When the pond had ice that was ready to harvest it was about January before cutting started. By this time, it's generally about 2 feet thick, maybe 30 inches.

Wallace would fire up the ice saw and start cutting lines in the ice. (The snow had been removed, if there was any). He could cut lines about 3 feet apart. Then go back at 90 degrees and cut about 2 feet apart.

A spade bar would start breaking rows apart. Then, the blocks are floated to an endless belt which takes them up into the ice house for storage.

In here, you use a short handle pike pole to "shag" these blocks around to spot them in a given space.

Standing at the end of the chute in the building when they come sliding in, was crucial. *Don't let them stop*! If you do, they stick right there!!

The water on the bottom (or sides) would "seal" within an instant! Then, while you're getting this one unsealed, more coming down the chute will start to back up, and they stick.

While we were standing there at the foot of the chute, a block came in. Wallace, with a pike pole and very nonchalantly, reaches out, snags the block, places it, comes back, and gives this pole to Stan. The block glides in, Stan reaches out, grabs the block and almost gets catapulted to the railroad station!! I thought I would never stop laughing, that is until I grabbed a block and flew about the same distance. They weighed about 250 pounds! Anyway, they didn't bother Wallace.

Wallace used to pick up milk cans on a route for the creamery. He could take two 40 qt. cans of milk, back the handles together and two more for the left hand, wind his hands through the four handles and walk off with two cans of milk weighing about 160 pounds, in each hand!

One cold morning, he came into the Cities Service Station near the bridge. Elbert Fullam asked Wallace what he could do for him.

Wallace said he needed a jump start – it was so cold, his tractor wouldn't start.

Elbert said - "Did you crank it?"

Wallace drawled, "Yeah, cranked it, till it boiled and it still won't start!!!"

Of course, Wallace had a route where he drove around town delivering ice for the customers who had ice boxes! In the thirties, ice boxes were very common. Taking a stab here, I would say it was around 1936 and on, the electric refrigerators became known and gained popularity. The early ones had that big round thing on top! Wallace was well-known about town for some of the feats he could do. I don't think *he* considered them feats!

For instance, one day he came into Windsor County Farmers Exchange. He ordered three or four bags of grain. Before he and Bob Noyes exited the office, Bob said, "Wallace, someone told me you could throw a bag of grain over your shoulder with a pitch fork! Is that true?"

Wallace: "Probably."

Bob: "Bet you can't"

Wallace: "What you bet?"

Bob: "Bet you double or nothing. You do it, the bag is free. You fail, you pay double."

"OK?" Wallace grabbed a pitch fork and tossed that 100 lb. bag of grain over his shoulder, like nothing!!!

Many products were delivered to your door.

Dana Clough, from Randolph Center, used to go around the village selling vegetables and fruit from his Model "T" truck.

The Model "T" was about a 1920. It had a canopy over it with side curtains that could be rolled up like an awning. I never saw them down because they would be in the way for him to work.

Of course, milk was delivered to the doorstep – so were groceries.

Mr. Rix from Sand Hill (I think his name was Bill) would walk from his house over to Whiting Milk Creamery on Pearl St., then work a full day. When finished, he would walk home. Then he walked around town selling berries he had picked, door-to-door.

Also, Harold Phelps used to go door-to-door collecting premiums for Met Life, some of which were a nickel or dime. He always carried his little book and most of the time, walked.

Also, various and many other sales people that sold products like the Fuller Brush Man, Rawleigh Products and, in later years, the Electrolux Salesman.

And then there was the story about the Electrolux salesman travelling the area in the late forties – after the war.

There were many areas around Randolph, where the population was quite sparse.

The Electrolux salesman stopped at one house, knocked on the door. When greeted by "the woman" of the house, explained what he was doing. So, he entered and proceeded to sprinkle fireplace ashes, sawdust, sand etc. on the living room floor. The he assembled his prize model of vacuum cleaner – not seeing an electrical outlet easily, he inquired to the woman where one was.

"Oh!" she replied, we don't have electricity yet!!

Most or some of these carried samples or a demo unit and later delivered the product.

In the thirties these people were common to see in any community. Don't forget the Depression carried well into the thirties.

Also, as mentioned previously, many hobos, as they were called at the time, used to wander away from the tracks into the residential areas looking for food.

Of course, the best known door-to-door salesman in Randolph was Barney Shapiro. He would sell door-to-door with all his products from dish holders, thread, buttons, etc. on his back! He had no store until later in life.

Day Dreaming

In school, I used to day dream when some subject came along that was boring. There were many instances when my mind was miles away.

One day, I was thinking about cars and how limited their speed was. At this year in the early forties, speeds were picking up – probably could get a car up to 80 m.p.h., especially down hill!

So I thought, why not take another transmission, turn it around and mount it backwards behind the first transmission. Think, front one in high gear – 1:1 – second one in low and backwards – 1:3!! Of course, this would work but actually it would require a lot of power (not in cars of this vintage). Also, I couldn't weld. I couldn't afford to pay for welding, so I stashed it mentally.

Ariel Jobes

One day, I ran into a fellow that apparently married a local girl and moved back into Randolph. Her name must have been Clara Call. His name was Ariel Jobes. He had built a unit like this on something like an old 1923 or 1924 Chassis, the make escapes me. Anyway, there was no body only a front seat on a frame. He was a welder and some way we hooked up and he gave me a demo.

We went by the (present) bowling alley site in hi-low. The engine was just barely "turning over" but we were moving! As a matter of fact, the engine was boiling, it was working so hard. He turned it into a drive, crossed over the road and "backed" it up at surprising speed. (This was pretty dangerous as later I surmised that the caster probably wasn't altered!).

This is 1943, and there is a war going on. I mentioned before about the aircraft lookout post on Braintree hill. There were other ways the general population pitched in to help the war effort.

Everybody was involved in gas rationing. Food rationing was in full force as was the fact that butter, sugar, and silk stockings were not to be found! Stan and I went to a round and square dance one Saturday night in East Barnard. There was one general store and in stock was most every item that normally could not be found or seen anywhere else! We made a couple girls happy and were quite impressed when they received a gift.

Scrap Drive

One big effort that the residents of Randolph, Brookfield and Braintree made, was a scrap drive. Scrap iron and steel were in high demand. So an area in Depot Square was fenced off and any and all scrap iron and steal was tossed there. This was right next to the depot platform on the north side. I can remember more than one Saturday riding on a volunteer truck going from homes in the village to farms in the country asking for donations.

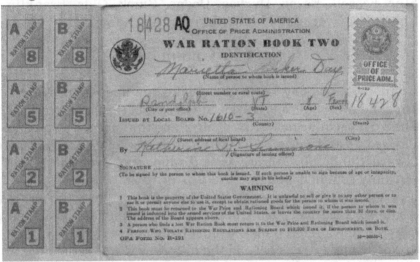

Typical ration book for food issued during World War II.

Also, another item school children used to collect was milk weed pods! These had a silky texture, and we were told, they were used in the manufacture of parachutes!

Cars in the River

On School Street, about four houses on the right in back of Bethany Church, was where Bob Ford lived. As you drove in the driveway, apparently there had been no garage(s) until the fifties. The driveway went straight into the "bank." Beyond the bank was the river. It must have been, that in the twenties, erosion was a problem.

So, to help slow the erosion, old cars were dumped there. To be more accurate they weren't all "dumped." Many were driven and others were pushed. The driver(s) would stop in the driveway, pull the hand throttle out, let out the clutch and jump off!

So, during this scrap drive, a wrecker was brought in and literally *dozens* of old vehicles were retrieved and hauled away for scrap.

Here are *some* of the makes: Ford (Model T), Hupmobile, Star, Kissell, Essex, Duryea, Dodge, Buick, Olds, Franklin, Chevrolet, Overland, Maxwell, to mention a few.

B 17 Crash

In 1943, one day I was on my bike and had stopped on the street near the railroad tracks, at the rear of the freezer lockers. I heard a peculiar noise like an airplane that needed a tune up. I looked up and saw a B 17 (Flying Fortress Bomber) going east toward Randolph Center. As it disappeared over the hill, it certainly sounded "rough."

I rode my bike up near Webster's Mill to watch it do the disappearance over Fish Hill to the east. From here I could get a better view. Before I moved on, it had made a circle from East to North while it was beyond the hill. Now it was returning. At this time, two or three parachutes were seen!

It was now flying in the southerly direction, I could follow it against the ridge. Only by now, it was puffing smoke. It appeared at least two engines must have quit and it was losing altitude! Good God, was this plane going to crash!? How can it not? It's getting lower and lower!! It quickly disappeared behind some trees near the Green Mountain Stock Farm. And then a crash and black smoke!

I was only 500 feet from my house, so I quickly pedaled home with my heart pounding all the way! Dad was home and I pleaded to "let's go." By now, the fire alarm had sounded. We drove to the Stock Farm and up Knight's Hill(??) and to the right you could see trees that had been topped! We parked. Dad was going to stay with the car. As I made my way into the woods, I began to see pieces of aluminum and other debris. The further I went it became thicker and was also emitting a peculiar odor, I was to find out it was aviation fuel. Then I came upon the tail section, later to learn the tail gunner was killed. The Vermont State Guard was flocking in and Jock Murray, who was the High School principal and also Captain in the State Guard, stood there. He had two cartridge belts on over his shoulders. He was standing, straddling a box. This box I found out was the Norden bomb sight. This was a highly secretive device that the U.S. had and was to be guarded at all costs! The plane was scattered all over the woods except a wheel, the tail section and a few other distinguishable pieces. The pilot and copilot were also killed.

What happened is this. These planes apparently leave Kansas and head to Newfoundland. Refuel, and then on to England. They were fully equipped ready to participate in the war and only lacked ammunition. There was belief that sabotage had taken place – something like sugar or sand dumped in the gas which could raise Hell. I don't know if it was ever proven.

Monument near the B-17 crash site. Photo 2001

Village Steam Roller

The village had owned for years, a big steam roller. This was stored in a two-bay garage building beside the coal office. Up to the war, they would fire this monster up and coax it out of its "sleeping" place. This was steam operated, and it took about three days of nurturing a fire in the boiler to generate enough steam to put life into the "ol Girl"!

It was big, heavy and, believe me, the railroad flat car that delivered it to Randolph in the twenties, must have groaned some when it was loaded on. No truck at that time could have carried it and if it were driven from the factory, that would have taken months. I don't think it did over 4 m.p.h. wide open!

For paved roads, they used to make a blade mix. By laying down a bed of small stones, then a big "tar truck" would heavily spray a coat of the tar and lastly a Grader (road machine) with a blade would actually mix this combination. Then a steam roller would "pack it down." Lastly, a coat of sand covered it while it hardened.

The point of telling this, is, I'm sure this steam roller was cut up and contributed to the scrap drive for the war. The rear wheels were solid steel and about 8 ft. in diameter, and probably 18 inches wide. There was a place to stand on the rear. Also, it had a big roof over the whole machine, and a scarifier on back, for ripping up paving, etc.

Kenneth Norton (Again)

Kenny Norton, of course, was getting a lot of action in the junk yard due to the high demand for scrap iron and steel. I don't seem to remember much about aluminum. It seems aluminum to recycle was also in high demand. However, let's not forget aluminum was not a popular metal at this time. About the only thing aluminum was used in was kitchen pots and pans, and not too much there, either. There was very little, if any aluminum in cars.

Gas was only about $.35 a gallon. The weight of cars was not a problem.

It was quite a common sight to see Kenny glide down Main St. Hill with a load of scrap. He took one of the Se-Lect bread trucks, cut the roof and rear doors off. Took another with the frame and rear axle minus cab and engine and made a trailer of it. By hitching it onto the number one, he would then take just the frame of a car (or truck) and bridge right between the two trucks!

When it turned, it cracked and groaned and made all kinds of funny noises. Then he would go to Rutland, VT to deliver the contents. If he ever got stopped, and, truthfully I bet he did (and often), but knowing Kenny, he would talk his way out of it and if he couldn't, he'd go to court and fight the ticket. I remember once hearing him saying he had been in 42 trials and won all of them except one!!

I know of one trip he made to Rutland. To get there, you had to go over Mendon Mountain. By the time you join Route 4, it becomes a hard pull. (Upgrading the road by now, has minimized the incline). However, he was well into the climb and either broke an axle or, something in the drive line, let go. As he was sitting there a Vermont Trooper stopped and soon became suspicious why a drive line failure should happen with basically sheet metal for a load.

Anyway, one way or another, it seems Kenny had dozens of auto batteries on the bottom of the load! That cost him a few bucks!

Everett "Spot Cash" Sager (Again)

In the spring of 1943, Sager ("Spot Cash") had bid on the coal for the "Aggie" School. I should explain here that the "Aggie" school in Randolph center is for the education and preparation of any student who wanted to be a farmer. Only potential farmers attended at that time.

When "Spot Cash" bid – I don't know if he forgot, if he didn't know or what – he never specified to have the steam coal shipped in a gondola car! The first car that arrived (spring 1943) was a two-pocket hopper car. It was spotted on the siding at the furniture factory. He didn't have a portable or movable coal unloader. He didn't have coal sheds he could use.

Some way, I was hired to help him, at least, on car #1. Know what we did? We climbed to the top of that car and started to shovel it from the top down. This meant that each shovel had to be "picked" first. Also, it meant that as progress was made, ultimately each shovelful was going to have to be tossed up and over the side!

Anyway, I picked, shoveled and grunted for days. "Spot Cash" just kept on going and finally we got down to where the pocket dividers started to show through. *I* couldn't throw a shovel full of coal and have it go over the side. It was too high. So, I picked and/or shoveled the coal into Everett's shovel. When it was full, he would toss it over the side. Then wait for me to load his shovel again.

I don't recall that I stuck with him for all the 240 tons that they usually took each year. I was paid about .35/hour!

Town of Randolph

I do recall, that by June 1, I had a job with the town of Randolph. This was *not* the village, it was the town. I was hired to operate a Cat D7.

It was interesting to me that to start this yellow "monster," the engine (which was diesel), had a two-cylinder gas engine built into it. You start the gas engine which then started the diesel. Electric starters weren't powerful enough as yet to start a diesel of that size (apparently!). This wasn't a bull dozer, it was a D7 crawler tractor without the blade. It was time to "hone" the roads. When you hone the roads, a road machine is pulled, in this case, by a crawler tractor. The roads that we are going to hone, are dirt – no hard top. By "operating" way over to the side of the road, the road machine operator can control the eight foot wide blade. By dropping the right end at a sharp angle, it will clean out the ditch at the side of road, by bringing all the silt, stones, leaves and crud up out of the ditch onto the road. It thereby, cleans the ditch and also crowns the road so rain water runs off and doesn't puddle. The tractor only runs about 4 m.p.h. and you constantly have to look back so you can steer accurately. Herb Sargent was the road machine operator. There were a few times he would holler at me. One time, he hooked onto a sluice, which meant a corrugated drain pipe going across (and under) the road. Of, course, this meant extra work to fix that. I didn't see it – guess he didn't either.

After the road was honed, then we had to walk in back of a slow moving truck and toss all rocks bigger than an egg into the truck. Everett Tyler and I always worked together on this. We all did many roads – many miles of road, under the guidance of the foreman, Lewis Chambers.

Somewhere around first part of August, we had honed Howard

Hill and was working the stone part of this operation. Howard Hill is quite steep. Out of the blue, Lewis said to me, "You, Wells. You haven't picked up enough stones to put in your pocket! You're fired!" Geez, I thought he was joking. He wasn't. "Everett is doing all the work! You're off the job. Your check will get mailed!"

Believe me, I was really so surprised. However, a quick assessment told me, I only had a couple weeks left before I had to start school anyway. I was about 3 maybe 4 miles from the village, with no transportation, not even a bicycle!

I don't know why, but I said, "No the check isn't going to get mailed to me. I'm going to wait right here for it to come to me!!" Man, I thought he was going to explode! Didn't say anything but in a moment or two, climbed into his pickup and headed down the hill, spewing dust and stones!

Within the hour he was back, gave me a check. I walked down off the hill, hung up a thumb for a ride into town.

I told Dad what had happened - I thought he would scold me, - - - but he didn't!

Also somewhere about this time, the United church, which had recently consolidated the Baptist and Methodist congregations, had decided to remodel the cellar of the Baptist church. This would end up with class rooms and various other rooms. Stan and I both volunteered to work on this project. Eugene McGee was the supervisor. We worked with a Gas Jack Hammer, plumbing, running wiring, and sheet rock nailing – no screws yet!

Pistol Packin' Mama

By now, I had bought a model "T" Ford from Ken Norton.. Age somewhere around a 1924. All it was, was a chassis, wheels, axles, and seat. There was no body whatever. There should have been a gas tank under the seat. I spoke to Ken about it and he said, "Lets go see if we can find one." So we did. Somewhere we found one in another frame – just needed to be removed. He said, "Stay here I'll go get a torch." A few moments later, he's pushing a cart with two tanks in it up the road or path.

"Here, hold your hand over the fill hole – the cap is gone." I offered more than a sprinkling of reluctance. "Not to worry, just keep your hand so no sparks jump in there." With that he cut the tank loose, shut off the torch and yanked the tank out. Someway, I forget how, but this vehicle ended up in the garage at home.

During the next few months, it required quite a lot of work. I was hoping to get it registered by fall – I would be 15½ then. So, it started to take on a rather distinct appearance. A pickup cab of some vintage was attached to the frame. That gave us doors, a windshield, floor boards, etc. Then a platform was built on the frame in the rear. That gave us some fenders in the rear. A hood was fashioned out of sheet metal. The "us" referred to was either Stan Gould, Wendell Smith, Oatey Smithers, or Bill Slack, whoever was around. It was registered with a plate and could be driven. It was named "Pistol Packin' Mama."

Don't forget, no work or play on this project until the 60 minute music session was completed in the house! I am still confused here about my age and driving on the road. I know I could drive this about town, it was registered. I know that I was only 15 by the year 1943. I suspect that the law was modified because of the war. Also, you were allowed to drive on the highway in Vermont at age 14, *if* you had a person with a Senior license with you on the front seat.

Montgomery's Farm

In my sophomore year, I used to drive this "vehicle," and cart four, five or six others out to the Elmer Montgomery farm on Route 12A. Elmer's son, Jeness, and grandsons, Dick and Loren Montgomery, all lived and worked this farm.

The potato crop was ready to harvest. It was fall – gorgeous days and cool nights. The potato digger would be pulled over the mound where they were growing. The machine whirred up the dirt and vines, shook everything apart leaving the potatoes loose on the ground. Our job was to pull or carry a bag, stop and gather potatoes. Bushels and bushels of potatoes were picked up, for which we were paid about $.40/hour.

After the bags were picked up, the potatoes were hauled back to a special room at the farm and were sorted and graded. These people did this by sight and feel as the potatoes passed by on a belt.

It was here that I learned, if a potato wasn't deemed good enough to eat due to nicks, appearance, etc., it was tossed into a separate location which ultimately was used to make vodka. (What was vodka?)

By now, most *all* cars had moved the gearshift from the floor to the steering column. It also should be said that 1941 was the last year of full fledged auto production. There were a few 1942 models produced, which had been designed and "tooled" prior. So, the 1942 model year did yield a few autos. I remember that Ford, Chevrolet and Plymouths were diverted to military use such as staff cars which were painted olive drab, or as some said s_ _ _ brindle brown!

Leon Webster 1940 Ford

Leon Webster had purchased a new Ford sedan in 1940 in Rutland, which was 45 miles away. He drove it to Randolph. It had the new position of the gearshift.

He had started out in first, then shifted up to neutral and up again to second. Somehow, when he again shifted from second down to neutral, he raised the shift lever and succeeded in getting it back in first gear. Again!! I'm sure it wasn't a *noiseless* effort, but he did it!! Drove all the way from Rutland to Randolph in low gear.

Glen Ducharme and I were unloading a load of coal, on Route 12, near the hospital. We heard a commotion, saw this car approaching and stopped at the curb in the street. The passenger window was rolled down as we walked toward him.

Leon: "Hey, either one of you know where the "go" gear is in this?"

Glen: "Well, Leon, you're doing all right. Go right along!?

Leon "No, no, you can't get any speed out of it without a lot of noise!"

Well, whether or not he found the "go" gear - the car went back to Rutland and the story was, the engine was replaced!!

Useless Auto Information

Back in the mid thirties, most cars started advertising about oil bath air cleaners. Up to this time, most cars had air cleaner insides that looks like an early pot scrubber – a real coarse metal, shaped to fit the air cleaner. By 1936, these cars started to ballyhoo about the oil bath cleaner. As a kid, it was a big puzzle to me on how they could run that air through oil!! When cleaning oil bath air cleaners and replacing the oil, it only served to puzzle me more.

The air doesn't go through the oil! As the air is sucked into the filter, it is deflected down and immediately up. As the dirt and dust grains have more weight (than any amount of air), they can't change direction, so they land in the oil and are trapped. That info, and a dollar, might get you coffee in some places!!

Model "T" Info

This is probably a pretty good spot to elaborate about Model "T" Fords. For anyone not interested, feel free to skip ahead. *But*, there are a couple unique features that should be brought up. One is the Model "T" coil. Unlike more modern cars, and, I guess, no other car, used these coils.

Every car has a coil – necessary to make the spark plugs fire! But one coil is used for *all* the spark plugs! On a Model "T," there is one coil for each spark plug (and thereby each cylinder).

The unique feature is that when the key is turned on, the battery is apt to make one of the four coils come to life (buzz), which then makes a spark plug, spark!

Very common occurrence to see a driver sit down in a Model "T," turn the switch on, and the car starts. If it didn't, the driver would move the spark control (under the steering wheel on the left side) up or down and then it might start. The reason for this is that this movement might accidentally find the spot where the "timer" is opposite the rotor and in doing so, would make the coil "buzz" for that cylinder, causing the plug to fire and the engine would start. This would eliminate the need of the driver having to climb out and giving it a crank!

Something else. It was customary, prior to shutting any Model "T" off, to rev up the engine and shut the ignition key off while the

This Model "T" view shows the 3 pedals, the parking brake and also, the black box for the 4 coil boxes.
Both Photos: National Automobile and Truck Museum of United States, Photo 2001, C. Wells.

Typical delivery truck. Photo 2001, C. Wells

engine is at a higher revolution than at idle. This was done to "load" the intake manifold *and* cylinders with a *correct* gas/air mixture. If this criteria was met, your chances for a restart greatly increased!

Although greatly diminishing, it was very common to hear many divers do this way up to the fifties and sixties. Even though the coil on newer cars won't duplicate a Model "T," having the proper mixture ready to go was probably an asset. Now that the "older" drivers are passing on, this act is less common. I had a neighbor up to about 1980, who would faithfully do this on his sixty and seventies Oldsmobile every time he shut it off. Well, this rev up was a carry over from the days of the Model "T"!!

Another thing "unique" with the Model "T," was the transmission. The transmission was called a planetary transmission and had no "stick" shift. Many other cars of this vintage (and even older) had a clutch and a stick shift on the floor.

The Model "T" had three pedals. The left pedal was a low-high (gear) pedal. If pushed down, you were in low gear. If you let up on it, you would pass through neutral and go into high gear. Now, the brake lever sticking up from the floor on the left came into play. With the brake pulled way back toward the seat, put the car in neutral (by placing the left pedal at the neutral spot). By releasing the parking brake, the brake would relax, put the vehicle in neutral (with no brake) and by allowing the brake lever to go way forward the left pedal would come into high. You had to develop a "feel" where neutral was with your left foot.

Your right foot was used on the middle pedal, which was reverse and also, your right foot depressed the right pedal which was a transmission brake and achieved the same result as a wheel brake would.

Once you got acquainted with the pedals, a Model "T" was fun to drive. You could also play "games." If you used the reverse pedal for a brake (and many did), on slippery "going" you would find that one rear (driving) wheel would go backwards while the other would go forward. This, of course, would accelerate a road spin around (without much concern which way the wheel was turned).

It was common to use reverse as a brake. The reason was that inside the transmission were three "bands." These consisted of a steel band about 7 or 8 inches in diameter or which was riveted a stiff "cloth or composition" belt. The band itself had terminates so a "bolt" could go through and also a recess for a nut (for the end of "bolt" which was actually a pivot rod with an attached pedal (one of three). Each pedal had a machined cam so as it was depressed, it would move to the left, and in doing so would move the appropriate band to the left. With one end fixed, as the band moved to the left, it tightened around a drum in the transmission. This drum dictates what's going to happen actually to the driveshaft and thus the wheels.

See, all this is information you can toss into the "so what" jug!

Before we hit the release button here on Model "T" let's talk for a moment about the coils I've mentioned before. A coil was a small wooden box which actually is a step up transformer. Inside, the transformer was encapsulated in tar. A set of points on top created the circumstances to allow this transformer to create about 20,000 volts to fire the spark plug. There were four coils in a box mounted on the inside of the firewall. Each coil had a high tension wire going to one of the four spark plugs. Each coil was controlled by a wire to the timer which told the appropriate coil to "fire"! You could vary the "fire" time by a hand controlled spark lever under the steering wheel. The only "gas" control was also under the steering wheel by a lever sticking out to the right. Typical operation was to hold both spark and gas "wide open" by one hand and steer with the other!

Here is a good place to speak about another one of my high school acquaintances, and friend, Harvey Hubbard.

Harvey had a 1931 Whippet when *he* was a junior.

One thing I *can* remember about that Whippet was the center of the steering wheel. Dead center was the horn button, which was surrounded by a ring of hard rubber. By turning this ring "of rubber," the various positions for lights would be seen. To the left – parking lights, to the right – high beam headlights, – another "notch," – low beams!

By pulling up on this "ring," was the starter!

One thing that used to really upset Harvey was *any* dog that "wetted" one of the wheels. More than once, I saw *and heard* Harvey let a shriek out – which *quickly* stopped any dog from lifting his leg *anywhere near* his Whippet!

One day, Harvey parked his Whippet on School St., near the High School. Before leaving the vehicle, he "actuated" his "dog chasing device"! *This* was a Model "T" coil that intermittently "charged" the car with hi voltage!

If, any dog sniffed a wheel, before he was finished, that coil would buzz and that dog was sorry he picked that specific car for a hydrant!!

I loved the old Model "T." We had many good times and much fun, you'll have to forgive me when I get started. After 1921, electric starters were added so cranking was eliminated or at least minimized. Too common, I was to see men walking around with broken arms, wrists and thumbs by cranking and *not* having the spark control up which was the retarded position. This would almost always prevent a "kick back" to the crank. Some people would jack up a rear wheel up and spin the wheel, or a push, or coast downhill was a common way to start a Model "T."

One thing I skipped was the fact that no second gear was many times a drawback. Ford didn't change this on any "T" that I knew about except on *some* trucks there was such a thing as a two speed axle! Imagine a two speed axle in the twenties!?

Garabaldi Barberi

By now, I had long stopped taking cornet lessons from Mr. Slack in So. Royalton. I had made pretty good progress with him but, for reasons unknown to me, my mother had found a man in Barre that taught trumpet (and cornet). They're both the same, play the same, are the same range, etc. The trumpet is apt to have a more brilliant tone where the cornet will have a more mellow tone. The popular instrument was the trumpet. The cornet was diminishing in popularity.

Garabaldi Barberi in Barre was younger than Mr. Slack, and knowing human nature somewhat, as I now do, I'll bet Mother's presence in the room while I had a lesson, was probably a piece of abrasion that "Baldi" could do without. It intimidated me also, as you can imagine.

Baldi insisted that you "keep time" by beating with your foot. OK, we can do that. And periodically, he would check to see if I was. He used to harp to me about my foot has to be even and equal. None of this uneven stuff – 1 down 2 up, etc. – no 1 down up 2. We dwelled on this or rather he and mother dwelled on how long it should be dwelled on! Round and round, while I sat there like a knob on a log!

Well, anyway Baldi played in the Barre City Band, also the Shriners Band of the Alleppo Temple in Barre. Baldi could play a trumpet!! He made me practice from an orange book called Gatti and I used to say to myself, "What is it with these people whose name ends in 'I'?!" This was taking place in about 1939 up to 1941.

Green Mountain Band

By 1941, "it" was decided that I could try out with the Randolph Town Band, known as Green Mountain Band. My first session was in the practice room in Sowles block over Grants Drug Store, in an empty room, above where Conrad Sault operated a barber shop.

Now, this band opened a whole new world. Many of the members I knew quite well, others I got to know as time went on. I had trouble keeping up, finding the (correct) place, etc., but I found out many others did. That's why there was a weekly rehearsal. Many of the guys became very close friends even with age differences.

Sax	Clarinet	Trumpet
Rudy Day	Bill Bachelder	Geo Hardy
Mike Pierce	Jack Lamson	Charles Ellis
Cliff Patch	Stan Smithers	Conrad Wells
Bill Clark	Bob Moore	Wayne Buck
		Clyde Estabrook
		Wendell Smithers
		David Angell

Trombone	Baritone	Snare Drum
Sherb Lang	Stanhope Brigham	Dick Phelps
Dr. Blackmer		Harold Terry
Charlie Hyde		Sonny Bachelder
Bass Drum	Tuba	Sousaphone
Lynn Hutchinson	Gerald Fish	Perley Slack

My apologies to others, I have overlooked.

Well, that named a few.

The first time I saw Rudy Day put his sax down, after we had played just a few bars, he opened his mouth and out popped a short cigar butt – lit. A few puffs and the smoke increased. I couldn't believe

Randolph's first schoolhouse was constructed at South Randolph in 1794. Two other facilities, one erected in 1818 and the other in 1835, served pupils before the substantial structure pictured was built in 1867. It closed in 1969 and its students moved to East Randolph. Photo courtesy of Wes Herwig.

Courtesy of Wes Herwig

my eyes, but I did see it!

Came time to start again, he rolled the butt back on his tongue, brought the sax up and played with only an occasional puff of smoke emanating from the bell. Rudy, at this time, worked for the Soil Conservation Corp., as previously mentioned.

Anyway, we rehearsed each week in the spring to prepare for weekly concert in Depot Square, etc. throughout the summer. We also did one concert each in Randolph Center, N. Randolph, E. Randolph and S. Randolph.

People sat in their cars on Saturday nights, ate popcorn, sat on their fenders and talked, etc. After each tune or, more appropriately, each rendition, they would honk the horns in appreciation!

The building pictured is the South Randolph school house, the band would setup in front of the building. Besides chairs and music stands, there was also lamps made of a wooden base, – a 6 foot length of pipe and a light bulb. The bulbs attracted every moth and miller in 4 counties!! One got sucked into my mouth when I took a deep quick breath on one occasion! It got stuck in my throat, cut my breath off and scared me enough, before I got my breath back to convince me I had been sent for!?!!

Selected Songs
Composed in 1943

All Or Nothing At All
GI Jive
Happiness is a Thing Called Joe
Lili Marlene
Oh! What a Beautiful Morning
Opus One
People Will Say We're In Love
Sunday Monday or Always
Surrey With a Fringe On Top

Prince's General Store

Stan and I were in Depot Square one Saturday. Jimmy Hunt pulled over to the curb and said he was going to Prince's General Store in South Randolph. "Want to go?" Sure, we jumped in and headed for Randolph Center. Up Slack Hill, his Model "T" growled and groaned in typical "T" fashion. This was a touring car and he had the roof down. I was in the back, Stan sat up front. As we reached the Center we turned right heading south. We were laughing and talking, having lots of fun. The turn to the left for the So. Randolph Road was identical to the turn into the church, which came first. As he yanked the wheel and entered the church drive, Stan said "cut through here" pointing to the tall grass on the right between the two roads. As we cut through the grass, all of a sudden the front just dropped followed by it coming right back up which, then prompted the rear end to drop also and pop right up again. *Geez what a bump*! Actually we crossed over a drainage ditch. Jimmy was wrestling with the wheel trying to settle this thing down as he went from ditch to ditch. Finally got it stopped. I ended up, on the back of the rear seat!! We got out to check the front wheels – both pointed out! The tie rod stuck through the middle of the front spring and axle! Jim put his foot against it and pushed. The wheels started to look much more normal as they swung in!! We jumped in and continued down the dirt road.

About three miles later easing over the crest of a long down grade, we could see Prince's General Store and all the people who had come for the auction. Prince's had been there for countless years. The last owner had died. The remains were going on the block. Compared to the stores of the nineties, this store was nothing. However, how many stores in the early forties could you go to and exit with a pound of cut plug tobacco (whatever that was), a set of piston rings for a Model "T" Ford, a coffin (pine box), some black thread, a shoe eye, and most everything in between, like a pound of cheese.

Jim's Model "T" had 30 by 3½ tires and it had to be cranked. Those two reasons meant it had to be a model prior to 1921. The exact year I don't recall. All of us had fun in the various Model "T"s and the fun wasn't over yet.

Model "T" Rebuild

I came out of Prince's auction with a set of Model "T" piston rings. Today I would ask, are they standard size or oversize and if oversize, by how much? But back then I doubt very much if cylinder reboring had been established.

Anyway, for $.15 I had a set of piston rings. Stan said he would give me a hand to put them in. The "Pistol Packin' Mama" did smoke and it seemed quite a lot more than usual.

When we got back to the "patient," we took the head off and the oil pan. This "job" provided a lot of experience, some good and some, – not so good!!!

After the pan was removed, it could be seen, there are four troughs, one at the low point where each connecting rod goes. Here it scoops the oil in each trough to lubricate the connecting rod bearing through the oil hole in the cap. There is no oil pump, and of course no oil filter.

We removed the head, peeled the old rings off and installed the new rings. We were careful to keep the pistons in the correct number for reinstalling. So, the head was put back on, the oil pan was reinstalled and oil put in.

Time to start it up. This Model "T" had a starter, so turn the switch on and step on the start switch. Step on it again – nothing! "Must be the new rings create so much drag, the starter can't turn it over"!!

"Maybe we could give it a tow."

So we hitched it up beyond a car and started a tow. This produced nothing more than the rear wheels dragging on the road.

"Hell, this thing hasn't got a body on back - we ought to put a little weight back there"!

So, we added four or five cement blocks on the platform.

That did it. No more wheels skidding along, the wheels turned the engine started and we're in business. However, after a few minutes, the radiator was boiling! God, it boiled and boiled some more. It was to the point we couldn't even put the radiator cap back on.

Finally it didn't boil, it also stopped smoking!

1934 Oldsmobile

In the spring of 1944, I bought a '34 Oldsmobile. By now I had a drivers license. I had passed age 16 in January. I had sold the "Pistol Packin' Mama" (which was painted on both doors).

My folks has some friends who came to Randolph during the summers. They lived on Hebard Hill, and their name was Hughes. One son, Rod still lives in town. So, I bought this car they apparently didn't need any more. The day "we" drove up to get it, I recall "we" had a pickup with "large" wheels. The "we" was Leon Hughes and whose pickup it was, I don't know. Anyway, the pickup left and Leon and I set about to get this thing "off the hill."

This Olds also had a straight eight engine and the car was heavy. Once we headed "north" to go down Howard Hill, we didn't go far. That monster sunk in the mud before we got to the hill! We were in mud up to, and even with, the running boards. Well, calling AAA was out, so was hiring a wrecker! Only thing left was the coal truck. I hiked down off the hill and thumbed a ride into Randolph. Backed the coal truck out (with Dad's permission) and headed up Route 12 and then up the hill to where the car was. (Dual wheels, plus the road up the hill being less rutty made a difference.)

Back up to the Olds and hitched on. Leon steered the Olds and I drove the truck. We dug and churned and dug some more. Geez – that car pulled like pulling a stone boat.

Anyway, I ran that for a couple months. It was a big car and heavy car. I recall it had independent suspension on the front. To me it rode like sitting and riding on a big marshmallow.

1931 Chevrolet

Next was a 1931 Chevrolet Convertible Coupe. This was only a fair car, small and even being a convertible, it wasn't great. However, I had a lot of fun with it. The car also helped me feel older.

Sister Takes on a Job

My sister has been around all this time, but I haven't mentioned her, only occasionally,

But in 1943, while she was in high school, some "official" from Gifford Memorial Hospital came to Randolph High School and asked Mr. True, the Principal for some help.

It seems the administrator in the hospital needed a vacation and there was no one to temporarily take her place. The war was going full tempo, so she had been two or three years without any time off. She was a registered nurse but was more an administrator, rather than floor nurse.

Someway, Mr. True arrived at my sister, Nan, to take time off from school and be her substitute.

In the hospital, she was responsible for admittances, discharges, all the patient files and countless other details in running the hospital—the most important of which was control of all the drugs stocked and used, which was tallied each Sunday.

I can't believe anybody, still in high school, would be allowed or rather given that responsibility—and I'm told she did it with flying colors, with only a reprimand (I recall) just once!

Dad's Lending Hand

"A.C." didn't lend me money to buy cars. He also didn't co-sign a bank note to lend me money to buy a car and then allow me to get soft on payments!

When I approached him for a loan, he said no. "But what I will do, is co-sign a note at the bank, and you can owe the bank." Well, that was a good arrangement. So we went to the bank when the time came. This means that up to this point at least, I had bought, sold and made enough so I didn't need a loan. However, an analysis later showed that my taste for vehicles was increasing faster than the profit margin! In other words, my desires were overriding my abilities.

Randolph Coal & Ice Co.

Now, I could drive to work which, at this time, was for Dad, or "A.C.," as he was called by everyone else. This is spring. "Spot Cash" either didn't bid or his bid was too high, so the Aggie School coal supply started to arrive at the coal sheds again. So, this year we ran "it" through the sheds which *was* easier than hand shoveling it off.

Most of it came in four-pocket cars with only a couple of two-pocket hopper cars. Some days we would do two pockets in one day. It was spotted at one pocket which filled one modified bin in the coal sheds. *If* we had time in the afternoon, we would start the second pocket.

A local freight behind number 468 has started across the long trestle over the Dog River north of Northfield. Note 4 pocket coal car. Photograph by Jim Shaughnessy, Courtesy of Robert C. Jones

R.R. Pinch Bar

We had a tool, which, when placed on a rail under a wheel would "pinch" the car along about an inch. There were two hard steel "blocks" that actually dug into the rail as you pushed that handle down. At the same time, a little pad came against the wheel and exerting up pressure moving the wheel up. Obviously the car was moved. You really had to be careful not to wrap your fingers *around* the handle. Always push down with the hand open! Do I need to say that with our fingers wrapping around the handle and *if* the blocks slipped (with pressure applied) the handle would drop right onto the rail! I can tell you first hand, that was a real ouch!

So-o-o we started a second pocket now and if it wasn't finished, that meant, up at 5 a.m. and finish that pocket before 9 a.m. (way freight time).

I can't leave this topic without mentioning that somewhere in this time frame and these circumstances, Glen was pinching a car along. On the same side of the car where the gate was manned, a

**Selected Songs
Composed in 1944**

Don't Fence Me In
I Love You
I Should Care
I'll Walk A Lone
I'm Beginning To See The Light
Long Ago And Far Away
Moonlight In Vermont
Saturday Is The Lonliest Night Of The Week
Sentimental Journey
Swinging On A Star
You Always Hurt The One You Love

five foot steel bar was leaning against one of the "ribs" in the car. Of course I was on my hands and knees sizing up the placement of the hopper as it moved into place of the unload slide. Well, you guessed it. The bar fell over. *LUCKILY* it just caught the end of the fourth finger, left hand. How or why (not all fingers) is unknown. So I took a trip to see "Dr. Frank"!! He took an X-ray. It broke the end, so that made my finger look like a lollypop. When he finished, I went down to work and we did pocket #2. It did heal, the nail came back *and*, I checked for shovels and bars from then on, and I still would today!

The Author in 1944 - Taken in front of Allen's Garage, Randolph VT. Note: Bandaged finger.

Furnace Conversions

Now, we're doing furnace conversions. Coal was a nuisance and *without* saying, it was dirty.

Harry Tatro was good sized, not tall, but "around." He did bookkeeping, oil burner servicing and installations. By this time, many people found out you turn that "whatchamacallit" on the wall and soon, feel heat! Keeping a wood furnace fed, kept you restrictive on how long you could leave the house. Wood also required a lot of work – cutting, splitting and stacking. Coal furnaces were also quite demanding for attention. Most coal furnaces (about 90%) required feeding, but also required ash removal. (Most ashes from any type furnace usually ended up on the sidewalk or driveway for traction, in the winter time).

The Iron Fireman

The furnace we had at 6 Prospect St. was semi-automatic. This means you had to fill a "hopper" with coal and you had to move a "barrel" receptacle for ashes when it was full. This baby was an "Iron Fireman," the only one I ever saw. This is surprising because it worked like a dream.

There was a steel "worm" that went from the base of the "feeder" unit into a boiler. In the firebox of the boiler was a steel unit that looked like a large flower. The coal worm went into the base where the "petals" met the stem. As this worm was turned slowly (and intermittently), the coal was forced up. At the top, about 12 inches high, the coal was burning. As it burned, more coal came "up" from the inside and also spread outward. By the time the coal reached the outer edge of the "petal" it was totally burned and as ashes dropped off the edge and fell to a vortex, which had another steel "worm." This also turned the same speed as the coal feed. So, you had timed coal feed and equally timed ash removal. As the ashes emerged from the boiler at the base, they were moved up a chain fed elevator and at the end fell into a receptacle. They were now cool ashes. The ashes were very condensed and ultimately were discarded.

Each night Dad came home, he would fill a large funnel shaped hopper at the top with a coal hod. This hopper was more than adequate to supply coal through the night and next day (24 hours).

The coal used was Anthracite, which is hard coal, and was called Buckwheat. Buckwheat coal was of equal size, about like a dime and hard with little or no dust.

Our water was heated by a small coal burning "stove" which burned Nut coal (short for Chestnut). Another hard coal and about chestnut size.

Here we had two heating units, two different types of coal and medium attention. The house boiler (not the water heater) was the first oil conversion I remember and I'm sure it was the first conversion for Randolph Coal & Ice.

Oil Conversions

The main part of the conversion was the combustion chamber. After dismantling and removing the Iron Fireman and the combustion "tulip" we had to build a combustion chamber for the oil gun to shoot the flame into. There were no ready-made chambers (yet) so we had to measure, cut, cement and install a chamber of bricks, only ... these were not clay bricks, they were asbestos bricks – 100% asbestos.

Harry couldn't reach through the feed (or sight) door of the furnace (or boiler). I could put my arms out and then stick my whole torso right in. (In those days, I was thin and weighed about 140.) Anyway, I would measure and Harry would cut each brick with a handsaw, mortar it and pass to me. After the "circle" was made, I would fill cracks or joints. A saw didn't last long cutting the *asbestos bricks,* they were abrasive and would wear the teeth right off the saw.

I really don't know of any repercussions from working with the asbestos bricks. It doesn't seem to affect me—yet! This brick was hard and, unlike some asbestos products, didn't release any dust into the air.

There was, however, in *every* steam or hot water heated house in those days, insulation on hot pipes that would certainly attract present day inspectors and make them go spastic. This was the large round insulation that looked like rolled cardboard and held in place by metal bands!

So with the combustion chamber done, Harry would set the burner which was an Esso Brand. He also did thermostat controls, etc. My next job was to start on two holes out through the foundation for a 2 inch fill pipe and a 1½ vent pipe.

This was the worst part of the whole thing. *If* it was concrete, the holes had to be made with a "star" drill. Don't reach for the carbide tipped drill bit. This was ten years plus before *I* heard of tool steel or hardened steel.

A star drill is held point first against concrete and pounded once by a hammer. Rotate drill and pound once more. As you can imagine, star drills didn't come with an instruction sheet!! God, what a tedious, boring job! You had to let your imagination paint pictures for you while you "ran" a star drill. OH, get too engrossed in painting these pictures and it was common to have the skin between your thumb and index finger (you know, the flappy part) cover the end of the drill. You know, the drill part where the hammer hits!!! Time for a short "Indian Dance" — naughty, naughty!!

OK, so now set up the threader, the black pipe, the tape and ignite the grunter. You *will* use all of them, and be sure to grunt unknowingly! The 275-gallon tank will certainly invoke a grunt or two. Also got to find a place where this will set easily. Yeh, just remember, the farther from the burner you "plant" the tank because "it's easier over there," the farther I have to run the copper oil supply pipe and cover it with concrete.

The job is done. I don't remember how much I got paid and to be totally honest, I'm sure my pay was the use of the car, or clothes that I didn't buy, you know trade stuff. I worked, my mother did the dirty clothes and believe me, *I got dirty*!!

The oil truck is still the 1936 Ford, almost identical to the 1935 Ford coal truck. The only visible difference to look at it, was the V8 Ford Medallion on the side(s) of the hood were placed differently. The medallion on the '35 was in the middle (front to back) and on the '36, it was moved toward the front.

There were three sections of the tank. Two held 250 gallons and the rear one held 140 gallons of Kerosene. It was necessary to flush the hose when going from fuel oil to Kero because the hose held 14 gallons.

Fuel Oil Bath

Fuel oil was stored in two 20,000 gallon tanks each tank had two compartments. One compartment was reserved for Kero.

So, this day I backed into the fuel oil loading dock. There were four fill pipe held up by chains with the spouts pointing up. They were spaced couple feet apart and the spouts on the shutoff valves would pivot. Each compartment in the truck had an adjustable marker (sealed) to indicate the tank stated capacity. I pull the spout down into the tank and pulled the rope to open the valve.

Strange I could hear it run, but nothing came out, so I pulled again. This time, or *by* this time, *I* was getting a bath, a bath of fuel oil. God, I got soaked. It was then, of course, I noticed the rope was on the wrong valve! So I hiked up Weston St., across Main St. and up the path beside Nelson Udall's place and came out on Emerson Terrace.

Once home I changed and showered! This could be mean stuff if left on the skin and irritated by clothing. So then, back down and finish loading.

*R C & O fuel storage tanks. Sprague's Dairy in distance.
Photo 1999, C.Wells*

Cliff Mix - Trumpet

Let's check the music and its progress. The Green Mountain Band had rehearsals through the winter. I've pretty well caught on, and it's a lot of fun. I'm quite well acquainted with most of the others. By now, we've "split" from Baldi, at least, my mother has! We've split because in Montpelier is a music store run by Cliff Mix. Cliff is an excellent trumpet player also, and I admit I can get along with him. So we really made some progress now!

Leslie Gilman Farm

In late Spring (1944), again I don't remember how I got this job, but I had one! I suspect Floyd Fuller might have been involved because I worked on Floyd's Farm and a neighbor a few hundred feet away needed help on his farm. His name was Leslie Gilman. Leslie's son Newell was in the service and farm help was hard to find.

1939 or 1940 Chevrolet ton truck similar to one Leslie Gilman owned. Described in text. National Automobile and Truck Museum of United States. Photo(s) 2001, C. Wells

I had my Chevrolet, so getting to the farm was not a problem. So for something like $.40/Hour, I spent a good part of the summer working for Leslie.

He also had two daughters (at home). Alice and Helen were older than I was.

Here again, I was hired to help primarily with haying. But as typical on any farm, there are always dozens of things to do.

Leslie was in with a group of farmers which allowed them to buy grain collectively, they would order a carload at a time. The grain bags had tags on them labeled Eastern States Farmers Exchange. When the car arrived, it was spotted either near the freight station or near Guy Catlin's feed store. Alice would drive the truck which was a 1942 Chevrolet flat bed. She would also help me (or vice versa) move the bags of grain. These were 100 lbs each. She was a good worker but she couldn't (and shouldn't) lift a bag of grain. Probably I could lift one, but I certainly couldn't move once I had lifted it. But, together we could load a two-wheel "truck" and wheel it to the truck. After it was loaded, we would deliver it to the participating farmers.

She was such a good a driver, that, one year, some insurance company had a vehicle that went around to schools for a demonstration of driver reaction. It was 1941 Chevrolet and had three marker guns mounted on the front bumper. One girl, one boy and the representative demonstrated. The rep sat in the rider's seat. This was done on School St. and was first driven by Alice. Students were on both sides of the street as the car came up School Street at 30 m.p.h. toward Main Street. Around Summer Street the rep pulled a cord under the dash. This represented a hazard in the road. When the driver's foot hit the brake, the rep pulled a second cord and when the car stopped, he pulled a third cord. Each shot fired a different flare gun pointing at the road and left a yellow sunflower mark on the road. This showed reaction time and travel distance, after seeing an object in the road. The demo was repeated at 40 m.p.h. and 50 m.p.h. with a female and a male driver.

Anyway, back to the job. We also did outside lawn maintenance on at least two summer homes on E. Bethel Road. One was owned by Dr. McLean from Chicago who would periodically show up for a few days in the country. The other(s) escapes me.

Then, as haying season approached Leslie started to build a

buck rake. This was a new approach to gathering hay in the field. After the field is mowed and the hay has dried enough to be picked up, it is "processed" by a side delivery rake which actually rakes the field in about an 8 foot swath. The hay ends up in a row winding through the field.

The buck rake Leslie was working on was on the front of an old truck he had on the farm. I recall it was a 1925 Federal. The body had been removed. All there was left was a seat.

Anyway, this involved about ten long wooden "teeth." They were rounded and tapered to a point. They were spaced about 10 inches apart and the wooden poles or teeth were about 10 feet long. There was a steel frame mounted on the front of the truck. This frame provided a "base" for all teeth to be mounted on with the tips leading. The frame was also "hinged" at the mounting point to the truck.

The operation was to drive into the hay field, lower the teeth which looked like a big comb, drive into a row of hay and as you scooped it, the hay would stack on the teeth. When enough hay had been gathered, engage the lift, pick the teeth up and drive to the barn!

It was a good idea and did work, until you tried to get the hay out of the bay. It was all knotted up, unlike tumbles that could be placed and stacked, this had no pattern, it was one long knot. So-o-o, that was only used the one year, the year I worked there.

Some farmer bought a silo and when it arrived by rail, Alice and I loaded it onto the truck, delivered it to its destination. I would have liked to work on putting it up, but that wasn't to happen.

One day as I walked past my '31 Chevrolet parked in the door yard, I noticed a pink bubble emanating from a tire!! Before I could let the air out, it had grown large enough to emit a swang-g-g!!! Well, I had to change that tire before I went home that afternoon. The tire had a crack which grew and grew. The tube stuck out and finally like all bubbles finally let go. Probably sitting in the hot sun didn't help!

One day, I was hoeing in the garden when Alice came running up from the barn. "Con, Con, Dad wants you in the barn. Hurry!"

So I scampered down to the barn. Leslie had finished milking and feeding the cows. As he released the stanchions so the cows could back up and walk out of the barn, it was typical of one or two to walk right in the gutter!! A gutter is a long trough at the rear end of the cows as they are locked in the stanchion. So when they raise their tails, any deposit they get rid of goes into the gutter!!

This would also be an appropriate time to mention that most farms have a "live" wire strung over all the cows as they stand. This "live" wire passes over the back of the cows. Apparently, internally in a cow, there is a sort of structural tie in, so that when a cow raises her tail, she also sends a signal for the back to raise in preparation for the dump! There is some leeway in the stanchions so cows can move forward and backward. If the cow is forward, when this dump action takes place, the result will drop on the deck where she lays down, and the udder (and valves) get all crudded up!! So-o-o the wire is placed as such, when the back arches, she gets a jolt and the cow always backs up until stopped by the stanchions. The deposit is dropped in the gutter and *extra* cleaning is not necessary. Now, tell me ingenuity isn't fascinating!

Anyway, as I went into the barn, the cows are gone, except one. Leslie is leaning on a hoe, looking at this one cow. She does look funny. Like she has no hind legs and this is because her hind legs are both sticking down through the scuttle hole.

The scuttle hole is in the gutter. Every 10 feet is a hole which has a cover. Typically, a cow will walk in the gutter instead of the walkway. This one did and stepped on a cover. Either it was not correctly replaced or else it was worn and not a good fit.

So, here we are, not in a good situation! Leslie says, "if you can reach down through and grab a flank, I'll pull on the tail and the object is to roll this old girl up and onto her side."

The first thing I did was to remove my wrist watch. I don't need that (and the cow certainly is not interested in what the time is!). Well, we tugged and pulled, again and again, till we finally got her up out of the hole! God, I was a mess up to my arm pits. Also, this was oat time and cows make funny "meadow muffins" during oat time. The "muffins" are quite soft and take on a greenish tint – just about the color of my arms right then!!

Vermont Liquor Licenses

For years, during the thirties and forties, Vermont had very controlling Liquor laws. This didn't affect my folks or especially me. As I have said before my mother would not even stop and eat at any restaurant that served "cocktails" or even beer. I don't know if my Dad didn't drink even beer because he didn't like it or knew it would tie his wife in knots, so he just didn't succumb.

As I rode in the family car, it was very noticeable to see a sign on a restaurant "Second Class License, or, First Class License." There were a total of four different class licenses.

I really don't remember how "they broke down," but, I think First and Second Class pertained to hard liquor. In some cases a bar could serve beer and wine only under one type license. Another license was issued to restaurants but, food had to be served also.

Third and Fourth Class pertained to those selling beer and wine, one you could drink on the premises, another you could not drink on the premises.

Something else, if you were sitting at a table drinking beer, and you ordered another "round" maybe because they gave a "last call," the waitress could not leave a full bottle without taking an empty! No way could you sit at a table with four or five others and have an array of empties on the table.

One other procedure that had to be complied with. If you were sitting at the bar (or table), and two or three friends came in. If you wanted to join them, you couldn't pick up your glass, part-full bottle, and walk to their table. You had to call the waitress, she carried your glass and bottle while you walked (or stumbled) over to their table. Talk about laws!!

In the later years, all alcoholic beverages were sold from State owned and controlled stores. For years, Randolph voted "dry" and no liquor store was there. Bethel, the next town, voted "wet" and the State store was there. Even if a town voted "wet," it took the State a year or two before they stocked a new location in that town for fear it would vote "dry" the following year.

Music Interests

I had progressed on the trumpet quite well. I guess I would call myself adequate and average. To be truthful, at this point I hadn't made up my mind or rather, if I wanted to become a good trumpet player. This was partly due to the fact I was not allowed to play music that really interests me. To elaborate, I had to play, "trumpet parts" of a choral group, or the obvious trumpet part of a music

192

group such as a high school orchestra. This was not what peaked my interest no matter who or how many told me I should play this. There was only one dance group that I should have fit into but I wasn't allowed to, why I'm not sure. (The other kind of music that was common was country or cowboy. Not much call there for a trumpet!)

High School Dance Band

There was a group that got together and presented some real good dance music. It was "headed" by "Bud" Sawyer who was about two years older than me. He played tenor sax and his group had about six musicians. They were called the "Royal Barons." They were the first group of musicians I ever heard who had some "polish" to their sound.

In Randolph, on Pleasant Street was Lamson's Hall. The ground floor was used for storage of various hardware products as mentioned previously. The second floor was an open hall (no posts) with a nice hardwood floor. Any dance held in Lamson's Hall was the tops. Most dances were held in the high school gym. But Lamson's instilled excitement.

It was standard practice to import a dance band. But, by 1943, Bud Sawyer's group had really progressed. I don't remember who was in the group beside Bud with the exception of Dick Phelps, on drums. I'm going to guess, Charles Ellis (trumpet), Bill Carey (String Bass), Harold Rogers (Piano). Trombone(s) and clarinet(s), I don't remember.

These guys played Glen Miller, Harry James and other big band tunes and really did a great job – at least to the high schoolers!

World's Fair - Tunbridge Vermont

I was in the Green Mt. Band, and this was fun. As typical when September rolled around, we supplied the music at Tunbridge Fair, otherwise known as the "Worlds Fair."

It was established as THE fair to see. I might add that the Rutland Fair, the Essex Junction Fair (Champlain Valley Exposition) were also about this time of year. This fair was 3 days long, usually Thursday, Friday, and Saturday. I think the

Tunbridge Fair better known as World's Fair, Tunbridge, VT.

Above, white uniform, visor cap is Wayne Buck.

Looking at the midway.

*Photo(s)
About 1941,
C. Wells*

schools were shut down for 1 or 2 of the days.

The first fair I participated in was probably 1941 (I was 13). We rode to Tunbridge, had to be there by 10 AM in uniforms. (I thought the uniforms were something!)

So at 10 AM we, (band only) marched through the midway. Everything or most everything was closed - but the band was the "signal" to open and get underway. There were some awfully red eyes, and a lot of people whose mouths probably tasted like the bottom of a birdcage.

This fair was quite well known for the fact that many "Guests" carried the brown paper bag. And an equal number just carried the bottle without this bag. There were still many "Guests" left over from the night before, that used Mother Earth as one big bed!

But, the band seemed to inject some life into everybody. So now we wait to play a concert at noon in the bandstand, which was located beside the stage, on the inside of the racetrack. The stage was in front of the wooden grand stand.

Early afternoon there was usually another "parade," led by the band, in front of the grand stand on the racetrack. This displayed various performers that were coming up on the stage. Also, tractors, farm equipment that was pulled by tractors, horses or oxen, various trucks with displays of products on them, etc., etc., and lastly, were the lines of cows, bulls etc. with the ribbons attached as they had been judged.

Harness racing took a while to complete. There was a stage show, which usually headlined a country singer or group - some Vaudeville acts and an "MC" who kept the whole show "glued" together! The band, by now, was sitting in the round bandstand at the side of the stage, and provided musical back up to the Vaudeville acts and "MC." This was not easy. The music was most always hand written manuscript - the melody had to be carried by the trumpet or clarinet section. The trumpet music was very likely to be violin music and dropped an octave as played - periodic abrupt stops meant the conductor had to watch the "act" very closely and at random get the band to burst out with a chord that induced applause from the crowd! The chord was to be a musical prize, for the acts as they were presented but were more apt to be a SURprise. A "C" chord seemed always to be confusing to some in the band - so it was apt to sound like hell (at best).

Believe me, this is a musical experience to anyone. There was no rehearsal and I'm sure, if I contributed to the presentation (which I did) I made some klinkers of my own. As the shows (2 a day) progressed, for a total of 6 shows, the quality did improve, if ever so slightly.

Late afternoon, the band could go out on the stage and watch the auto thrill show. The first one I remember was "Lucky Teter" - he then, used mostly 1940 Dodges. I couldn't believe what those guys did!! In later years, "Joie Chitwood" performed for the crowd. Actually, Lucky Teter was killed, somewhere, while doing a "T-Bone."

Then we were "free" till 7 PM when a concert was played in the bandstand. Then a repeat vaudeville show at 8 PM and the auto thrill show. We finished up at 9 or so, went home and had to be back at 10:00 AM and start again. I recall for one of these years, I was paid 10 dollars a day, but this was not supposed to be a money making event, but to be a community service.

This WAS a good way for the band members to get better acquainted with each other and it was fun.

The bass drummer was Lynn Hutchinson - a thin and frail, VERY senior citizen. The drum was as tall as his 5'4" height. As he played that drum, each time he made the mallet hit the drum, his head would shake and his pinch nose glasses would jiggle!

The Bandstand was "2 story" with the band exposed, naturally so we could see the stage. "Downstairs" was the dressing room(s) for the stage acts. As Lynn pounded the drum once, his glasses fell off and slipped through a crack in the floor. Luckily, this happened near a break coming up - so Lynn got a coat hanger, was on his hands and knees "fishing" for his glasses.

Bart Camp, a big man and the deputy Sheriff, liked to always stand at the top of the stairs of the bandstand so he could see all around. Someone told Bart, Lynn was being a peeping Tom, so Bart went over and picked him up by the belt just like a suitcase and lugged him off, lecturing him as they went down the stairs with Lynn's arms & legs "swimming" the air!

During one break, George Hardy and I were in an open area standing beside a sideshow tent. This was a girlie show and these were apt to be placed somewhere other than directly on the "midway." Let me explain; outside of a fair, strip shows or a show of "moral indecency" were not allowed anywhere in THIS state. The only thing close were the "Burley" houses in Boston. We knew what was going on inside, or at least thought we knew. They always brought "the girls" out on a stage in front. The barker would sell the show. The girls would go inside. Finally, the barker would go inside - he would beat a drum for the dances and the "Bump and Grind." Inside there was also a State Police or two, or a deputy or two *and* one or two guys with bare arms, each bigger than my leg! You know, the type of guy when not on duty would wait probably in a cage and dine on a banana or two!!

There were always guys that showed up at Tunbridge Fair that were "different." Some guys would come down out of the woods once or so a year. They were apt to be trouble looking for a place to happen! So, the bouncer(s) needed to be equally talented.

Anyway, George and I stood by the tent, it was getting dark, when one of us spotted a hole in the tent - a little high but low enough, so I had to stand on my toes to look through. We took turns until, as I was looking through, I stuck my finger in the hole. So did George and as he pulled against my finger, that hole went rip-p-p. The music stopped and someone inside said - "Get those guys"! Not us! We peeled out and as George was running and pouring on the power, he struck enough "cow flops" to make himself look like all arms and legs!! But we ducked enough corners and disappeared into the crowd.

I didn't try many of the temptations of the midway but it amazed me to see the fists of money these guys had. Most all wore carpenter's aprons to keep change and bills in. It was an experience - one I saw in 1940,1941,1942 and 1943. In 1944 I was not around so that stopped the annual Tunbridge Fair for me, for at least a couple years.

Incidentally, Tunbridge Fair was where I first saw a chain saw. This "first" chain saw was a two-man unit, the cutting bar must have been nearly 4 feet long and the engine was large. For all I know, they could have used the 60 HP V8 engine from a 1937 Ford I have previously mentioned! I'm sure it wasn't, but believe me this thing would CUT wood, it was also heavy and I think the engine had to remain upright. The cutter blade rotated for a horizontal cut. (It had to be around 1946).

In the late nineties (1998) the Fair is in its 127th year.

Lyndon Institute

In late August (1944) my mother and I drove to Lyndonville, VT or rather we drove to Lyndon Center.

By now, I'm ready to enter my junior year in High School. A man by the name of Walter True was the principal in Randolph High School for, I recall, 23 years. Walter had left 2 or 3 years previously. He had been replaced by "Jock" Murray as principal, and Walter went to a school named Lyndon Institute.

My folks had been in contact with him and found out that L.I. was a highly rated semi private school that served Lyndonville and a couple surrounding communities. Along with that, there was room for about 13 boys in its dormitory and 15 or 18 girls in the girl's dormitory. As L.I. was the school for students locally, the tuition and board was very reasonable.

Shwon above is the boys dorm on the left, a private house beyond and Mathewson House (girls dorm) is in the center. Photo, C. Wells

Up to this point, I know there was quite extensive research on other "schools" or whatever, including Mount Hermon and some military location in New York. I have to say that for the first grades, I went through them like a dose of "salts" through a sick kitten. Grade 8 was different and very little was accomplished, until Mrs. Perry took over about midway.

However, High School was a lot different in as much that I couldn't settle down. Grammar or English was a bore, Foreign Language like French or Spanish would be a waste of time, don't even mention European History! I was between a rock and a hard place by my sophomore year!

Here's partially what I did like, cars, trucks, airplanes, buildings, houses, music, girls and peanut butter sandwiches. Unfortunately you can't get a High School diploma with only those. So, - back to the rock and hard place. As a matter of fact, I liked so many things - I couldn't settle down to study just one thing and then another. I didn't know what I wanted to do to earn a living and at this point I really didn't see what the hurry was! (Wrong Idea!)

There were guidance teachers but that didn't seem to answer many questions. Of course, at this time I really didn't apply myself.

For that reason, (and others,) I'm sure is why I was looking out the window at St. Johnsbury VT as we continue on to Lyndon Center.

I might add, that one teacher, Kay Phelan, had also left Randolph and was now at L.I.

Well, to boil this down a bit faster - I was enrolled and present on the first day of school.

Bear in mind, by this time, we were deep in WWII. Many or most of available young men had enlisted. Some were my age and some even younger, but my folks would not sign for me to enlist (THEY were right, I was only 16).

The papers were drawn and now I was a junior at Lyndon Institute living in the boy's dorm known as "Ye Olde Tavern" in Lyndon Center.

Walter "Prof" True greeted me (probably) the first morning - ushered me right by the arm into his office. I remember wondering if I might be in trouble already!

He shut the door and leaning toward me he softly remarked "All right, Mr. Wells, Let's don't forget you're here for the sheepskin and not the wool, so keep your eyes off the sweater girls"!!!

As I left him and wandered down the hall, a very small gentleman with hair only at the eaves trough area was very close. I asked him where (U.S.) History class was. He pointed and said "3 Doors." Also, - "say you're going out for football, a young man of your size?" I replied, "God, no - I don't know anything about football!" Which was the truth, we didn't have football, track, skiing, only basketball in Randolph – that coupled with the fact that I wasn't sports minded anyway.

So, I found a desk in history, sat down and got introduced to the history teacher, Mr. Lewis, a very small gentleman with hair only at the eaves trough area!!!

As you can guess, I really couldn't do very much right in History the whole year, at least that's what my marks used to say.

I won't bother to go ahead and explain or detail the whole year, but it was eventful.

Connie Allard

One person I met, who I liked, was Conrad Allard. He lived only about 4 houses from the school, in Lyndon Center. If you remember back a few paragraphs, what I liked and disliked, you'll know what Connie Allard also liked, and disliked. One thing I didn't mention on the list of likes was motorcycles - for both of us.

He and I were to become known as the "Gold Dust Twins." Soon, we were in the High School Orchestra, (we both played trumpet,) we were both in the Lyndonville Town Band and we would both have motorcycles! (and other similarities).

We were at his house one Saturday which was easy to find. It was right in front of the puking pig! At a "Y" intersection in Lyndon Center, is a copper (or bronze) statue. It is a pig sitting on a large base with water coming out of its mouth! "Homeliest damn thing you ever saw." (Quote from Connie Allard.)

One Saturday morning, I went to his house. As we were about

to leave for someplace, his mother said it was his turn to take out the garbage. Normally he or his sister would take the garbage across the street, across the large field and dump it into the river. This morning, it was his turn. As he stopped at the door, you could see he was thinking.

He went upstairs and came down with a shoe box and some paper. Dumping the garbage into the box - smoothed it out and proceeded to wrap this eye catching paper around the box and then topped it off with a ribbon!

Out the door, he placed the box at the edge of the road near the "puking pig"!! As we watched, soon a car went zipping by and then stopped. You can tell by that statement that traffic really wasn't very heavy! The driver looked both ways and then backed up - got out, - looked both ways again, scooped up the box and placed it on the floor behind the driver's seat, then drove off. Wiping his hands, Connie said "that takes care of the garbage for this week!" We went out!

His living room was quite small with a big easy chair in one corner facing the center. Right at the feet area was a big round

The Famous "Puking Pig" in Lyndon Center. Connie Allard's house is in the background. Photo 1984, C. Wells

register in the floor. This register was a "one pipe" "system" to heat the whole house. Upstairs was heated by register(s) cut in the floor, so the heat would rise to above rooms.

One day he sat in the big chair with a cigarette in his mouth. As the ashes grew longer they took on a droop! As I swore it was going to drop off, the furnace blower came on producing a noticeable *up draft* from the register. Very casually, he removed the cigarette from his mouth, extended his arm over the register and flicked the ash. In one very smooth operation, the ash started to drop - slowed up - then rapidly rose toward the ceiling. His arm reached for the ashtray on a side table, extended toward the front, the ash slowed up its travel, stopped and proceeded to drop------------- into the ashtray! I looked from the ashtray to him, he was already looking at me - with a grin!

Connie had practiced a simple ditty where he put his cigarette (lit) on his right hand in a split between his index and middle fingers. Then he would slap the heel of his hand with his left hand. In doing so, if his "motions" were all correct, that cigarette would do an end flip on its way up, to end up between his lips, at which time he would puff and blow a puff of smoke out. Then, invariably he would remove the cigarette and blow two or three nice round smoke rings!

I couldn't smoke in Lyndon, at least anywhere in Lyndon Center where Mr. True might see me, because my mother wouldn't sign a document to be on file, allowing me to smoke.

We also found out Mr. True wasn't receptive to us both, parking our motorcycles just inside the girl's entrance door to the school building. After that, I was limited to parking mine in a shed in back of the boy's dormitory, to be used only when I was headed to Randolph on a weekend. This, meant only in early fall or late spring - due to snow or ice. I remember one trip, I lined my jacket and pants with layers of newspapers to cut the wind - it was cold!

In our Junior year, Connie developed an attraction to a girl who stayed in the girl's dormitory by the name of Jean Hall, also a Junior. As we progressed through the Junior year, I also thought Jean had been sent from heaven but I wouldn't try to date her, mostly because the two of them were quite steady.

Both Connie and I were in the Lyndonville Town band. As

202

Covered bridge between Lyndonville and Lyndon Center, VT, Prior to 1960. From Secord Collection Cobleigh Library, Lyndonville, VT.

A COVERED BRIDGE SAILING UP MAIN STREET. It may seem a bit odd but in 1960 the bridge was saved and moved north about a mile-and-a-half from its original location, spanning the Passumpsic River between Lyndonville and Lyndon Center, to make way for a modern concrete bridge.

Courtesy of Harriet Fletcher Fisher

the winter progressed, Rod Darling, who played trombone, asked me if I would like to come to his house Sunday, spend a little time, have a bite to eat etc., which I did. And I started to date his older daughter - Bunny Darling. I now suspect his motive. However, it was great, they treated me like a son and I spent a lot of time with them. Bunny was two years younger than me. Also, she could play the piano. This lasted through my junior year and beyond.

Getting back to Connie, we both played trumpet in the high school orchestra. Each Monday the day started with an assembly and the orchestra set up on the floor in front of the stage. All the teachers sat on the stage.

Connie was apt to comb his hair forward so it ended in a straight line over his eyebrows. It was a perfect replica of Ish Kabibble, a trumpet player in Kay Kaizer's band, who was

WILLEY'S RESTAURANT
LYNDONVILLE, VT.

Specials for Today 1944

Tomato Juice	or	Prune Juice	.10
	Consomme		.10
	Hot Rolls		

GRilled Top Round Steak	.85
Grilled Native Calf's Liver	.75
Roast Pork--Brown Gravy	.50
Pot Roast of Beef--Brown Gravy	.50

Mashed or Boiled Potatoes
French Fried Potatoes 15¢ Extra
Spinach or Lettuce

PLATE SPECIALS

Fried Baby Beef Liver	.50
Fried Honeycomb Tripe	.45
Potted Beef with Vegetables	.40
Chipped Beef in Cream and Boiled Potato	.30
Hamburg and Onion Sandwich	.25

DESSERTS

Apple, Custard, Pumpkin, Blueberry, Raspberry, Lemon, Mince Pie	.10
Grapenut Custard Pudding	.10
Vanilla, Maple, Chocolate Ice Cream	.10
Lemon Sherbert	.10
Chocolate Sundae	.15

Tea	Coffee	.05
Milk	.06	

Courtesy of Willey's Restaurant, Lyndonville, VT.

1944

EMMONS & HEBERT, Inc.

Plumbing, Heating & Hardware   Paints, Oils, Lime & Cement

Fine Tools for Mechanics, Painters, Carpenters, Etc.

Tel. 242   Lyndonville, Vt.

SANDWICHES

3-DECKERS ON TOAST

Burke Mt. .... .55
  Ham, Swiss Cheese, Bacon, Lettuce and Mayonnaise

American Club .... .55
  Chicken, Tomato, Bacon, Lettuce, Mayonnaise

Pickwick .... .55
  Bacon, Lettuce, Tomato, Chicken Salad

Tux .... .55
  Chicken Salad, Ham, Lettuce, Mayon.

2-DECKERS ON TOAST

Junior Club .... .45
  Chicken, Tomato, Bacon, Lettuce, Mayonnaise

Dutch Club .... .35
  Ham, Cheese, Bacon, Lettuce and Mayonnaise

Hamburg Club .... .40

Depot Street .... .30
  Bacon, Lettuce, Tomato, Mayonnaise

SANDWICHES

Jelly	.15	Hamburg	.20
Bacon	.15	Ham and Egg	.25
Western	.20	Bacon and Egg	.25
Sliced Ham	.20	Fried Egg	.15
Salmon Salad	.30	American Cheese	.15
Crab Meat Salad	.35	Lettuce and Tomato	.20
Sliced Chicken	.35	Cream Cheese and Olives	.20
Chopped Chicken	.30	Lettuce and Mayonnaise	.10
Bacon, Lettuce, Mayonnaise	.25		

Sandwiches Toasted 5c Extra

Home Made Pies .... .10

Plain Ice Cream .... .10   with Sauce .... .15

Coffee or Tea .... .05   Pot of Tea or Coffee .... .10

Bottle of Milk .... .06

Our Sunday Dinners are unusual. Why don't you form the habit of taking out the family occasionally? It always assures you of good food, well cooked, and attractively served—and best of all, you do not have to bother preparing the meal. Come often.

WILLEY'S FOOD AND COFFEE SHOP

Main Street   Opposite State Armory   St. Johnsbury, Vermont

Milk Served Here is Fresh from Our Own

LONG MEADOW FARM

E. C. McNALLY, Prop.

Its Pure Pasteurized Guernsey Milk

Phone 26-R-11   Lyndonville, Vt.

1944 Menu Insert courtesy of Willey's Resaurant, Lyndonville, VT.

206

DINNER SELECTIONS

1.25

Tomato Juice
Broiled Steak
French Fried Potatoes, Rolls and
Butter, String Beans
Coffee & Dessert

.80

Tomato Juice
Broiled Native Calf's Liver and
Bacon
Hashed Brown Potatoes, Rolls
Coffee and Dessert

.75

Cranberry Juice
Two Pork Chops
Hashed Brown Potatoes, Rolls
and Butter, Beans
Dessert and Coffee

MISCELLANEOUS

Prunes	.10	Buttered Toast	.10
Crackers and Milk (Bottle)	.20	Plain Omelette, Toast,	
Dry Cereals with Cream	.15	Fr. Fr. Potatoes	.40
Hot Cereals with Cream	.15	2 Eggs, any style, Toast	.35
Orange, Tomato or		Ham or Bacon and Eggs,	
Pineapple Juice	.10	Toast	.60
Griddle Cakes with		French Toast with	
Maple Syrup	.30	Maple Syrup	.30
Griddle Cakes with		Half Melon	.15
Maple Syrup and Sausage	.50	Chilled Half Grapefruit	.10
Milk Toast	.20	Cream Toast	.30

Meat orders include Potatoes, Rolls and Butter

SALADS

Egg	.30	Tuna Fish and Sweet Pickle	.45
Fruit	.45	Sardine and Egg	.40
Potato Salad and Dill Pickle	.30	Waldorf Salad	.35
Salmon and Egg (hard boiled)	.45	Cold Meats with Potato or	
Tomato, Lettuce, Mayonnaise	.35	Vegetable Salad	.50

Chicken Salad .65

We are authorized agents for the famous Maple Grove and Elizabeth Chase Maple Products, and we also have Fancy Maple Syrup from the finest sugar orchards in this section. A fine way to remember a friend.

All Food except ice cream is prepared in our own Kitchen and Food Shop

Courtesy of Willey's Restaurant, Lyndonville, VT.

popular in the nineteen thirties. The hairstyle coupled with his ears that had a tendency to protrude noticeably - also a pointed chin could make every person in the room snicker - including teachers!

And then, he would place the "bell" (large end) of his trumpet on the floor, place the edge of his foot over the edge of the bell, then proceed to imitate shifting a truck by grabbing the mouthpiece and moving it like a gearshift while his left foot worked a clutch pedal! It took on more laughter, especially, when the music (the rest of us were playing), varied its speed within different sections of the song.

Junior Year

The first year, I was busy at trying to produce a decent scholastic record. I was busy with French, Algebra, History etc. I also had signed up for typing which I felt would be an asset.

The mimeograph machine, which has long faded into oblivion, was a machine that made copies. It used a chemical process, made from a master, which had to be a special type paper. (The copier of today is years away.) Kay Phelan asked me to apply some effort to correct a couple of problems,-this took a week.

Although I could play the piano (without looking at the keys) I certainly had difficulty typing without looking at those typewriter keys. I apparently finished typing to the extent it went on my record. This topic will show up again, later.

"Mr. K"

I had a course in Physics with "Mr. K" as the teacher. This not only was a total disaster in learning anything, it was also a breeding ground for calamity! "Mr. K" was also the "live in house father" at "Ye Olde Tavern." There were "a couple" of theories on what took place prior to his arrival at Lyndon Institute, that is to cause his "presentation" to be such as it was. I don't want to "peck" at that topic, it being pure speculation on what and how.

So, with that said, I have to relate an instance or two on "Mr. K." He was a big man, about 6'5", but very awkward - perhaps

clumsy would be a better description. There were times you could
tell that the brain was either not writing any "orders" for the
limbs - mouth or eyes, or, the "orders" were confusing or just not
being delivered!

For instance, each door in the dorm required a hasp and
padlock. He came up to the second floor where all the rooms were
- strode to his door and lifted the padlock. Anything about that
padlock being different or unusual would throw him askew.
Something like a coating of Vicks - he knew THAT shouldn't be
there, but what was it, how did it get there, etc., etc., all with his
hand in such a position, and how the hell do I get this off?

I know this sounds like what anyone should do and of course
it is. Only with him - you could almost "see" the thoughts passing
by. And as someone said, he had to learn all the basics again. I
can't imagine how he got this job, it was his first year here and it
must have been his first year at everything. (Remember, WWII
had taken all men in the service).

One of the first days in class, he said, "Physics - who can tell
me what Physics is?"

A subdued voice from the class somewhere said - "Its
something to make you shit!" Everybody heard it, everybody
laughed but he stood there, either didn't hear it, heard it and
just didn't emit anything. Looked at the floor, and took 2 giant
steps, as we found would be a common reaction.

In laboratory, someone would hook a rubber hose to the
propane outlet and lay it in the sink trough that ran about 10
feet in both experiment tables. Propane being heavier than air,
would settle to the bottom of the trough. Then shut the gas off,
and toss a match into it. Who-o-o-o-s-h, the flames would rise 2
feet and travel that sink in a flash! All the while "Mr. K" was
bending over the bench, with the sink about a foot from his head!
Never saw it! And of course, no smell etc. - by the time he raised
his head - gone!

Some students would enter the class 5 or 10 minutes late - he
would send them to the office for a signed tardy slip. Connie A.
would stand out in the corridor with a fistful of blanks, and soon
had perfected an authentic replica of W. F. True, (which "Mr. K"
never suspected).

One day "Mr. K" turned around to write something on the

blackboard. Every time he did, many flask stoppers would fly through the air. They were live rubber, quite soft and very bouncy. As he wrote on the board, with his face very close to it, a stopper zinged by his ear, hit the board and bounced off narrowly missing his other ear. Never saw it, never stopped writing!!

His desk was also a table for experiments or demonstrations. There was a small sink on one side, with a faucet. A tall spout reached up with a sharp curve so water would go into the sink. Also, a small tube protruded from the spout just above the faucet. This was used as a vacuum source when water was turned on. Except, if a wooden plug (like a pencil) was stuck into the spout. Now, this small spout spewed water as "Mr. K" found one day. As he flipped the faucet on, a stream of water got him in the pants right in the front! This puzzled him momentarily why water did that!! He didn't turn that faucet on again for weeks.

Another time, "Mr. K" was demonstrating how a certain type of "metal" would burst into flame as soon as it came in contact with water. This, seemed to catch everyone's attention.

He stood behind his desk, which also served as an experiment desk. He took a small wafer dish and added about an ounce of water. Then, from a small bottle, dug out a piece of this "metal" about the size of a head of a pin. Using a pair of forceps, he urged that piece of metal into the water. It looked more like yeast cake than anything else. Also, it was stored in a bottle that had a special liquid in it.

As soon as the small piece hit the water, sparks started to fly off - and as it scurried around, it left a trail of smoke. Shortly, a loud pop with a flash, and it was over.

Later, Connie said, "that was something" as he climbed over the half partition into the chemical stockroom. Momentarily, he came out the door with a "hunk" of "this stuff" the size of your thumb on a pair of tweezers. Out the classroom door and across the hall into the boy's room. We headed for a stall - there was no one else around. He snapped that hunk into the toilet and immediately it started to swim around. Also, BIG sparks came off it and smoke, lots of smoke - then a humongeous amount of smoke. We were both startled and shrunk back. By now, the stall was full of smoke, sparks were jumping over the side and a peculiar noise was really noticeable as it "swam" around.

210

B-A-M!!! That did it, we're outta here!

So, we took cover in the girl's room (also empty). Later, as we came down the hall, Mr. True and Lenny Burns, the janitor, had the door open so the smoke could clear. Connie asked Lennie if they caught someone smoking and if so, what the hell was he smokin?!

Daily, "Mr. K" would take an attendance for school records. He would call names out for a reply - I don't think he could tie a face with a name all year long! Most of the time, he didn't even look up.

(Example) "Conrad Allard" he asked.

"I'm not here yet" replied Conrad Allard.

So, "Mr. K" marked him absent!

Or if Connie or anyone actually wasn't there, someone else would call out "here" and "Mr. K" would check him off as present.

"Mr. K" was always discharging someone from class with the verbal order to report to "Mitter, Ta-Rue"!!! And the more excited he was, the more he stretched that order. "MITTER ———— TA - RUE" really indicated the dischargee was in big trouble!

And he was very apt to start taking large strides — meaning his large shoes could cover the classroom frontage with very few

Boys Dormitory 1944 - 1945. Mr. "K" is the tall gentlemen in the rear.
The author is sitting in front - right. Photo, C. Wells

steps!! Or, his hands would start a rather peculiar demonstration as if he was holding a clarinet, and his fingers would be doing a mid air dance. This would be coupled with an additional motion as if he was also playing a slide trombone!

Geezus, this was quite a sight to see, all these appendages in motion at one time. And of course, this was apt to be an enticement for many students to shoot for "the big one" - the mouth going, but no sound emitted, the long steps and turn arounds, and, both hands with flying fingers rendering a silent display of a slide trombone!!

Seeing all that at once, you knew he was <u>REALLY</u> aggravated.

Members of boys and girls dormitory 1945, Photo, C. Wells

Charlie Chase

We had two students in the class who where ahead of all the others. One was Charlie Chase, who, always came to school with a suit (and tie) and, always had his homework done. And, I should add always right! Charlie carried a round slide rule and had thorough knowledge on how to use it. Even found a mistake in a book (which was never heard of then), notified the publisher who sent a reply accepting the correct math answer promising to correct future printings! At that time, <u>THIS</u> was totally unheard of.

Jack Davis

Jack Davis was the other, and you knew that Jack would end up in a responsible occupation.

One day, Jack and I were partners in the lab, on assigned lab projects and, of course, knocked them off in short time. Jack says "we ought to make a torch!" What kind of torch? An Acetylene torch. We'll make an oxygen generator for half of it and the other half we'll make acetylene.

I'm not going to elaborate, but I will continue. So we took the two rubber hoses, one for oxygen on the bench, and in his left hand, held the flask with a cap and a hose. Tied these hoses into a glass "tee." "Ok, Con, Light it." So I did. A nice blue/orange flame emitted from the tee. We both knew that both gases were giving the desired mixture. We watched as the flame changed from "just right" to grow shorter and shorter and disappeared. It hadn't disappeared long when there was a <u>Wh-ooo-m</u>!! Jeez - that flask just disintegrated! All Jack had left in his hand was a rubber cork with the glass neck attached! Luckily, no one was hurt...nobody. We decided that we should probably not do a repeat.

Of course, interspersed with some of the fun times were hours of not so good times meaning, either classroom or study times.

Lyndonville Town Band

Another one of the good times was the Lyndonville Town Band. Once a week, the members got together to rehearse. Having some experience, I decided to try out in this band. I don't recall what the dormitory rules were about something like this but I think that some "some latitude" was allowed.

Connie Allard was in the band, as was another classmate, Edgar Kellaway. Another seat for trumpet was made available. I have to say that the level of professional ability was higher than Randolph band. This was probable because of a few strong musicians, and a really good leader (conductor) named Harris.

One was Paul Aubin, who played Trombone. Paul was a very good - rather excellent musician. His father played trumpet, a brother played clarinet and another brother Jerry played

213

VERMONTERS

and concerts on the green, that staple of small-town New England life, depend on a sense of continuity. And the Lyndonville Band definitely has continuity, thanks to **Gerald Aubin**, who has been playing with the band for 70 years.

Aubin began in 1929, when he was 13. His chosen instrument then was the cymbals. He later played the trumpet and today plays the baritone horn or the double-belled euphonium. He has played in town bands from Barton to Barre, and his stint with the Lyndon band is probably one of the longest anywhere in the U.S. But Aubin is modest about his long musical career. "I'm still looking for the right notes," he jokes.

The Lyndonville Band plays throughout the summer, Wednesday nights at 8 p.m. on the village green. If you happen to miss Aubin there, you can hear him Monday nights in nearby St. Johnsbury, where he has been playing with the town band for a mere 50 years.

Check your local public television listings in October; you may find Tunbridge cinema star and retired dairy farmer **Fred Tuttle**. The Public Broadcasting System will offer director **John O'Brien's** film *Man with a Plan* to affiliates across the country that month. That, notes O'Brien, could bring

Fred Tuttle heads for television sets across the country this October.

Tuttle, the movie's star, into a million or more homes. The exposure won't bother Fred, 79, who has already been in *Life, People, The New Yorker* and on the front page of *The New York Times*. Meanwhile, O'Brien continues to work on *Nosey Parker*, his next Tunbridge film, which he describes as "The first mystery-love story-comedy made about property tax assessors." Fred has only a supporting role in this one.

Brattleboro writer **Karen Hesse** has won the Newbery Medal, among the highest awards for children's literature in the U.S., for her novel *Out of the Dust*. The book, published by Scholastic, traces in blank verse the bleak life of a teenager during Dust Bowl days in Oklahoma. Barre's **Katherine Paterson**, the winner of two previous Newbery Medals (for

The Lyndonville Band's Gerald Aubin.

Jacob Have I Loved and *Bridge to Terabithia*), this year won the Hans Christian Anderson Award, a prestigious prize recognizing an author's entire body of work.

When **Arlene Degree's** husband, Paul, won more than $1 million in the Tri-State Megabucks lottery last summer, Arlene couldn't celebrate immediately. She is the Williston Town Clerk, and the town water bills had to be sent out. "We went over to the store and checked the numbers, and I went back to work," said Arlene. For the time being, $1 million or not, she plans to keep working as town clerk, a job she has held for 25 years.

Catherine Robbins Clifford, one of three young women who made headlines in 1927 when they hiked the length of the Long Trail unescorted by males, died last July at the age of 96. She and her two companions were known as the Three Musketeers, a title that seems to have summed up their sense of adventure and fun. Memorial contributions can be sent to the Green Mountain Club, in care of Robert Lincoln, RR 1, Box 650, Waterbury, VT 05677.

Robert J. Alzner, a photographer from White River Junction whose photos graced the pages of *Vermont Life* for many years, died in July. Bob was known as a warm and friendly man who delighted in capturing Vermont's landscape on film. His photograph of the Grafton Cornet Band [Autumn 1996] was part of our 50th anniversary retrospective of *Vermont Life* photos.

A Canine Star

Montpelier's Chundo, hard at work in the studio.

If you're walking in Montpelier's Hubbard Park, don't be surprised if you catch a glimpse of a celebrity. That's because **Chundo**, the handsome Weimaraner who stars in Sesame Street's "fairy tales" segment, lives nearby. Chundo's owner, Pam Wegman, says she chose Montpelier for its proximity to New York City, but also for its dog-pleasing qualities. "We wanted a combination of country and city."

Pam Wegman's brother, William Wegman, came up with the idea of using dogs in his photo/video work in the 1970s when his pet Weimaraner, brought to the studio to keep him company, kept nosing her way into the shots. On current projects, which include coffee table books and children's videos in addition to Sesame Street appearances, Pam Wegman serves as costume designer. "Dogs don't have shoulders," Wegman says, explaining how she alters thrift-store purchases to accommodate the models.

— CAROLYN CORY

Reprint courtesy of Caledonian Record, Autumn 1998

Euphonium (Baritone Horn). Jerry was music director somewhere in Barre and used to drive over to Lyndon each week.

Also, a fellow named Bill Lang played solo trumpet so you know HE could cut the mustard. Two more, Ed Kellaway, trombone and Rod Darling, Trombone, and many others whose names escape me.

It was really fun when Bill Lang and Paul Aubin played some novelty numbers, one of them being "Ida and Dottie" polka with a band backup!

Sunset Ballroom

I thought this was Crystal Ballroom, but I could be mistaken - so let's call it the Sunset Ballroom. Another highlight while being in Lyndonville, was the Sunset Ballroom. Saturday nights were always something to look forward to. Dorm rules allowed us to attend on Saturday night. During the winter, it was cold in Lyndonville. Zero degree nights were normal. This Sunset Ballroom was on the second floor over a garage right on Main Street. Climbing a set of stairs outdoors and then entering the hall was a breath taker! Of course, the lights were low, the crowd totally filled the hall with a ring of onlookers always standing near the dance floor. The music was varied and good - and right in the middle of the ceiling was a crystal ball slowly rotating and throwing sparkles at random over the ceiling and walls. If the door was open, steam would pour out in droves!

Every Saturday night, it was packed mostly with teenage high school students. Remember, most 20 year olds and up were in the service.

Perhaps the Crystal ball was added later, and maybe induced the name, Crystal Ballroom.

Pie In The Living Room

One Saturday morning I was at Connie Allard's house. His folks were not home. As I sat in a Living Room chair, he came in from the kitchen with a lemon pie balanced on his fingertips. Leaning against the door casing, he said, "watch this!" And with that started a series of spins, ups and downs and more spins. I

Lyndon
INSTITUTE

Alumni Newsletter

Winter 2000

Mason General Store, Lyndon Center, VT.
Coutesy of LI Alumni Association

1935 Dodge Coupe - Similar to one Kay Phelan owned.
(Her's was a 1936 4 door). National Automobile and Truck Museum
of North America. Photo 2001, C. Wells

flinched more than once expecting that pie to fly off his fingertips at any second. He ended up at the door casing again and said, "Betcha thought I'd lose it!" And with that gave it a Frisbee toss toward me - I flinched again and, you guessed it, on the floor bottom side up!

I have to spend a few more moments about Connie, (rekindle the memories).

Halloween - 1944

The second year I was there at Halloween time found Connie and I were on the track which was in front of Lyndon Institute building. Standing at the track, you had to look in the distance, and up at L.I.

This was Halloween night and the school had hired a deputy to cruise around the circular drive of the school, around the boys and girls dormitory and also to keep an eye on Sanborn House which was a girl's residence for Lyndon Normal School.

The building of L.I. has been conditioned so access could be

Lyndon Institute from the "Track." Photo 2001, C. Wells

achieved. In back of the boys dorm was a shed, and in the shed was a surrey with fringe around the top, shafts and all. This surrey was pushed across the street, up through the cemetery and close to a fence on a hill besides the L.I. parking lot.

Slowly and painstakingly this surrey was dismantled and the parts went into the assembly hall. Once all the parts were inside, it was reassembled on the stage! There were 4 or 5 students who participated, most of them from the boy's dorm.

The next morning, after the deputy reported "nothing abnormal," there was a student assembly meeting in the assembly hall.

With the surrey on the stage there was not enough room for the faculty without many (6) sitting in the surrey!

Cheers and laughter started the assembly off!

After it was finished, Connie and I came out and headed down the hallway. As we rounded the corner we felt a person move between us and take each of us by the arm.

We were guided by Prof. True, into his office, I knew at this point we were both in BIG-G-G trouble! He closed the door, and said, "How did you do it?" There was no point in saying "Us, Mr. True?" "What makes you think it was us?"

He was concerned about the access into the building - but we left with only a reprimand!

New York - New York

One weekend I had the good experience of going home with another dormitory member, Stuart Birch. He lived on Long Island somewhere near Floral Park as I remember. We rode the Long Island R.R. and, Saturday we took the train into Manhattan. Just to see the buildings and the sights was quite a thrill. This was the first trip I had ever been to New York City. I won't take the time or space to describe where we went or what we saw except for a couple of sights. One was the Empire State Building and one was Rockefeller Center. The elevators and their speed knocked me over.

Undoubtedly, I was like the story of the country boy who visited New York City. He stood on the sidewalk looking up in awe at the Empire State Building; somebody stopped beside him and looked up also.

Soon, many people stopped, looked up and could see nothing unordinary. Someone asked him what he was staring at and he replied that he was trying to estimate how much hay it would hold!

One other place that I requested to see was an Automat. We didn't have a car so all of our sights were confined to a small geographic area. (We did use the subway.) In the Automat, I wandered along the doors looking at all the food. The doors would open with nickels or multiple nickels.

I was especially fascinated to watch the (human) coin changer as she sat in the small booth near the entrance. There was a small granite sill the customer came up to. Behind the sill was a fair sized "tub," rectangular in size, full of nickels. The customer would lay a dollar bill on the sill. With the left hand, she scooped that dollar up and with her right hand would scoop a handful of nickels. Just as she would deal cards - she made 4 hand motions. Out would come 5 nickels per pass, not 4 or not 6 - 5 every time and with the speed of lighting. The sill had 4 distinct wear spots where those 4 groups of nickels would land! (It doesn't take much to keep my attention, huh?).

I also remember the 1941 De Soto taxicabs (most were 1941, a few 1942 and equal 1940 probably). The rear window would open and from them they had little canopy awnings, and supports with flags on the top. All yellow, as they were Checker taxis.

Someway we returned to Lyndonville, from an fun weekend in New York City.

Girls of 1944

Although Prof. True alluded to the sweater girls in his remark when I first enrolled, let me tell you that if or when the girls wore sweaters, they were not tight and were provocative mostly in your imagination. Dressing for both boys and girls was conservative. Boys would wear shirts, sometimes with ties. Some had sport coats or sweaters and I think, regular dress pants. I only had 1 pair of dungarees, if I had any. I think corduroy pants were popular but not with me. (I had to wear corduroy knickers sometimes in the grade school and they made so much noise, it made dogs bark when I walked!!) Girls wore saddle shoes and loafers a lot, as I remember and skirts were always at or below the knees. Probably SOME lipstick was worn etc. but, if it was excessive Prof. True would send you to the girl's room to remove some or all of it! I should probably add that nylons were worn but were very scarce, also high heels were worn on dates etc., but clothing worn in school was very conservative and non-startling. Both boys and girls wore I.D. bracelets. Also, girls were wearing anklets. Cosmetics were very scarce (except lipstick). Jewelry and earrings were very conservative.

Cold Day In Lyndonville

The winter in Lyndonville used to be an experience. It was cold through January and part of February. This was part of the reason why L.I. had a ski team for participation in winter sports, especially in ski jumping.

One morning I hopped out of bed, went through my usual morning ritual, and headed out the door. My pajama top was something like a sweater with stretch cuffs. Ditto for the bottoms. I used to pull a pair of pants over the pajama bottom to act similar as long johns. A light jacket on top would get me to school - it was just a short distance. Immediately I knew as the air hit my face - this was cold. I accelerated up the hill to reach the building

220

faster. Inside everyone was talking about how cold it was, as it was 62 below! Not Wind chill - - - - - actual temperature!

For years, I carried an article I clipped from the Burlington (VT) Free Press - and pulled it out of my wallet many times to substantiate my stories in the future about how cold it was in Lyndonville, VT.

Cutting Ice

A couple of weekends in January 1945, 3 or 4 of us boys in the dormitory got a job with Handy Ice Co. cutting ice in a small pond somewhere in Burke, VT.

The ice was nearly 3 feet thick - the owners cut it with a circular saw as Wallace Hill did, etch this top into 2 x 4 blocks. We had a small elevator loader bringing the blocks into the truck. The truck was loaded while sitting on the pond. On one occasion, they drove the truck off the pond and just before they reached land, there were a few "cracks" heard and the rear end of the truck settled into the water. I was in the back of the truck, but up near the headboard. The driver "gunned" it and luckily got it off the pond before water got into the engine. It was really cold and I had no desire to get wet and then have it freeze. I think we earned between $.40 and $.50 an hour.

Campus Life

Life on campus during non-school hours was somewhat flexible.

Study time in the evenings, on weeknights, occupied from 7 to 9 PM. This was quiet time, you had to be in your room. Of course, TV wasn't around, radio was but you couldn't have one on during study hours. Permission was easy to obtain for such things as a visit to the town library or for town band practice, even during study hours.

The boys ate at the girl's dormitory for all meals. The seating arrangement changed each week. I suppose this was done to prevent "clicks" and to overcome shyness on anyone's part.

One girl was exceptionally smart, and could very easily make you feel like a Dodo. But, away from a book or outside the classroom, a few felt that she didn't know shit from apple butter!

Naturally, I sat beside her on more than one occasion.

Very often we had ice cream for dessert and for some reason this also meant two cookies.

I'm not a great cookie lover and found I could stash them on an extension support under the table. Actually, I found I could stash many undesired items there.

One day, this girl was seated next to me when, for dessert, ice cream (and the cookies) were served.

She conversed with other people at the table and as she ate a cookie, I supplemented hers with one of mine - sort of a "now it's gone, no, there it is"!!

That worked so good, I planted a second one of mine on her plate. Never slowing up, that one disappeared! So, now, I fumbled around wondering if I could find one under the table on the extension support! Bingo! I found two. One at a time, one of these was placed on her plate. The other students knew what was happening and continued to extend the conversation.

I know she ate at least six cookies, the last two of which were hard as hell, before she started to wonder!!

Well, that took a little monotony out of that meal.

Dorm Rules

The boys could stay in the girl's dorm until 7 PM in the evening, but only in the rec room.

No boys were allowed on the second floor at any time.

The house "mother," these two years, was Mrs. Emerson. She was very pleasant and very fair, but she did rule the roost! Don't break the rules.

The boy's dorm occupied only the second floor and a very small third floor. A total of thirteen boys stayed here. A chaperone had the ground floor apartment and in my junior year, the chemistry teacher, Mr. K had a room on the second floor. There were two baths on the second floor. Apparently, at times this might not have been enough. There were a couple of times during my first year and in the winter, Mr. K and Lenny Burns were seen standing on the front porch trying to figure out how a small area, about 4 or 5 feet from the side of the dorm had yellow snow! The

puzzling part was that there were no footprints in the snow!
Is there a need for an explanation?

Snow in West Danville

Sometimes, Kay Phelan, the typing teacher, would go to
Randolph to visit friends for the weekend. This might happen
once a month, and she would ask me if I wanted a ride. I think
she liked to have me drive the old Dodge so she wouldn't have to.
I liked to drive, so this worked pretty good. Once in awhile, I
would take a bus. Vermont Transit Bus Lines used to run from
Newport to Montpelier. On one bus trip around March we made
the usual stop at the General Store in West Danville. In West
Danville, was a small body of water called Joe's pond. There were
many camps around the edge. As the bus left the store, it had to
cross a set of railroad tracks - snow was piled high. The wind had
really blown some drifts and was still blowing. Just beyond the
tracks was a cottage, the corner of which was about 4 feet from
the road. The bus had to stop, the driver opened the door and
that cottage looked like one big snow bank. You'd never know a
cottage was there! Also, you would never know there was a pond
there either! Needless to say, this trip took a long time before I
got home.

Connie Allard's Dad

Connie Allard's dad was a truck driver. He worked for
Speedwell Farms, a local dairy, and his job was to deliver milk
and other dairy products to Boston.
The tank, which was for bulk milk, was different than a
regular tanker. This tank was inside a "box" trailer with space
around between the tank and the insulated sidewalls. Here, they
would place 40 qt. jugs of cream, or other dairy products. This
trailer in comparison with others was very heavy. Connie used
to say "the damn thing pulled like a 'stone boat'!!" Connie A's
dad had worked here as a driver for years. Speedwell Farms had
a "fleet" of Internationals. This was a fine "tractor" but it was
really worked as it headed for Boston.
One day, management asked him to stop at Manchester (NH)

Connie Allard graduation photo - 1946. Jenks Studio, St. Johnsbury, VT

1938 International K-11 similar to 6 or 8 units Speedwell Farms had.
(Including Connie Allard's dad). National Automobile and Truck
Museum of United States, Photo 2000, C. Wells

Mack to look at a Mack they were considering to purchase. When he stopped (reluctantly), he hooked his thumbs behind the straps of his bib overalls (picture this and the fact he was about 5'2"). Kicking the tires, his remark was – "I don't know why they think it's necessary to buy anything as big as this."

So, he expressed to management that even though he was impressed with the Mack, it was just a lot bigger than was necessary.

So-o-o-o, they bought one for trial, and of course gave it to him to drive.

Upon return of the first trip with the Mack, Connie asked his dad how he liked it. "Best damn Truck they've ever had - wonder why they didn't get one sooner!!" So this was the beginning of a new era for him!!

There were a few "pulls" in New Hampshire that taxed trucks and drivers those days. One was in Glencliff, a SHORT but steep pull. This is on Route 25, which goes through the edge of the

Ozzie Gilman drove this Speedwell Farms truck.

The Creamery, Lyndonville, Vermont

box with a pink clover on it. The butter and cheese were made right there at the creamery.

In 1890, W. Irving Powers, clerk and treasurer of Theodore N. Vail's Speedwell Farms, organized the Lyndonville Creamery and was its general manager. He was also president of the Lyndonville Board of Trade, the forerunner of the Chamber of Commerce. The creamery provided an outlet for milk from Theodore N. Vail's more than 100 thoroughbred cows at Speedwell Farms. Milk and cream from other dairies were handled here too. In time even small farmers from Lyndon and area towns made their living by sending or taking their milk to this creamery.

The creamery association owned and operated a chain of fourteen creameries in Vermont and New Hampshire with a large branch near Boston for handling its own products.

This was a successful separator creamery, the first in this area. Butter made there in the morning was shipped by rail in ice chests and reached restaurants and hotels in Boston by

evening meal time. Later, milk, butter and cheese were shipped by refrigerated trucks.

From 1933 to 1938, Osmore (Ozzie) Gilman was one of several who drove a Speedwell Farms refrigerated truck from the creamery, to Watertown, Massachusetts. Back then it was a six- or seven-hour drive to cover the 200 miles. The drivers worked seven days a week including holidays—to Massachusetts one day, back the next.

The truck had a 125 gallon tank for milk. Doors on the side opened where milk jugs holding 85 pounds were carried. Cheese was carried in the back. The creamery made cheese with olives, cheese with chives, cottage cheese and butter. The skim milk from the creamery cheese and butter making was fed to pigs kept in a piggery back of the creamery.

The buildings are gone except the one that was the office. It was moved further from the road and remodeled into what became the Town and Country Restaurant. It has again been moved and remodeled and for a while was the Highwater Cafe. The building is not in use at present.

From Harriet Fletcher Fischer Collection

New 1946 Mack (Con's 1937 Lafayette). Photo 1946, C. Wells

White Mountain National Forest. Route 25 was then a main route on the trip to Boston.

Summer Off - Randolph

By now, spring had arrived, this school year was over and I returned to Randolph for summer vacation.

Dr. Frank Retires

As I settled down for life in Randolph, an announcement was received in the mail addressed to Mr. & Mrs. A. Wells.

This announcement stated that "Dr. Frank" was retiring after 50 years of practice in Randolph - 1894 to 1944

This would mean that I could no longer visit "Dr. Frank" for any mishaps or accidents. Now, this could present a problem, but "Dr. Frank" had a son who was also a doctor. However, "Dr. Bill" was in the Navy and as I recall, was on an aircraft carrier and with a "pretty good" rank! I was to see him in the future but not for a couple of years, at least!

Incidentally, going to the doctor's office was different in those days. Regular office hours were 2 to 4 and 7 to 9. Most of the time, there was no "greeter" - you selected a chair and sat down. Dr. Frank would open a door and beckon - if multiple persons were waiting, he'd ask who was next. You never knew how long you would wait.

And, I might add, doctors did minor surgery, put in stitches or whatever needed to be done to help the patients, right in the office.

I don't know how he got paid, I didn't pay him - I guess he ran a tab and a bill was sent out each month for "services rendered."

1894 ----- April ---- 1944

Fifty Years in Practice

Frank C. Angell, M.D.

228

Also, doctors used to make house calls. He would sandwich a house call (or two) in with his hospital visits in the mornings but, he or other doctors were apt to show up at your doorstep, in the evening.

Later on, I recall Nellie Wilcox was in the office. She worked as a receptionist, doctor's helper, bookkeeper and what ever else was helpful.

By now, it was standard practice that someone be in the room with a woman patient during doctor examinations. I think also, there was a law backing that procedure.

3rd Battalion Band

While I was in Lyndonville, I was a member of the Lyndonville town band for about 2 years, I was also in the Vermont State Guard 3rd Battalion Band.

This unit was based in Lyndonville and was comprised mostly of the same members in the Lyndonville town band.

We had scheduled meetings, rehearsals and, in addition, military training and uniforms.

As I "enlisted" on Dec. 5, 1944 and was "discharged" on June 1, 1945, this solved any problem which would be coming up for summer recess in 1945.

I suspect the discharge was sort of a surprise because of World War II ending about this time, that is, in Europe.

Hopping Stove

Sometime during the 2 years I spent at Lyndon, Stan's mother and father bought a house on Weston Street, right next to Tewksbury's "Corner Store."

It was only about 14 feet from Tewksbury's house attached to the store. A narrow driveway in between had a small garage at the end.

Stan and I would work on various and many cars in the garage.

You could hardly get in (or out) of a car inside, the garage was so narrow.

Stan bought a new sheet metal stove - it was oval shaped and quite thin metal. He paid less than 4 dollars for it new at Lamson's Hardware Store.

One day, I was with him and it was late fall - chilly. He lit a fire in the stove, and once it was burning wood, he chopped up an old tire and chucked about half of it in the top lid. Not very long, that stove was getting cherry red, as were the two sections of stovepipe nearest the stove!

Then it started making funny noises - fortunately, the small feet had a hole punched in the middle, so we nailed it to the floor! Didn't seem to bother him - scared the hell out of me.

I'm quite sure; Stan's car at the time was a 1928 Erskine, which was in excellent condition, only one I ever saw.

1927 Erskine (Studebaker) Identical to 1928 Erskine Stan G. had in 1945. National Automobile and Truck Museum of United States. Photo 2001, C. Wells

A Small "Pop"

It was during one of these sessions Stan was telling me about the following incident.

As I was "away" during school year, Stan was still in Randolph and, of course, in school. He knew many people - probably most of the people in the whole damn county and, the next county.

Anyway, a small town business owner from someplace like Tunbridge, Chelsea, Sharon or South Royalton had his brother from Connecticut come up for Christmas. It was very common to have snow in central Vermont by Christmas.

After a day or two of "getting caught up," Harley (the businessman) said "Jack, you'll have to see my deer camp - it's only 3-4 miles up the road." Jack said "Well, let's go."

So they drove to it, got out and traipsed over a snow bank and through quite a few inches of new snow to the door, a few feet from the road.

Once inside, the "main room" had cans of paint, stain and sealer in the middle of the floor. Also, a gas log was there, so Jack knelt down to light it.

Harley said "You better let me light that, Jack, it's apt to "pop" a little when it lights." So Harley knelt down, lit a match, and the resulting explosion blew the walls out, the two of them, and the roof dropped onto the floor. Both of them ended up in the snow bank - stunned, but not seriously hurt. Jack said "By God Harley, You're right, that sure does pop!!!!"

1930 Chrysler

By early spring, (1945), someway I heard about a car for sale - it was stored in a shed at the greenhouses on Sand Hill. So, I went up to the greenhouses. I don't recall if I have sold the Chevy convertible or what the status of it is. Well, let's say I drove up to the greenhouse in the '31 Chevrolet. When I found this car - let me describe it!

It's a 1930 Chrysler convertible coupe with a rumble seat. It's a tan color with chrome bumpers and large chrome headlights. The wheels are orange spokes with chrome hubs and large white wall knob tires. The dash is loaded with instruments and chrome. If the rumble seat is open, there is an access panel across the front of the rumble that lifts for easier access to the rumble seat. There is a black and chrome luggage rack on the back. Inside, the seat is split, 2-bucket seats, which are leather and is similar in design to a Bostrom truck seat! The engine is a 6 cylinder. Man, WHAT A HONEY! It seems the owner was in the service and in Europe. The price is HIGH - the most I ever paid for any car. Can I raise 80 dollars? Well, yes I can! I sold the 31 Chevrolet - registered the Chrysler and put the wheels on. What a machine! It was HEAVY, but it rode like a cloud!

I should say that registering a car at that time was simple. Attach a plate and send the application and check. I don't think there was even an inspection to contend with. There was no compulsory insurance - no insurance at all was more the norm than the exception! Everything was a lot simpler. If an accident happened, it most likely was resolved on the spot or at least quickly. Lawsuits were very rare!

1931 Chrysler - very similar to the 1930 Chrysler described in text.
Courtesy of Mr. & Mrs. Jack Saylor and Reminisce Publications

So, through the summer, I drove this car and loved every minute of it! Of course, it caught the attention of many people, at least for the first couple of times they saw it.

One of the people whose attention it caught was an ex G.I. who was attending the "Aggie School" in Randolph Center. He had been in the service and had received a medical discharge. He had hand, arm and head wounds somewhere in active service. (This was becoming fairly common to see G.I.'s who had been injured and discharged even though the war was not over).

This car caught his eye and he wanted to buy it. "Would I sell it?" Well, I really didn't want to, but I did realize that a monthly payment was a "hard bite" for me each month. I owed about 50 or 60 dollars. I said I would sell it for 150 dollars. This didn't seem to slow him up too much. How about if he gave me 80 dollars and the balance when his next disability check came in?

I agreed, collected the 80 dollars, wrote a receipt and gave him the keys and the car.

Never saw him again! He took the car, packed his bags and I was told headed for Texas!

Of course, what I lost was profit only but also, one great car! This was a quick short lesson I had to chalk up to experience. So, I paid the note off, but I had to replace it with something.

Info - Unimportant

Through the winter, I also had made good progress on the trumpet even though I only played during rehearsals. When you play an instrument such as a trumpet, if you are the weak link in the chain, by surrounding yourself with strong musicians, the net result is that you will improve rather than others being degraded. This is true not only in music but in sports etc. So, when I came back to Randolph in spring 1945 I had a lot more confidence in myself! One other item of interest here, is the fact, that your progression in music or anything you work at, will look like a set of stairs. You will make progress through practice or applying yourself and the result will be some improvement (the riser), and will level off for a variable length of time (the tread). Both the "riser" and the "tread" length of time (or improvement) will be dependent on many factors such as application of one's self, sincere interest and desire.

Teep Stoddard

When I was back in Randolph, someway I got acquainted with "Teep" Stoddard. Teep had just been discharged from the Marines. He received a medical discharge, as he had been involved in some frontline action. He didn't tell me this and he, also, didn't talk about his "experiences" in the service. Someway he bought an Army truck known as a 6 x 6. This was a full-fledged Army vehicle, color and all. It had a "hard cab" and a 6-cylinder GMC engine. (Actually, of course, it was made by GM).

Teep had built a body on the frame in his dooryard. It was a wooden flat bed which was now finished and wanted to try out.

He had negotiated with Clifford Dustin who owned one of the 3 local feed stores, (mentioned previously.) Cliff needed enough

234

fertilizer to constitute a load. Teep was to go down to Middletown, CT, pick up the load and deliver it to Randolph.

He asked me if I wanted to go with him. After receiving permission I jumped in and away we went.

This was not a difficult destination to get to, mostly Route 5 until just below Hartford, CT.

We found our way to the "plant" where the fertilizer was produced and backed up to the loading dock. This place loaded so many trucks, it didn't take much time before we were loaded. This is where a problem showed up. Teep hadn't given quite enough thought to building this body! One of the body cross pieces was over one of the axles. As the truck was loaded, the weight made the body settle and this cross piece settled on to a tire (on each side) so the truck would hardly move. These dockworkers didn't want any part of unloading this or even partially unloading it. So, Teep and I removed bag after bag on to the ground until he could finally use an ax and cut most of that cross piece out of there (both sides). Then, we had to reload. I think we worked

Gas stations received motor oil in bulk and from this dispenser, glass quart bottles were filled - 1940's. Photo 2001, C. Wells Courtesy of National Automobile and Track Museum of U.S.

more than 4 hours. Also, the load was heavy enough in the rear, so the front end was very light!

Well, this really didn't hamper us as we drove along the highway. However, we were heading north on Columbus Ave. in Springfield, MA.

As you approach Memorial Bridge, (a 4 street intersection) there was a traffic box at the intersection. We had to turn left as Route 5 directed you across the bridge. This was just a little different as the box was offset in the intersection meaning our left turn meant we turned left prior to the "box." This box was actually open on 4 sides but had a roof on it, and some casters to move it.

Now the combination of the uphill start, the light front end, the left turn (and maybe some drag on the rear wheels) were working against us. Teep started up in 2nd gear as the traffic cop motioned him to turn left. This would require a lower gear yet to start up. So, Teep pushed the clutch and dropped into 1st, muttering something about old Grandmother gear, let the clutch out and proceeded right toward the traffic box!

As the front wheels came down, each bounce helped to steer to the left - but not enough, not quick enough! As the traffic cop literally bailed out the further side, the right corner of the front bumper seemed to nudge that box quite out of position! Then the whistle blew and the traffic cop was running after the truck, coming around the rear end with his arms flying (so Teep said later). After a short discussion, Teep climbed in and we started again - the cop repositioned his box and we continued up Route 5 to Randolph. I don't recall how many hours this took, but I scatted home.

Later, I was to run into Teep again, when we worked together for another employer.

The Pool Room

Facing Sowles Block from Depot Square, there were two storefronts. One, over Grant's Drive was a storefront, which at one time was home to Sault's Barber Shop. This was during the sixties and seventies. Another barbershop also used it.

But, on the right side, next to the double doors for Sowles

Hall entrance was another storefront. This storefront in the 1920's and early thirties was a business called Buck's printing. When Mr. Buck died, his daughter (and wife) moved the equipment to the cellar of a house on Prospect St. The house was owned by Cedric Clark, the railroad station agent, mentioned previously. From that time, up to about 1938, the store was a funeral parlor run by Robert Mayo. But sometime after that it became a pool room.

This was operated by "Dell" Scribner for some thirty years, the exact year(s) I don't know.

I used to spend time here starting when I was about fourteen. That would be about 1942.

There were 4 pool tables and one billiard table.

It certainly wasn't very "ritzy," just plain bare walls, a tin ceiling and a hardwood floor.

There was a counter that offered a few goodies - peanuts, a few candy bars maybe but not much because the war made snacks scarce.

However, there were quite a few "punch boards," from very small to very large.

These contained pieces of paper, accordion folded and sandwiched in between many layers of cardboard. A "punch" about the size of a six-penny nail - and flat on the end was used to push the top foil and the paper out of the hole through the bottom.

The small boards have about 200 holes while a large one could have many thousand punches. Each punch would be a nickel up to a dollar.

Very seldom, would I push a punch - it seemed like a fast way to separate a few coins from my pocket. Earning a few coins by shoveling a little coal or whatever else, also seemed to be a slow way to put a few coins in the pocket. And, at this age I really didn't have much earning power.

But others played the boards - there weren't too many ways during the war, to spend money.

Also, I sensed that these might not be legal, especially after watching the two guys who periodically would trudge up the steps with a large case, and then spread these boards on the counter for Dell to examine.

Also on the counter, or in the large case were cigarettes, cigars, pipe tobacco and stuff called cut plug. Most of the cut plug was Beechnut brand - maybe a couple others.

But, I saw many a game of pool interrupted by someone, who's turn it was to shoot, stop, reach in his pocket, and take out a white package with red stripes. Then, open it up and proceed to take a pinch of this, and put it in a place where there should have been some teeth! Quite often a couple (or even a few) teeth might show, but those that did, were apt to be in desperate need of some "body work."

And I can't let this go without mentioning that another reason to interrupt the game, was when one of these "players" would wheel around and "discharge" a wet mass on its way to one of a few spittoons strategically placed near each table. Each one of those had a big flare top about 12 inches in diameter. Believe me, some needed a spittoon the size of a bathtub and would still miss!!

Dell would have to clean up periodically and I'm sure he didn't relish that, even with his monkey face gloves on!!

I wouldn't do it by any manner short of wearing hip boots, apron, oil resistant gloves and a pair of long handled tongs!!

I very seldom played pool for any money as mentioned but there were others who did - and for surprising amounts. The game they played was either 9 ball, rotation, or straight pool.

My playing pals and I stuck with eight ball, nine ball, or rotation, also.

Dell would often rack the balls so he could keep track of the number of games per table. When you finished, the players would square away with each other and then pay Dell.

Here, I learned about credit. Dell would let some players "run a tab" by writing on a piece of card board from a candy box, how much you owed and then stick it between the cash register and the wall. I always paid Dell before it went over three dollars.

During 1944 and 1945, I was away, so I didn't spend as much time in the pool room - also, my mother didn't give permission to go there.

Dell told me, in later years, "she was afraid you might hear some bad language" and added, "I didn't have the heart to tell her that you could learn some of those guys a new language!!"

238

One time, about 1945, I was home, Dell and I were talking. Someway, I mentioned I had a date with Barbara Day and couldn't go "wherever" because I didn't have a car.

He tossed me the keys to his 1935 Ford which was always parked in front of those steps. So, I used the car, brought it back around ten and thanked him.

The pool room was a gathering spot for a lot of the town (or village) characters, mill workers, farmers, business men and male students used to gather at the pool room and very rarely was it empty or nearly empty.

Contrary to what my mother used to think that I might learn here, quite the opposite actually took place, as I now look back and analyze.

I learned to respect people, all people regardless of their background or appearance. When you're using a cue stick - all that is irrelevant. Most of these people didn't have much money in their billfolds, - but they had a wealth of pool ability in their hands!! Also, you really learn when to give a person "space," which is quite important.

1931 Harley

Somewhere along the way, I had found a motorcycle I wanted to buy, if my parents gave their permission.

It was a 1931 Harley Davidson "45 Twin." When I bought this from "Rat" Tabor, I didn't know how to operate it, so, I put down the stand which raised the rear wheel off the ground. Motorcycles of this age, had two stands, the kickstand and a rear stand. This one was light enough to lift it up on the stand. The clutch, gearshift and gas weren't that difficult to learn just by watching the rear wheel. So, after a few moments, off the kickstand and down the road. I don't recall how many miles this had on it but it was about 14 years old, so it had quite a few. And it was in need of tender loving care, which I gave it.

One of the first persons I gave a ride was Russell Day, better known as Buster, who, later would be my brother-in-law.

There was another brand of motorcycle, I'm sure was still being made. It was an Indian which was made in Springfield, Mass. An Indian owner really did not like Harley's, and vice versa.

It seems whichever one you started with you stuck with. They were quite different - the Harley shift was on the left side, the Indian shift was on the right. Harley had a left foot operated clutch and throttle was controlled by the right grip. I don't remember how Indian allocated those functions - I really wasn't interested - I was a Harley man!

The Indian also had a 4-cylinder engine, where Harley stuck with 2 cylinders. When mine was made, I'm sure that was the only size engine. More on that later.

There was an Indian owner in town (which was also a 4 cylinder) by the name of Harvey Hayward which I will also come back to.

Stan and I had a lot of fun "tooling" around on the Harley. I don't think his folks were totally happy about it, they wouldn't give in to the reality of him owning one.

It really didn't help though, when he would come home with the heels on his shoes worn down! When we banked on a few corners, his heels hung off the rear of the foot rests.

The foot rests were hinged, so if they dragged on the pavement during a hard bank, there would be less pressure on the road. However, the rear rider had to put their feet on these foot rests - with the foot trailing off the rests. This position made the heels drag on the pavement.

I had a lot of trouble with the clutch. It slipped a lot and required almost constant adjustment. I knew there was an oil leak, but I didn't have the money to get that done at that moment.

One day we were at Stan's house on Maple Street. His house had a driveway going to their garage. Beside the driveway was a strip of grass about 10 feet wide and the neighbors had a driveway also. Across Maple Street was the Eastern Star Home (A large residence for elderly Eastern Star members) and directly across the street, they had a long garden that paralleled Maple Street. We were on this strip of grass and Stan asked if he could take a trial spin on the motorcycle. His mother wasn't totally opposed, the motorcycle was heading toward the street.

Sitting on the seat, he turned the switch on, swiveled the kick starter out, rose up and brought his weight down on the kick start. (No electric start here).

As he started to roll very slowly he gave it a little more gas -

then he looked down and realized the clutch wasn't fully engaged. As he stepped on it, the throttle was about half way, he quite suddenly shot out of the dooryard toward a good sized Maple tree near the sidewalk! Just missing this tree, he crossed the sidewalk (with both legs and an arm or two doing metaphor signals), crossed Maple St., and into the Eastern Star garden. I thought surely this would impede or stop his jaunt - but it didn't! Over squash vines, through radishes, carrots and finally you could see cornstalks giving way.

By this time, I'm running after him and then I saw Reverend Engel, beyond the garden, watering his lawn. HE also heard the commotion, glanced, dropped the hose and ran. The nozzle less hose looked like a long green snake gone berserk spewing water. This is where Stan was headed for Rev. Engel's woodpile and managed to climb most of it before it came to rest near the top, in a cloud of smoke. He wasn't hurt, (neither was Rev. Engel), but the Harley suffered a couple of dings and the loss of a mirror or two - they were probably in the same place as Stan's pride.

There were a few other incidents, as a matter of fact, about each ride yielded an incident (or two), that I won't bother to reiterate here both for lack of time and more so, for lack either of intelligence or common sense - that damn motorcycle didn't seem to have a normal amount of either! I'm sure you can see through the fallacy of that theory and that is why I shudder when I see

Con - 1931 Harley 45 twin. Note broken headlight lens. Photo 1944.

the machines of the nineties. So fast, so powerful, so quick that any instance of poor judgement can lead to discomfort or worse.

Like this incident, Stan and I were coming out of the parking spaces at George Allen's Garage. As we came down the slight incline on to Pleasant St., we leaned right to follow the street. At the same time, I "gunned" it to pick up speed. All of a sudden the rear kicked around, whoops too far, lean to left, whoops again - headed for the post office, lean right - lean left, lean right - legs flying, finally got it tamed down!!! We went back, looked like and felt like Prestone or oil - something got on the tires which was really slippery.

Anyway, two or three people confided they really thought we were going through the bay window of the Post Office.

Last thing I'll speak about in relation to this motorcycle, and then we'll move on.

One day, the engine made a very disturbing noise and then failed to run. It also failed to even "turn over." This is not good. I knew there was a shop in St. Johnsbury on Route 5 that repaired motorcycles, so the smart thing was to let him evaluate it. How were we going to get it there?

Stan had the use of his folks 1937 Ford Sedan. Stan's father was a mechanic and kept this car in top shape. Anyway, we decided to tow the Harley to St. Johnsbury.

We tied a rope around the handlebars, sort of an "evener" and tied the tow rope to it, the theory being the tow rope would "travel" the "evener" rope when cornering etc. Before we started Stan asked how fast I wanted to go, so I replied that "not too slow and not too fast!" So we headed north on Route 12 and it didn't take long for me to realize that anytime that tow rope wasn't perfectly straight - it "pulled" and my arms would tighten up. So it took a few miles to get used to this.

By now, we're going "up" through Northfield Gulf - a twisting, quite narrow road that follows a brook in a ravine that becomes quite high. It also becomes quite twisty before you reach the top. So we reached the top, traveled a few miles and started down a long and fairly steep hill. Knowing I wanted that tow rope to stay "tight," I had reached for the foot brake and that's when things happened!

That tow rope "evener" was long enough in slack, it dropped

down and got caught "across" the front wheel and stopped it dead.

Over I went and down I went! Stan (later said he was doing 50 m.p.h.) saw me go down, but didn't dare stop fast for fear of me sliding under the car. I got my right foot caught between the foot brake and the crash bar as it bent back! So I was getting dragged down the paved road and couldn't get free. Stan was slowing up as fast as he dared to, and just before he stopped I freed myself from the crash bar.

I didn't have anything broken and I wasn't hurt too bad with the exception that the front headlight broke and the glass from it didn't *ALL* go by me. I picked up many pieces, my right shoe on the right side was "street burned off," so was my right pant leg, my jacket right arm, my shirt - etc. Worst thing was my hands where they dragged. However, I was ok enough so we left the Harley in someone's barn - drove to Northfield where some Doc used a box of Band Aids and a few stitches and also removed a fairly large piece of glass from my leg!

We did have to replace a piston (which broke) and a couple other things to the Harley to get it running again. I fixed the accident damage.

**Selected Songs
Composed in 1945**

Day by Day
Give Me the Simple Life
I Can't Begin To Tell You
It Might As Well Be Spring
It's Been A Long Long Time
Laura
Love Letters
The More I See you
Till The End Of Time

Exhaust Whistle

Stan and I also came up with an exhaust whistle. I don't know where it came from, but we decided to put it on the 1937 Nash. This apparently could be installed to your own personal desire.

We chose to install a "tee" in the exhaust pipe very close to the manifold. At the time we built in two valves - one in the exhaust pipe and one in whistle inlet. One pull control would shut the exhaust off and also open the second one to the whistle.

By this time; the Esso station in Depot Square, was operated by Alton Rogers and he let us install it using the pit in the station.

After we finished we took a "spin" up Route 12 to East Braintree, (E. Braintree had one general store - they also sold beer which was not available in Randolph).

The whistle sure worked, and when we got back, Alton Rogers said if he knew we were going to E. Braintree, he would have asked us to bring back a six pack! The whistle sounded just like a train whistle. Surprised, we asked him how he knew we went to E. Braintree.

He said he could hear it up the valley all the way and the turn around (E. Braintree is about 4 miles)!!

Dating Advice

It was about this time in my life that Dad gave me his advice about dating girls. When I would go on a date, or when I left to go to Lyndon (back to school), he would make a statement.

"Keep your nose clean." This was the total advice I ever received about sex! My mother gave me even less - she said absolutely nothing! As I have stated before, you didn't even use the word "pregnant" in the house and there were no "giggly" stories told, or off color jokes either.

On other things besides sex education, such as using the car, treatment of other people or other people's property - Dad also gave me instructions.

"I don't want to ever look up and see you standing in front of my bench." This was just a reminder that he was a Side Judge in the County Court where I would appear on any serious charges.

Believe me, that was all he had to say to me, coupled with the fact that I highly respected him AND his wishes. I knew exactly what he meant, and, *most* of the time, I lived within the boundaries.

Model T Racer

The Harley had been sold and by now I had bought a vehicle that had a racing body on a Model "T" chassis.

Someone had started with a Model "T," stripped the body off and then made this racing body in its place. It had a cockpit (no doors) with a windshield in front and the rear tapered to a vertical point. There were no fenders and, it *was* a pretty good job, (for those days).

At the time I ran this Model "T," I certainly couldn't have had any amount of claustrophobia. When you were sitting at the wheel, it was so tight you couldn't sit there if you had a pimple on your butt! You had to get in from the other side and slide over – the seat was fixed, so where you sat was all you were going to get. When Wendell Smith and I were both in, there was absolutely no room to jostle around!

This thing would go anywhere, mud, ruts, snow banks didn't stop it - just slowed it up! No fenders and high ground clearance put it in about the same category as a mountain goat.

When fall came, it got a little chilly with no heater. So I decided to put in a hot air heater. I installed a piece of sheet metal wrapped around the exhaust manifold. At the rear end was a piece or two of plywood which allowed some hosing to capture the heat. A hole was cut in the floor board (about 2" in diameter). Then the hose directed the heat through the floor.

Of course, it would have required a hose of at least 12 inches in diameter to supply enough heat to feel anything! But, Wendell and I had fun - and you could feel a little heat, that is until we could smell smoke! Then on Maple St., right beside the hospital, a couple small flames emanated from the hole right between Wendell's shoes. I pulled over so we could stop what was burning! We knew this was right near the carburetor and also, right under the gas tank in the cowl. Wendell jumped out, unhitched the hood side panel which went flying and then grabbed the metal

1921 Model "T" Ford Racer. All photos 1945, C. Wells

All photos - C. Wells, 1945

piece around the manifold including the burning plywood.

Those items landed on Fred Preston's lawn where the snow extinguished the small fire, and also ended the life of the heater.

Good try, just not successful! We had numerous experiences with the racer and a lot of fun, such as the day Stan and I were getting some gas at the Esso station. After shutting the pump off, we started the engine and it sat at the pump, idling.

Then a very metallic thud was heard and it almost looked like one side of the car actually raised up as it stopped so quickly.

After removing the hood side panel we saw what caused that rather peculiar noise. A connecting rod had come loose from the crankshaft and stuck right through the engine block!

Well, anyone familiar with engines at all knows that one solution is to replace the block. Welding at this point of time is out, no one around here could do that.

So, one possibility left was "Smooth-on" furnace cement. I had seen this used on boilers.

We asked a couple of mechanics and they both laughed. "It would leak," "it wouldn't hold," "the grit in it would get into the oil" etc., etc. Well, we didn't have anything to lose, and everything to gain. We also came up with the couple dollars to buy it. Lamson's Hardware had it, so we proceeded to mix some up, - place the 3 or 4 pieces in position and patch them with some "Smooth-on" (furnace cement)!

We helped the curing process along some with a blowtorch - - -never had leakage or other problems.

Of course, we had to replace the connecting rod which meant head and pan removal.

We drove the car for months and continued to have fun with the "racer."

Company "L" 2nd Battalion Infantry

This was another "hitch" I did in the Vermont State Guard.

Here I enlisted on July 16, 1945 and was discharged on August 27, 1945 which was only for one month!

Here, again I don't recall the reason it was only for a month. In addition, this was Infantry so I probably wasn't too disappointed it was short lived.

Honorable Discharge
From the State Guard of Vermont

To all whom it may concern:

This is to Certify, *That* Conrad J. Wells

_____ *as a* TESTIMONIAL OF HONEST AND FAITHFUL

SERVICE, *is hereby* HONORABLY DISCHARGED *from the* STATE GUARD *of*
(Entrance To Special Schooling)
Vermont by reason of Business Interference

Said Conrad J. Wells _____ *was born*

on 26th of January, 1928 , *in the State of* (Randolph) Vermont

When enlisted he was 17 *years of age and by occupation a* Student

He had Brown *eyes,* Black *hair,* Dark _____ *complexion, and*

was Five *feet* 11-3/4 *inches in height.*

Given under my hand at Montpelier _____ *this* 27th *day of*

August _____, *one thousand nine hundred and* Forty-Five

Col. Geo Bn
Commanding State Guard

ENLISTED RECORD OF

Wells	Conrad	J.		Private
(Last name)	(First name)	(Middle initial)		(Grade)

Enlisted 16th of July, , 19 45 , *at* Randolph, Vermont

Character: Excellent _____ Married or Single: Single

Remarks: None

Signature of soldier: Conrad J. Wells

PEARL H. LASKEY, 1st Lieut., VSC.,
Co. "L", 2nd Bn., INF.,
Commanding

AGO-Vt.
Form No. 47
1000

2nd Batallion Infantry discharge

Fire in Bethel

So, one afternoon in December 1945, I had finished work at the Coal office.

About 4 PM I heard the fire alarm blow. Man, that horn is loud when you're near it. (It will carry for miles)!! Anyway, I found out the fire was in Bethel, in the business district. Now, a request for Randolph assistance wouldn't be sounded if it wasn't a good sized fire, or had the potential of being one!

So, I drove down to Bethel, had to park prior to the bridge somewhere around the "old" high school. I walked down the bridge and south on Main St. Just past the railroad station, was a block of stores. A wooden building with about 7 storefronts on Main St. and two more on the right end facing the parking lot of the railroad station.

The onlookers packed the sidewalk across the street, and also filled the street.

In the store fronts on Main St. were various businesses, only two that I distinctly remember. One was a State Liquor store. In

The Building in Bethel, that replaced the block which burned as described in the text. The burned block covered from about the left end of the building, to the right end of the iron fence. Photo 2001, C. Wells

Vermont, all liquor, at least at that time, was sold through a state controlled store. Beer and wine could be purchased at other stores such as grocery stores. Bethel had a State Liquor store - Randolph did not, as it continually voted "dry." Even so, if it did vote "wet," any town would have to vote wet two or three years in a row before the state would spend the funds to set up a store. The other store was a First National store. This would be a grocery store and I doubt it was a supermarket. This is the store the fire seemed to be in —facing the block, the store is on the far left.

I recall the building to be 3 floors high on the front - the stores on the right end would be considered in the "cellar." There were porches on 2nd and 3rd floors across the front.

Once in awhile, you could see a flame inside the First National Store. It was about 5 or 6 PM and looked like the fire was about out. Bethel, Randolph, and So. Royalton appeared to have "nailed" this one.

The crowd still milled around. I groped my way around the right end, and found myself standing among quite a few people, in front of a storefront in the cellar. It certainly was unoccupied, door locked and dark. What the hell was the attraction here? I went back up front, - on the sidewalk I ran into Stan. Asked him why all the people were around the unused store on the right side. He said that was where this liquor store stored all the stock!

As it approached 7 PM, Stan and I were standing on the sidewalk across from the block. There was a lot of people here, but not nearly as many as previously. I'm sure that many headed for home as the excitement was over. There were still fire departments from Bethel, Randolph, So. Royalton and I think Tunbridge. Mostly as a precautionary measure.

Out of the blue or rather, black, a good sized explosion came from inside the First National store. Within seconds we had a fire! And how it did spread! There was all kinds of action now, including Stan and I - also all the other people watching in front.

Not knowing what was going to come down out of the sky - or, how many explosions would follow was a GOOD reason or reason(s) to clear out. I know I was pushing on someone's back who was blocking my way. This was a common act of many at this one instance. Well, no one was hurt and everyone had scurried. I stopped, in front of Washburns store (beyond R.R. station).

Didn't see Stan - I knew he had to be near, because we both started from the same spot and "you" were limited on the ground "you" could cover. Not seeing him close at hand, I started to scan further away. About the same distance again - there he was.

He caught up to me, but couldn't explain totally how he got so far! No one will ever know, short of flying, how he covered that distance!

As we made our way back, we had now concluded that no more serious explosions would probably take place, so we stood in front again and this time, the number of spectators had really reduced. The fire, - *man, there was a fire*! The inside of the First National store was a full blaze and by now, the State Liquor store was being consumed and spreading fast throughout the whole first and second floors. This building was old, the wood was dry and was a perfect setting for a fire, waiting to happen!

After a few minutes, Stan and I worked our way again to the end of the building near the R.R. station. We stood in front of the vacant store, along with 15 or 20 other people. There was a door and a big bay window.

Stan was in line, I was behind him and behind me was "Cakkery" Smith, who we both knew. Cakkery said - "If you get in before me and get a case - pass it on to me!" "If I get one first, I'll pass it to you!" Sure Cakkery I thought, - if I gave him a case, no one would see him for 4 days!!

Word came that it was ok to "break the door and window - the whole building is going up."

Bang - Crash! Someone broke the flanker window of the bay unit - also the door had been pushed in. Stan didn't wait for anyone to pass out anything nor did he wait for an invitation - he jumped through that window in a flash. Broken glass around, still sticking out of the sash - I took a couple seconds to "clean" and then I jumped through the window.

Inside, it was dark as pitch, but you knew that MANY people were around. God - flies on a dead horse?! Everywhere. As I poked my way toward the rear, cases of liquor were moving towards the front of the store. There were cases and cases and cases stacked on the floor. Back to back, and an aisle. Again, back to back and an aisle. It was dark - the further in I went the darker it got! I took out a lighter, flipped it, so I could read labels. Whoa, this is a poor place for a lighter, one wrong move and the whole damn building could go up! - Wait a minute the whole building IS going up!!!

Here's something that looks good, wish I knew more about this stuff but I didn't, so, take this and run with it. Out the door, and ran into Stan (coming back). "Take it down to the tracks, Dad is there and will watch it." Down to the tracks, Stan's dad, Merville, is standing between two sets of tracks - has a case at his feet. The fire is so bad now, no trains are allowed to pass, and for about the next two hours.

Back I went into the store, out came the lighter as I made my way down an aisle. I didn't know what this stuff was, but I noticed that the further in I went, the better the boxes or cases presented themselves. I was so engrossed I finally noticed no one else was very close to me. Something dropped - I looked up. Above me was a big hole in the floor - - - and above that, big flames! Whoa, no place to be. Grabbed something else and dashed back to Merville. He now had 4 cases in front of him with what I just dropped off! We lugged them along the tracks and to the car(s).

If anybody had told me about the hole in the floor etc., I would have doubted it could happen. But thinking about it - all the fire and therefore all the heat and smoke was above the cellar. I think the window and door open in the cellar probably created a draft up through the floor which blew everything up further.

WHITE RIVER VALLEY HERALD

THURSDAY, DECEMBER 20, 1945

DISASTROUS FIRE CUTS SWATH IN MAIN BUSINESS SECTION IN BETHEL

Three Mercantile Blocks Destroyed in Fire That Raged for Hours; Three Fire Departments Join to Control Blaze

LIQUOR ABOUT ONLY ITEM "RESCUED" IN BETHEL FIRE

One of the few items to be rescued from the Bethel fire was an undetermined but considerable amount of liquor from the State Liquor store. Heroic bystanders saw the imminent danger to the liquor store in the Gay building before it became a mass of flames and acted—fast. Unfortunately, the rescued liquor probably will not be returned to the state since it disappeared in a number of directions, tucked under overcoats, in automobiles and even, it is reported, some case lots were carried to safe places in trucks.

The date was December 19, and that very day, the liquor store received a truckload of stock for the Christmas holidays so it was chocked full. We didn't drink any of the stuff but a lot of people "got holiday cheers" - and apparently someone did give permission to "salvage" the stock. You could hear bottles popping and something like propane explosions through the fire!

2 Model T's

Stan had a Model T sedan and Bill Slack also had a Model T sedan. Stan had a nice 4-door sedan with wooden spoke wheels and Bill's was a 4-door sedan with wire spoked wheels. They were both a 1927 year, they must have been a standard body and a deluxe. There were very few that had wire wheels so I would assume that one was a more expensive model. We spent a lot of time running around in one Model T or another.

Randolph Businesses

In Randolph, at the intersection of Main St. and Pleasant St. were two or three blocks. Within these blocks were various apartments and at street level, were stores.

Smith's Store

One of two stores, was Smith's, a variety store. It was across from the Methodist Church (which is now vacated). Being near the (only) village school building, it sold a lot of candy bars, peanuts and especially "penny" candy. The store was operated by Ed Smith and his wife. These people were elderly but they had the door open every day. Ed Smith is the same gentleman I mentioned before. He delivered freight and railway express packages from the Central Vermont Railroad Freight House. (I used to help him, when I was about 10 or 11, mostly by keeping him company)!

A whole counter top display of penny candy - it could use up quite a few moments trying to decide what was worthy of your couple pennies.

"Randolph House" - a multi tenant building replacing one known as Barney's Block as described in text. Photo 2000

Barney Shapiro

Next to "Smith's Block" was another that was similar - apartment or two over the street level store, also more apartments down below the street level. This was the norm for at least four blocks in a row due to a large drop off from the street. Next door, just prior to the library was a similar block which was owned by Barney Shapiro. Barney came to town years earlier and made his living selling door to door, from a pack he carried on his back. Needles, thread, knives, jackknives, anything he could carry. Over the years, he progressed until he opened a store which sold clothing etc. He ultimately bought the whole block. It is now replaced by an apartment for senior non-assisted living.

Patch's Studio

Another Randolph business was Patch's Studio on Pleasant St.

It was there in 1934 when 2 other businesses were in the same block. One was Bert Day's grocery store nearest to Randolph Avenue. And, a fire (in 1934) took his business out, but was stopped before Patch's suffered serious damage.

At that time, Herbert Patch was the owner. How much time he was there before that, I don't know.

As the years passed, his son Cliff was working there, as was Cliff's wife Dot.

And, after more years passed, their son Donald joined in.

It was a full service photography studio and was well known, and well respected for all types of studio portraits to full service local film developing and printing. And, of course, all types of cameras, film, and accessories were sold.

At this time, the business is closed - its time has come and gone, but thousands of prints, pictures and portraits by Patch's Studio will be around for years.

I used to be in the Randolph Band with Cliff where we shared some lasting moments. One being at World's Fair in Tunbridge. And which, I won't cover at this time.

Former Patch's Studio on Pleasant Street, described in text.
Photo 2000

L.W. Webster Employment

At this time, I was 17 and with a Driver's License. My Dad and Leon Webster had a conversation which led me to be hired to work at L.W. Webster's. This was one of three mills in town that was apt to be in need of new employees.

This was 1945, the war was still in full effort and thanks to many "G.I.'s," from around the world, the allies were getting a handle on the war!

Leon was the owner of Webster's mill along with his son, Kenneth. They were "short" a truck driver, a driver for one of their log trucks, of which there was four. These were all long wheel base Fords, early forties. I think mine was a 1940, "Hap" Carrier and Teep Stoddard both had a 1941 and Pearl Laskey's was a 1942.

Pearl delivered a lot of the finished product to Massachusetts, New York and New Jersey. This was a long trip in the forties. I remember, the truck ("his" truck) was loaded in the afternoon and he would leave at 3 or 4 AM the next day. Once it was loaded, someone believed it was beneficial to place 2 pieces of 2x6 vertically under the frame and down to the ground and then they would back up a couple of feet. This would take the weight off the springs until he left.

I didn't have any experience in driving a log truck but I did have some idea from previous "trips," I made with Bucky, or Bill Rogers.

The procedure to start the day, at Webster's, was a short whistle blast at 6:50. This was notice to employees to "punch in" at the time clock. It was also a wake up call for the whole village! At 7:00 AM, another blast signaled employees to start work.

Bill Barcomb

Although this incident didn't happen on my first day, this is a good time and place to bring it up.

Leon (L.W.) used to stand by the clock and watch the "punch in" line as it moved along. This prevented others from punching in for "others."

The line had ended, and Leon stayed there for 10 or 15 minutes. Bill Barcomb came straggling along about 7:15, punched in and started away when Leon said, "You know, Barcomb, we start here at 7:00 AM."

Bill replied "I know Leon, and if I'm not here, you start right in without me!"

Bill Barcomb Again

On another incident, Bill asked Leon for a raise, as he had many times before.

Leon replied, "Alright Barcomb, you've been here a long time, so I'll give you a nickel an hour more. BUT DON"T TELL ANYBODY ABOUT IT!!"

To which Bill added, "Don't worry Leon, I won't, I'm as ashamed of it as you are!"

Bill didn't get fired that I heard, but I bet there were times when Leon was working on an ulcer.

"Hap" and "Teep" gave me some background about the trucks and geographics where we went to pick up loads etc.

"Little Stoney" Brook

My first trip, I followed Hap (only), we went to Bethel and on toward Rutland. Shortly after Gaysville, Hap slowed down, made a left turn into a small field and stopped after allowing me enough room to be clear of the paved road. I was really surprised he turned here, the only place to go was straight in front of him and surely he (and I) weren't going "up" there. "Up" there was a narrow one lane trail for horses with stones in the wheel ruts - bushes etc. sticking out, surely he wasn't going there!

As he got out motioning me to do so, he knelt down and removed tire chains from under the body and laid then out in front of the driver wheels. We're putting tire chains on around July 1!! We are, We're putting

Road described in the text. As it says, within the text, the road has been "reworked" and upgraded greatlysince 1945 as this picture shows. Photo 2001, C. Wells

chains on and we ARE going up that burro trail!

Sometime, between 1945 and around 1988 this "road" was reworked and in doing so, reduced the dramatics!

This location is called "Little Stoney Brook" and I would find very quickly why we needed tire chains. It was quite steep, it was "dug out" of the side of a hill with a very long drop down into a valley which had a brook at the bottom. My first trip up didn't allow me to view "down" as it was on the rider's side. I couldn't believe we were driving up this "road" or trail. It was steep, it was narrow, it was bumpy, it was full of stones AND ruts - surely we aren't coming back down here!

Finally, after about 1000 to 2000 feet we came to a place to turn around near a "header." A header is a structure made from logs that elevate and allow the logs on the ground to be stored and also rolled on. Then heavy planks are put down so the logs can be rolled and stacked on a truck.

These two trucks, similar to the trucks described in the text, are both loaded to a minimum of six feet above the cab. Both are long wheelbase and appear to be a 1 1/2 ton rating. Probably are Ford's, being at a Ford dealer and are each estimated to be carrying about 16 tons. Its difficult to determine what "year" they are, probably between early 1940 and early 1950. the late 1940's saw tandem driving axles with dual wheels on both axles. Also, small mirror suggests up to early 1950's. Courtesy Harriet Fletcher Fisher.

Hap was loaded and he put the chains on the load and then installed the chain binders, which took the slack out of the chains and made the load secure.

The truck was parked in some ruts in front of the header and the load was about 4 or 5 feet above the cab. This was a pretty good load for this ton and a half Ford. It was a long wheel base and had a "donkey axle" added to the body to the rear of the rear wheels. This only helped carry the load - they were not driving wheels and also, didn't have brakes on this axle. It was an axle from a junk truck that was added to each and every log truck - for it to comply with state weight laws. The "donkey " or "tag" axle had to be lowered and locked down prior to loading and raised and locked up after unloading.

Shortly, a crawler tractor came out of the woods pulling a dray full of logs. He unhitched from the dray, then came down in front of the headers and hitched onto Haps truck. The first few yards were so steep, the truck didn't have enough power even in its lowest gear to move away from the header without having an assist from the tractor!

I should mention 1940 or 1941 was the first year I'm aware of Ford trucks had a 2-speed axle. It was manually operated by a second shift lever that came up through the floor board on the drivers left side, was offset toward the door a few inches, and then extended up about 14 inches. Way forward was high range, back about 3 inches was neutral and back again about 3 inches was low range. In low range the lever stuck up in front of the door and you had to content with it to get your feet by.

So with Hap out of the way, it was my turn to back "in" and get loaded. Getting loaded meant each log was rolled on the two moveable planks to its best place within the load so it was stable. Back to get the next log. Rolling a log involved using a Peevee or Cant Hook. You could bite into the log to grab it and roll it, or to use as a pry bar which would "kick" the log in order to change direction.

All logs at "Little Stoney" were hardwood so a load consisted of Birch, Maple or Beech. Beech was very hard to handle, especially if it was wet - it was very slippery. The load was stacked up, one log at a time, but with two people, one working at each end of the log, the job went faster and much easier. As the load went up, it required a little more planning where and how to place it. As you near the end, the load was somewhat rounded at the top. Two chains were tossed over the top and secured at each end. A chain binder "took up" the chain slack and minimized any load shift. I couldn't stand on the ground and toss a chain over the top - I didn't have enough strength. Hap could, and with such ease, it was embarrassing!

The tractor pulled me "up" the incline to a stopping place (I might add, the truck was also working, in first gear low range). Hap said if I didn't want to descend as a driver, just say so and he or someone else would drive it down. Well, I knew that wasn't going to solve the situation especially on subsequent trip, so I declined, determined to handle this on my own. I had made quite a few trips to this location, so by now, I was reasonably experienced.

One Saturday, Stan was available and rode with me to "Little Stoney."

As we made the climb up, we both were bounced around inside the cab. He didn't say much especially when we were passing a stretch where on his side – it was quite a ways "down" to the brook.

At the top, he was sure, no truck should haul logs out of here – down the "road."

When we did start down and came to the same area again, he decided to open the door and bail out. We really were doing under 10 m.p.h. – so it was safe to jump off.

He walked down, and followed the truck. Later, he described watching the descent in quite flavorful description.

I soon found out that even vacuum boosted brakes didn't offer enough braking power to stop this thing or in some spots even enough to slow it down. The descent speed was always under 10 m.p.h. but this rolled and pitched. It would stutter in sound as the traction would vary because stones or stoney gravel offered only questionable traction. Going over an angled drainage ditch was a combination of pitch, roll, stutter, etc. The big thing that really bothered me, was the fact the donkey axle was as much as a hindrance as it was an assistance. When you came to a pothole, the "driver" would drop into the hole and the donkey wheel would carry more of the weight. This meant the driver wheels momentarily lost their speed retarding ability (under compression)

260

and the donkey wheel on that side carried more of the weight. Then, the driver wheel would find traction, as the hole passed by, and resume its compression to hold back again. There was no control on speed for an instant or two you went over the pothole. So all of this contributed to the "ride." Many times I would pull the parking brake on with little effect. Also, I would put the right foot on the brake and my left foot right on top of the right foot! The fan at times would scream as the rpm went high and higher and the breeze was so strong, there was always a lot of dust and leaves being generated. At times, even clumps of wet leaves would get blown from under the truck.

As we approached the last incline we had to stop prior to the main highway and remove the tire chains. On one trip, as "Hap" started down this "pitch," a tire chain got crossed up on the wheel and tore a hydraulic brake line out. He went down this trail - right across the highway and stopped in a field across the road. Luckily, no car or vehicle came along. (Or a commercial bus)!!

Each load was about 4 feet above the cab and would vary in weight from 10 to 14 tons.

It was very common to replace a radiator every 3 or 4 months. This was due to the frame movement. As the radiator was mounted on the frame, it was subjected to a lot of motion, so the tubes would break or loosen up and then leak.

It can easily be seen how a loaded truck going down this incline would certainly surprise any vehicle coming from the right. Photo 2001, C. Wells

Easy Unloading

Back in Randolph, unloading was an easy job. Remove the chains (very carefully), we didn't want any log movement until the chains were totally off. Pry off the logs, one, two or three at a time. Mostly they went on the ground in a "bare spot." If we didn't unload them directly into the pond, they were very near the pond. The pond was a concrete swimming pool where all logs went prior to cutting them up. This washed all the dirt, gravel and crud off, so the saw would not saw stones or whatever stuck on the outside. In winter, ice was also removed and that is why the pond "steamed" because of the hot water. It wasn't scalding hot but it was very warm. Logs were moved about or lined up by someone using a pike pole. This was like a long handled spear with a reasonably sharp point on the end along with another point sticking out at 90 degrees - like you can do with your first and middle finger. You could spear a log and then pull on it enough to move it as it floated in the water.

Leon Takes A Swim

One day, Leon got frustrated at the "fisher" - the guy using the pike pole, grabbed the pole out of his hands and went to spear a log. He missed the log and of course, this upset his balance and he ended up in the pond, clothes and all! Boy, he was red as hell when they fished him out. A trip to the hospital was necessary to ensure he was ok!

To my knowledge, there was no such thing as medical coverage for employees. If an employee got hurt on the job (and many did), they were taken to the hospital (or doctor's office for medical treatment). The hospital or doctor would send Leon a bill.

There was no vacation pay and no holiday pay.

Also, there was no workmen's compensation. If you were out of work, due to injury, you didn't get paid, which was standard for many, many small businesses at that time.

Making Bobbins

So let's go back to the pond - the logs were guided one at a time over to one end where they were lifted out by a chain conveyor. Here, they were dumped in a waiting area - waiting to be cut by a huge round saw about 6 feet in diameter. It was so big, the teeth could be replaced individually with new teeth which

I had never seen before. This saved buying a new saw if something happened to an individual tooth (or more). The saw cut pieces off the end about 16 inches long instead of sawing the log lengthwise.

The big round pieces then passed to one of three or four large vertical splitters. These looked and operated like a large guillotine, and ran continuously. The knife was about 2 feet wide and would raise up about 24 to 30 inches. The operator would put a round chunk on the "table" and then push it in to a fixed stop as the knife went up. When the knife came down it would split off a piece. The piece would drop below and after it was totally split, the operator would refeed the piece(s) so they ended up about an inch and a half square for the small size or about 2 and a half inches square for the large size. This blade just kept going up and down all the while, the big steam engine was running. All the machinery ran from the big steam engine by many, many flat belts overhead.

The square pieces would drop on a conveyor where they went to one of four or five manual lathes. They were inserted by an operator who then stepped on a pedal and in one pass were "turned down" into a round bobbin. These bobbins were then shipped by truck or rail to North or South Carolina where yarn was wound on them. These bobbins wound with yarn or whatever would find their way to looms in the textile industry. Later, wood bobbins were replaced by plastic ones, but that didn't happen until probably in the sixties.

Imagine, operating one of these machines. You couldn't allow your mind to wander for a second - you could lose a finger or hand! Fortunately, there were no female distractions in this section of the mill - none allowed!

This part of the mill was cold because of the continual stream of logs that had to come in. They operated from 7 AM to 12 Noon and I very much doubt a mid morning coffee break took place.

So here was a mill and stable employer that employed up to a hundred people. It turned out products such as bobbins, kiddie car seats and bowling alley flooring. All of the products were made from Birch, Beech and mostly Maple which were dependent of logs arriving at the mill, on one of 4 company trucks or, one of many independents working as suppliers to Webster's.

During the war there was even one woman that I knew of

who worked for Webster's and she could handle a Cant hook and a log truck as good as any man!

Over the River

One time, Hap, Pearl and I went over near Washington, VT. This was my first trip bringing logs from this location. Believe me when I say that Washington is very small and there is not much there, but logs! Or trees that became logs!

I followed at the rear because Hap and Pearl had both been here before. Each time we turned off a road, the next road became smaller and worse. After crossing a field then into some woods, we came to a fairly wide riverbed. There was water in the middle and about a foot to 15 inches deep. The water was about 15 to 18 feet wide with a noticeable current. Surely we aren't going to drive across here!! We were now going very slow and Hap didn't stop! We WERE going across. Being in back it was difficult to see where we were going.

As we crossed the river, it was certainly different to look out both sides and see water and almost up to the running boards! And as might be expected, the riverbed was not totally flat - there were good sized variations which made even an empty truck throw you around some inside! It was solid gravel, good gravel on each side.

We came up a slight bank on the further side and now I could see the headers where we were going, and also I could see why 3 trucks came over - the headers were FULL and logs, many logs were on the ground waiting to be put on the headers. These guys cutting here were really in "high gear."

But, I was also thinking about the return trip. Beside the river (I certainly didn't know if my truck could swim, especially loaded), there was also one wicked climb up a hill. This would certainly tax my truck for all its worth! Bear in mind, the engine was a V8 and, looking back, I would say it HAD to be less than 150 horsepower! That is really very little to be powering a truck toting around 10 tons or even more!

So we loaded each truck, which with three people, didn't take much over an hour or two. All the while Pearl is puffing on a cigar butt and throwing out the orders because he was senior driver. I was just a kid and a kid with very little experience. Hap was a powerful man - he could take a chain binder in each hand and hold it straight out with hardly any effort - I could hardly lift (a large) one with ALL my effort! Hap also had one glass eye, but that didn't seem to hinder him.

I was the last one to be loaded and Hap told me to keep my hand on the door handle crossing the river. (This didn't boost my enthusiasm much)! He also told me that once in first gear low range, heading up the hill out of the riverbed, keep the gas on the floor - let it up for nothing - let it scream - and also I could get another quarter inch of gas by pushing down on the floorboard!!

So Pearl headed the decline toward the riverbed while Hap and I stood and watched. Pearl had a fairly new truck compared to the other three because he used it mostly on long runs delivering finished products. Mine especially, and the other two were beat up from various experiences in the woods etc.

As Pearl entered the water, you could then see how much this rolled from one side to the other. Hap said he was too far downstream, off the direct route for a straight crossing and was saying - keep right - keep right when the truck took a slow lean to the left and didn't stop. - God, he rolled that sucker over right in the water! There it laid on its left side like a big elephant! Pearl opened the right door (now on top) and climbed out.

We grabbed a hook and by prying at a "monkey link" or two in each chain, got the load chains to break away so the truck was free from the load. Pearl had shut the ignition off when he realized he was going over so the engine didn't get hurt.

We hailed the tractor driver who came down into the river - hooked on and righted the truck, then pulled it back to dry land. There was motor oil available, so a couple quarts was added to the crankcase. It started up with very little damage anywhere, so he was reloaded again. The logs in the river were hauled by the tractor back to the header.

Hap was next after Pearl's second attempt, which was no problem this time. Hap stayed more in direct line which had fewer potholes in the river and even though he rolled from side to side, he crossed successfully and stopped on the further side.

I started across and knowing that Hap had not rolled excessively, I tried to follow exactly where he had gone. My trip was successful and I pulled up in back of them on the further bank. I won't' try to say it was duck soup, because probably my heart was in my mouth!

Tough Climb

As we headed back, the "road" improved, the further we went, but we still had a tough pull up one hill.

As we approached, I had the throttle to the floor and then got that extra quarter inch out of the floorboard! (Actually speaking, wide open throttle was wide open and the floorboard bend could or could not have made any difference - it depends on throttle linkage). But anyway, I had the old girl "wound up" and was "getting all it had" as I went into the bottom! I should say here that downshift timing is on the top of the list - as soon as that speedometer gets NEAR a certain speed, you better be in the act of going for the next gear! (I don't recall what the speeds to shift gears is now) - but if you wait a couple seconds too long, you're going to lose your momentum! So as your speedometer keeps coming down to slower speeds, dropping a gear will sustain your speed momentarily, and you can capitalize on your maximum horsepower.

Apparently, the power, the load weight, and the momentum and the shift time paid off because, I did crest the hill ok!

We, ultimately made quite a few trips to this location and it was always by two trucks at a time.

Teep Jumps Off

I had a trip with Teep one day – we had been to Little Stoney and were returning loaded. Teep was in front of me as we started down Main Street Hill in Randolph.

Teep had a medical discharge from the Marines and had been involved in a lot of front line fighting. I don't know why he was discharged but I do know it was legitimate.

As we came down the hill, I was probably in 2nd gear and as I passed Pierce's Garage, my truck backfired. Teep was right at Weston Street intersection – and as that backfire took place, Teep's door opened and he literally dove out onto the road! He no

266

sooner hit the pavement (where he probably realized it was not a shell), he got up and started to chase his driverless truck as it passed the theatre. Jumped in, slammed the door and we continued as if nothing happened with the exception I started to laugh, as it was quite a sight!!

Sleep on the Porch

As a typical teenager, I used to sleep like a log. This was the time of the year I slept out on a large screened porch. During the summer months, Dad used to sit on the porch and read during the evening. I'm sure he enjoyed it very much – God knows he certainly didn't do much for his own enjoyment. Anyway I slept out there and once I started, I hated to quit in the fall when it got chilly. A couple years, Christmas came and went and I was still sleeping on the porch, (without an electric blanket!) By this time of year, the temperature could get down to 10 – 15 degrees.

A couple mornings I heard a car drive up and a door slam. I had no idea what time it was. But it was Leon Webster. Wanted to know if I was going to work that day! So, I would get up, grab a doughnut or something and get a ride down to the mill in his car.

Former Wells Residence 6 Prospect St. Randolph VT.
Showing porch as in text. Photo Approx 1980, C. Wells

Hot Tire

One trip I was coming to the mill from the "Rabbit Track" which was about 5 miles east of East Randolph in quite a desolate area. Rather than climb the mountain with a load toward Randolph Center, we "went around" and up through Bethel. As I started into Bethel, I could see smoke in the mirror. I stopped in front of the Creamery in Bethel and just as I got out, the tire caught fire. I bummed a hose from the creamery and squirted it early enough to put it out. A tire fire is quite common if a tire goes flat and is driven on far enough. I certainly was lucky to get the burning stopped – I didn't want a truck fire there on South Main, especially with a load of logs. (A fire that size could have roasted enough marshmallows for the whole state!!)

The Rabbit Track

It was raining one day when I went to work and Ken Webster sent me to the "Rabbit Track." He felt there were enough logs for a load even if the woods crew weren't working. Driving over there, I was thinking it wouldn't be easy loading alone (and it was also dangerous, especially alone). When I arrived, I drove up to the header and got out. Nobody around, no noise and then I spotted Leon's car (in the brush off the road where he had parked it). And in a couple minutes I spotted him coming down out of the woods toward me. It was a fair incline from the header up to where he was. I also noticed a dray full of logs up about 100 feet. As he approached, he said for me to get a "hook" and bring him one also. Which I did. As he took one from me, he said for me to go down a little way in front of the logs loaded on the dray and he would pry one off and for me to "catch it."

Believe me, this idea held no appeal for me whatever, and I found myself saying something to the effect of "to hell with that, I'm not going to catch any log!!" This is something I'd seen done a couple of times and tried it once. When a log is rolling toward you, you stand with a hook in preparation to catch it with the hook. If you're good (and lucky), you'll stop it from rolling, but only after it gives you a good snap, especially in the neck. This was VERY dangerous, and by now, I had decided if I ever saw a

268

log rolling toward me, the ONLY thing I was going to do would be to get the hell out of its way!!!

Well, this really irritated Leon, he certainly didn't want that truck leaving here empty, and with a few logs there that could be loaded, I was over ruling his plan.

"Well, you pry them off and I'll catch them" He belted out as he passed me on his way to position.

"Send the first one" he shouted as he planted his feet. I tried to talk him out of this idea knowing he was too old and not physically very strong.

Again he commanded me to "send the first one" – and so I did. And I watched as it started very slowly and then picked up some speed, as it rolled toward him. It also bounced around some as it rolled, but he stood poised and ready to catch it. Just before it got to him, it bounced in the air and when he went to grab it he missed! Believe me when I say, he's in a VERY poor position right now. That log hit him – rolled up his leg, knocked him down and rolled right over him. I don't know how heavy it was, but a good 300 pounds might be in the neighborhood. Well, his neighborhood right now was sharing the neighborhood of that log!

It apparently didn't break his leg or anything else except his pride! There he was on the ground, moaning with pain (and probably fright), we're miles from any help. I could picture myself loading him on the back of the truck and bringing him down to civilization.

Well, after a while he came around enough and the cool rain of course got him soaked but also helped to make him rally at least enough to get him in his car and away he went! I never saw him again at any loading area, but I wasn't around very much longer either because summer vacation was nearing the end.

Light Front End

On one trip coming in with a load, I blew a tire on the donkey axle. I was so near the mill, I decided to cure my problem not by changing the wheel but to jack the truck up enough to pull the pins that locked the donkey axle down. That would let the donkey axle just trail without carrying any load. For that short distance, the drivers would carry the whole load, also it wasn't far enough for the flat to heat up and catch fire. So, that's what I did. When I had removed the jack with both pins out, you could tell that the front end was pretty light. The space between the front fender(s) and the front wheel(s) was increased because more weight now hung over the rear axle, with no donkey axle carrying any weight. As a matter of fact, it was so light, I could turn the steering wheel with just one finger, where it normally required a lot of effort. (no power steering)

I had to be careful finishing the trip into Randolph and to the mill. The front had a tendency to wander so I went very slowly. Down hill was all right so when I started down Main Street Hill, that was no problem. I did find that when I crossed the tracks and then had a 90 degree turn, I had to back up a couple times in order to follow the back street along the tracks. On the first attempt to turn right, I almost wiped out the little building that was the original Randolph National Bank. Luckily I got it stopped in time.

Street along R.R. tracks as described in text. Photo about 1987.

Hill Beyond R.R. tracks with L. W. Webster mmill on left as described in text. Photo about 1987.

Coming up was a hill on South Pleasant Street for which I had to travel about 250 feet. So I turned around before the tracks and backed up the hill. Then I turned on to Pearl Street. Kenneth W. came out of the office and signaled me to stop. He came up to the door and wanted to know why the front end looked so light. So I told him why and what I did. He cautioned me about steering being light etc. and then directed me to unload at the pond. I agreed, slipped it into first gear and as I let the clutch out, gave it a fair amount of gas. Of course, this brought the front end up with the wheels completely leaving the ground! As the front bumper came up about 4' above the ground and with the truck moving ahead, the stunned look on his face was probably similar to him seeing a tiger coming at him.

So, I stopped at the log pond and proceeded to remove the chains. With them off, a couple of pries at a key log and then jump back and watch the action. That truck would get jounced around like a toy as a few logs came tumbling off with most rolling into the pond making a splash of hot water.

Right after the War ended in 1946, surplus U.S. Army trucks

were available. Websters bought a few of these 6x6 - mostly made by GM. After removing the dump bodies and putting on platform bodies, they made good log trucks.

Summary

For this job, I was paid $.50 and hour which had the week start on Monday. Most of the time, by sometime Thursday, I was on over time. Also, this mill provided steady employment for many townspeople and for years. While I did talk about 3 or 4 very hazardous jobs, most of the other jobs were safe within reason, providing the employee used some degree of common sense (and self protection).

Plans For Future?

At this point in my life, I wasn't having the greatest results with school. I really didn't know what I wanted to do for work or as a profession in my life. What I did know was that there was a lot of professions I didn't want in my life.

I was working this summer at L.W. Webster's in Randolph and it was a job to get me through the summer of 1945. I really did enjoy the trucks, the trips into the woods, the freedom from the repetition of doing the same thing day in and day out.

I thought of Ed Berry operating the splitter machine. Just think, no matter how much sleep you got the previous night, you were going to run that splitter for at least 8 hours today. If you don't pay 100% attention to what you're doing or if your mind wanders for a couple of seconds, you could lose a finger (or two) or worse! So, naturally I had to think of something different than that. I didn't want to dwell on anything long range, but, by now, I was getting "crowded" into decisions.

This was complicated further by the fact that, a term of some length, was probably going to be spent in the service. The war was still in full force, I was now 17 and soon the draft board would be looking my way. The draft board wouldn't be knocking on my door because that wasn't the way it worked. I recall it was setup that by age 18 you were to sign up at the local draft board. This meant that half way through my senior year, I would have to register with the draft board and probably go in the service soon after graduation. Many classmates (and younger) had left school and enlisted in the military. So, for the next few months, my life had an undetermined goal, with an undetermined time frame.

Sometime early in August, I was either fired or "let go" from employment at Webster's. I don't know if they were upset with me, my work, or whether they had someone else that needed a job and "right now" or what.

So what? I had to quit very soon and go back to school – it didn't make much difference to me, one way or another, whether I left in August or September.

The Three Musketeers

During the summer (1945), Stan Gould, Stub Howard and I spent a lot of non-work hours together.

I don't recall what work Stan was doing, but Stub had a full time job in his folk's farm on Hebard Hill. He put in long hours starting with morning chores, regular farm chores during the day and, of course, evening chores of milking the cows.

Stan and I didn't go to the farm very often. But, one day we were "up" there and for some reason we climbed over a fairly high wood gate, into a large – very large field. We were 200-300 feet away from the gate when Stub made a loud shout to get our attention.

We turned and read his gestures enough so when we looked 180 degrees away from him, we quickly found out why he shouted.

We were in the field with the bull- - - - a large bull,,,,,, and he was in the overdrive heading straight for us about 100 feet maybe 200 feet away.

In no time, both Stan and I headed toward the wood gate.

As we ran, Stub had picked up a long handled shovel or a hoe, climbed the gate and was in the field. He was yelling to "run" and faster.

He stood 40 or 50 feet inside the gate and as the bull came, it shifted to him and away from Stan and I.

Stub merely stepped aside and swung the shovel handle which, crossed the bull right on the forehead.

The handle broke, the bull was stunned, Stan and I scrambled up the gate and then so did Stub.

Lot of action for the moment which, thanks to Stub, it ended ok.

Stub knew the bull well and also knew he didn't like visitors especially unknowns in HIS pasture!

Stub had a 1941 Dodge he kept in A-1 condition, and of course, it was only about 3 years old.

We had a lot of fun that summer, and we also took in many dances in surrounding towns, far and near.

Back To Lyndon Institute

I returned to Lyndon, on the Harley and during the fall I could leave it at Connie Allard's house.

One day, both Connie and I rode our motorcycles to school and once, we parked them just inside the north entrance. One, or more likely, both of them dripped some oil on the floor. We were very strongly told not to park the bikes inside! (Again!)

This school year was a fairly routine year.

Academically, I certainly didn't blaze any trails I was actually riding very close to failing in a couple of subjects. I had absolutely no interest in French (which I was taking over from the previous year), I also lacked anything over a minimum desire in English – History, I could take U.S. History, but, European History, to me, was a waste of time. Strange, time was one commodity I seemed to have!

I still had no idea what I wanted to do in life, but also, there wasn't much emphasis put on a career. It was more just financial survival – which meant get a job!

As I said, I was poor in French, poor in English and History.

But I was good in technical subjects such as aeronautics and I could puff out good smoke rings! Speaking of aeronautics, this was a temporary and filler subject, only taught for part of a year. I liked this subject and recall an "A" was easily achieved.

One other item here, the fact I didn't do as well as I could of, was in no way a reflection of poor teachers or teaching. On the contrary, *all* the teachers at L.I. were "top shelf" and I'm sure, still are!

This is a good place to mention that all the people I met or encountered, in Lyndonville and Lyndon Center were warm, friendly, helpful and courteous. I wish I could spend more time and text in exploring this community, as I have in Randolph. However, if I did, this text would be much thicker and that is not something that I can do at this point in time.

In the spring, seniors had it quite easy and, of course, we're all looking toward graduation. It was also time that Connie A. would skip a day of school and hitch a ride down to St. Johnsbury airport. If we heard a plane that sounded like it was right over the roof, and his seat was empty, there was not doubt who was in it! He had a couple of friends that were pilots and would let him take over the controls.

Jim Allard – Flying Tigers

Flying must run in the family because his brother Jim, was also a pilot. As a matter of fact, Jim had been in the Flying Tigers. This was a group of flyers that was a U.S. splinter group who were flying in China. Using P-40 planes they were helping the Chinese to give the Japanese a tough time. Japan was trying to invade China at the time.

Boys Dormitory members 1945.

Class Outing

We had a class outing that was held at Lake Morey. Connie had just landed a job driving a truck, picking up milk, so he missed the outing.

Graduation was held without any problems. As I lived in the boy's dormitory, we had to be out of there within 2 days after graduation. I wanted to stick around for the Saturday night dance at the Crystal Ballroom. So for Saturday night, John Phelps, Arthur Robinson, and I had to find a place to sleep after the dance.

Vail's Mansion

Up on a hill in back of the "Institute," was a large house. It was huge with many (many) rooms and it was also vacant. It was called Vail's Mansion. A gentleman named Theodore Vail built it and used it during the summer for a residence. Theodore Vail was the founder and CEO of AT&T. He would arrive in Lyndonville by rail in his own private observation car. This contained kitchen, sleeping quarters, and a "living room" with a crew of three or four to keep him comfortable. He used to give each student that graduated from eighth grade, a brand new bicycle.

This mansion was an interesting building. I had been in it a couple of times. One room was a large "silo" about three stories high and standing in the middle of the floor it was easily distinguished as the library. Stairs took you up to a balcony where you could walk around the outside – and every inch of wall space was bookcases. Imagine the carpentry required to build this room. All woodwork was something like Walnut or Mahogany. I think this was at least four floors high with the center open.

There was a staircase made of glass. The risers and treads were heavy pieces of glass! There were so many rooms you could get lost (seriously). This was no place to explore after dark and the whole building was empty and deteriorating for at least the two years I was around. I don't know how many acres of land it had, but by this time, Mr. Vail had long gone and apparently there were no heirs. It was later torn down and is now the location of Lyndon State College.

So, after the dance, I recall 3 of us stayed for the night without benefit of blankets or anything else. It was supposed to be "haunted" but we didn't gather incidents to support that belief. The three of us had to be "residents" of the boy's dorm, because everyone else had a regular place to sleep.

Vail's Mansion, Lyndon Center, VT Courtesy: Harriet Fletcher Fisher

Graduation

So now, I'm out of school, I have a graduation diploma. Many colleges would accept a student graduating from L.I. without an entrance test providing your record showed marks of some given level. (What, I don't recall). This wasn't going to affect me because my marks weren't high enough – I also had many other factors that would preclude college. My mother insisted I go to college. I knew my father couldn't afford to pay for college, and I also knew I could work to get through, but this seemed crazy because I didn't know what to study for.

Con, Mother, Father. Photo 1944.

So, I worked for Dad at Randolph Coal and Ice Co. for the summer waiting to see what the local draft board had in mind for me.

Randolph Coal and Oil Co.

Somewhere in here, Randolph Coal and Ice Co. became Randolph Coal and Oil Co. Ice was no longer sold and hadn't been sold since 1928. Oil sales were rapidly becoming equal to coal sales.

This should be a welcome change because the coal end of the business required a lot of manual work. By now, some of the coal was loaded INTO a truck easily from the coal sheds. However, getting it into the coal sheds from the hopper cars could be a lot of work depending what kind of coal it was and what time of year it was.

In the winter, Buck (Buckwheat) was wet down when loaded into coal cars at the mine but was frozen by the time R.C. + O

278

(L) Con, (C) "A.C." (R) Glen Ducharme
Track side of Coal Office.

(L) Harry Tatro, (C) "A.C." (R) Glen Ducharme. Photo(s) about 1946

received it – for that reason, it was best to receive this in the fall. Steam coal (which went to the Aggie school) and also to the Randolph School building (on Main Street) was very labor intensified. Stove, nut, buckwheat were easy – Coke wasn't too bad. However, from the truck to the coal bins at destination could be a lot of work! Most of the time a coal chute would be used, but with no dump body, all of it had to be pushed or coaxed out of a scuttle hole where the chute was attached.

One in 25 deliveries probably involved a basket. This meant 2 men – I (or someone) would fill one of two "baskets" which was actually a canvas "pouch" on a heavy wire frame. When full, the "carrier" would back up to the tailgate, put one hand up grab a handle – over the shoulder and carry the basket on his back at shoulder height. It typically would weigh about 60 pounds. The problem was, and also why, a basket was used, meant it probably had to go to an upstairs apartment or one "out" back so the truck couldn't get close enough or whatever reason.

The "Dustin" block had a couple of tenants on the third floor which at 60 pounds per "basket" – a half ton of nut coal could require 15 or 18 trips up at least 2 flights of stairs!! Sometime during the early forties, I decided I could carry a basket of coal up 2 flights to help Glen. By the time I got to the 3rd floor – my strength was totally gone and Glen grabbed the basket just in time or I

**Selected Songs
Composed in 1946**

Anniversary Song
Five Minutes More
Laughing on the Outside
Linda
Sunday Kind of Love
Tenderly
There's No Business Like Show Business
They Say Its Wonderful
Things We Did Last Summer

would have dumped the damn thing on the customer's kitchen floor! This would be difficult for a 50 year old man! By the time I had reached 16 or 17 I could help "lug" – we would swap duties!

But, any type of coal shoveling at age 50 and up wasn't easy and many of the previously employed men were that age. Ernest Rattie, Elbert Fullam, Glen Ducharme, Arthur Huard, Harold Simmons, and Harry Tatro to name a few.

As oil gallonage increased, fuel oil deliveries of course also increased, as many homeowners found it was easier to adjust only a thermostat than it was to shovel coal into a furnace, and, also to contend with ash removal and discarding ashes.

Manual Labor

EVERYTHING in those days was very labor intensive. Naturally, a large operation or business had bigger and better equipment than a small one. Another labor intensive operation was lumbering. The chain saw hadn't been invented yet, so all logging and pulp cutting was done by an ax or cross cut saw. I knew quite a few men making a living either cutting pulp or cutting logs – it was work. There were still many horses used in the woods (during the forties), to "snake" logs or to pull a "dray" of logs. After WWII, tractors started to become popular.

1936 Harley

About mid summer in 1946, I heard about a Harley for sale in Barre VT. The owner was a relative of Norm or Pat Woodward in Randolph.

I drove to Barre and found the Esso gas station on Main Street where the machine was.

After looking it over, the owner asked if I could handle a "bike." I said I could and had sold my "45 Twin."

"Take it out for a spin"

So, I started it out and headed out of the lot on to the street.

This one was a "61," and I knew it had more power than my "45" – what I didn't know or realize was, - how much!

Once on the street, I twisted the throttle, the extra power made that bike jump ahead, and conversely made me slide off the

1936 Harley "61" described in text. Photo C. Wells

seat toward the back fender – more accurately ONTO the fender!

I did have one BIG job getting that bike back under control but, a few people on the sidewalk stopped, held their breath and watched the show for a couple moments!

I also remember that incident also elevated my voice at least one octave!!

Regardless, I did buy the motorcycle.

One day, Stan and I went down School Street and kept on going until the road went from paved to a "dirt" road. Dirt roads were very common and, depending on what time of the year it was, could be a very good road. This was probably mid summer, so spring mud season was long gone.

The Green Mountains run north and south in Vermont so traveling north to south was quite apt to be in a valley (such as Northfield Gulf or Williamstown Gulf). East and west travel always meant if you weren't going up, you were going down!

Climbing Mt. Cushman

Well, we were going west, which meant up and also meant the further you go, the worse the road and the steeper you climbed (within reason). It wasn't long before we were making our way up Mt. Cushman and the road had diminished to the point it certainly wasn't a road anymore, it was a trail! Over a brook or two, through some tree branches, rocks, stone and mud. This would be a great run for off road vehicles today! But, at this time even a Jeep would be heavily taxed, and they were the only vehicle that had 4 wheel drive.

Anyway, we made it to the top, had a picture or two taken at the base of the fire tower. The tower at this time wasn't used. I can only imagine that when it was built, the materials had to be pulled up there by a crawler tractor. The elevation of Mt. Cushman was 2,700+ feet. Nothing spectacular, but not just a "hill" either.

Con on descent from Mt. Cushman. Note: quality of "road".

Photo- 1946, C. Wells

When we were back in Randolph, somehow the local paper (you know, the Drysdale paper) heard about it and did a write-up for the next weekly run!

After that, Stan's folks were a little warmer about motorcycles.

During the two years I was "away" to school at Lyndon

Con at base of Fire tower. Photo - 1946, C. Wells

Institute, Stan Gould and I weren't in constant touch. I used to return to Randolph during my junior and senior year on the weekends, but not every weekend so Stan and I would get caught up on events when I came home. Stan was a year younger, so he wasn't quite as concerned about the draft as I was.

Stan's 1947 Pontiac

By fall of '46 Stan had a 1947 Pontiac convertible coupe which in my eyes was about utopia in automobiles. This car was a tremendous step up from previous cars either he or I had owned previously.

One of the first times I rode in it we were driving in South Pleasant in Randolph toward "Beanville." As we went down Beaudoin Hill we saw 2 eyes at the foot of the hill reflect in our headlights. We knew it was a deer so Stan slowed up as he approached. The deer was mesmerized by the lights so we were able to drive within 6 or 8 feet. At which point, the deer turned around. But before he ran off, proceeded to kick at the light – damned if he (or she) didn't kick the headlight out and then – ran off!

Draft Dilemma

January 1, 1947 was celebrated with these facts on my mind.
A) 1946 brought the end of World War II, - in the Pacific.
B) The draft was still in effect. (I had to Jan 26, to enlist or gamble that I wouldn't get "called."
C) If I enlisted, probably the draft would be cancelled.
D) If I didn't enlist, I end up in the Army infantry.
E) If I enlisted, I could pick the branch of service.